EXILE AND THE JEWS

JPS ANTHOLOGIES
OF JEWISH THOUGHT

UNIVERSITY OF NEBRASKA PRESS
LINCOLN

EXILE AND THE JEWS

Literature, History, and Identity

Edited by Nancy E. Berg and Marc Saperstein

THE JEWISH PUBLICATION SOCIETY
PHILADELPHIA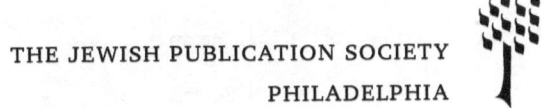

© 2024 by Nancy E. Berg and Marc Saperstein

Acknowledgments for the use of copyrighted material appear on pages 231–37, which constitute an extension of the copyright page.

All rights reserved. Published by the University of Nebraska Press as a Jewish Publication Society book.

Library of Congress Control Number: 2023046421

Set and designed in Charis by N. Putens.

Contents

Acknowledgments..xiii

Notes about the Cover..xiv

Introduction...xv

1. Exile as Human Condition..1

BIRTH AS EXILE

Midrash Tanḥuma, Pekudei 3......................................3

EXILE FROM EDEN

Genesis 3...5

Moses Maimonides, *Guide of the Perplexed* (ca. 1190)............7

Don Isaac Abravanel, *Perush ʿal ha-Torah* on
Genesis 3 (late 15th century).....................................9

Amos Neufeld, "Exile" (1988).....................................10

2. Exile in Ancient History..12

EGYPT

Exodus 1:8–14..13

Ezekiel Landau, "Exile in Egypt versus Exile in Persia" (1782)...15

BABYLONIA

2 Kings 24:8–25:21 16

Psalm 137 19

Tanḥuma, Yitro 5 (8th–9th century) 20

Pesikta Rabbati 31:4 (ca. 845 CE) 21

Yalkut Shimoni, Psalms, *Remez* (section) 883, no. 16
on Ps. 137 (11th–14th century) 22

Israel Mattuck, "How Shall We Sing" 23

Amir Gilboa, "By the Waters of Babylon" (1953) 25

Lea Goldberg, "Night" (1955–56) 26

Yehuda Amichai, "If I Forget Thee, Jerusalem" (1968) 27

ROME AND THE LONG EXILE

Yalkut Shimoni (ca. 13th century) 29

Shir ha-Shirim Rabbah (ca. 7th–8th century) 30

Eikhah Rabbah (ca. 500 CE) 30

Profiet Duran (the Ephodi), "Epistle of Lamentation,
Grief and Consolation" (1393) 31

Judah ben David ibn Yaḥya, "Me'orah" (ca. 1428) 33

Don Isaac Abravanel, "Letter to Yehiel of Pisa" (October 4, 1482) .. 36

Don Isaac Abravanel, *Ma'yenei ha-Yeshu'ah* (1496) 37

Don Isaac Abravanel, *Zevaḥ Pesaḥ* (1496) 38

Abraham Saba, "A Debate over Which Exile Is Worse" (ca. 1500) ... 40

Abraham P. Mendes, "The Sorrows and Consolation
of Jerusalem: A Sermon for Shabbat Naḥamu" (1855) 43

3. Exile and Holidays ... 45

TISHA B'AV

Lamentations 5 ... 47

Pesikta Rabbati 30:2 (ca. 845 CE) ... 49

Anonymous, "A Derashah on the Haftarah for the Ninth of Ab" (ca. 1700–1900) ... 50

David Einhorn, "For the Anniversary of the Destruction of Jerusalem" (1896) ... 53

Mordecai Ze'ev Feierberg, "Whither?" (1900) ... 57

PURIM

Book of Esther 2:5–22 ... 63

Amīnā (Binyamin ben Misha'el), *Commentary on the Book of Esther* (early 18th century) ... 65

Abba Hillel Silver, "But Mordecai Bowed Not Down" (1936) ... 67

4. Divine Presence in Exile ... 68

SHEKHINAH

B. *Megillah* 29a ... 69

THE DIVINE PRESENCE AMID GENTILES

Zohar I, 84b–85a ... 70

R. Nachman of Bratzlav, "The Lost Princess" (1816) ... 72

PROVIDENTIAL PROTECTION IN EXILE

Isaac ben Yedaiah, "Commentary on the Aggadot of the Talmud" (late 13th century) ... 74

Saul Levi Morteira, "Dust of the Earth" (ca. 1623) ... 75

Saul Levi Morteira, "Guarded Him as the Pupil of His Eye" (delivered 1631, published 1645) 79

Menasseh ben Israel, "To His Highnesse the Lord Protector of the Commonwealth of England, Scotland, and Ireland" (1655) 81

Berr Isaac Berr, "Letter of a Citizen to His Fellow Jews" (1791) .. 83

ABANDONMENT BY THE DIVINE PRESENCE IN EXILE

Hayyim Nahman Bialik, "In the City of Slaughter" (1904) 84

5. Exile as Penance and Atonement 86

NATIONAL EXILE

Leviticus 26:31–45 87

Deuteronomy 28:64–69 88

Sanhedrin 37b (4th–6th century) 89

Zohar III, 115a–b (13th century) 90

Don Isaac Abravanel, *Perush ʿal ha-Torah* on Leviticus 26:38–39 (late 15th century) 92

Don Isaac Abravanel, *Perush ʿal ha-Torah* on Deuteronomy 28 (late 15th century) 92

Hermann Adler, *A Course of Sermons on the Biblical Passages Adduced by Christian Theologians* (1869) 94

Alexander Altmann, "Sermon for Rosh Hashanah 5695" (1934) 96

INDIVIDUAL EXILE

Genesis 4 98

Augustine, "Reply to Faustus the Manichean" (ca. 400) 100

Tanḥuma, Bereshit 9 (ca. 400–600 CE) 101

Israel Brunn, *She'elot u-Teshuvot* (Responsa) nos.
265, 166 (15th century, published 1798) 102

Don Isaac Abravanel, *Sefer Naḥalat Avot*, Pirkei Avot 1.11 (1505) ... 105

Moses Cordovero, *The Palm Tree of Deborah* (1588) 106

Israel of Koznitz, "Avodat Yisrael to VaYetzei" (ca. 1750–1810) ... 107

6. Life in Exile 109

ADVICE AND REBUKE

Jeremiah 29 111

Dunash ibn Labrat, "Reply to an Invitation to a
Feast" (10th century) 114

Benjamin of Tudela, "Exilarch" (late 12th century) 116

Solomon Levi, *Divrei Shlomo* on Va-Yetse' (1573) 117

Aaron Berechiah of Modena, "Shemot," *Derashot
Ma'avar Yabbok* (1619) 119

Saul Levi Morteira, "The People's Envy" (1622) 120

Charles Reznikoff, "Babylon: 539 B.C.E." (1934) 124

Myron Ernst, "Exile" (1988) 129

7. Internalized Exile 131

COMMUNAL IDENTITY IN EXILE

Yitzhak Baer, *Galut* (1947) 132

Eliezer Berkovits, "Galut, or the Breach between the
Torah and Life—the Real Problem" (1943) 134

Eliezer Berkovits, "Galut and Eretz Israel" (1943) 134

Eliezer Berkovits, "Galut" (1973) 135

SELF-IDENTITY IN THE DIASPORA

Isaac ben Yedaiah, *Commentary on the Aggadot of the Talmud* (late 13th century) 139

Judah Leib Pinsker, *Auto-Emancipation* (1882) 142

Amy Levy, "Captivity" (1889) 144

Hayyim Nahman Bialik, "Indeed This People Is Grass" (1897) ... 147

Joseph Hayyim Brenner, "Self-Criticism" (1914) 149

Jacob Klatzkin, "Boundaries" (1914) 151

Max Nussbaum, "To Travel and to Flee" (1939) 154

Natan Zach, "An Exile Poem" (1966) 155

Eli Amir, *Tarnegol Kapparot* (1982) 157

Joshua Sobol, *Soul of a Jew: The Last Night of Otto Weininger* (1983) 160

8. Exile in Medieval and Modern History 161

MUSLIM SPAIN

Moses ibn Ezra, "Ad An ba-Galut" (11th century) 163

Moses ibn Ezra, "Aḥar Yemei ha-Shaḥarut" (11th century) 166

CHRISTIAN SPAIN

"An Anonymous Chronicle of the 1492 Expulsion" (ca. 1492) 167

Y. L. Gordon, "In the Depths of the Sea" (1884) 171

EXILE FROM ELSEWHERE

Bābā'ī ibn Lutf, "How the Grand Vizier Found a Pretext against the Jews of Isfahan and Drove Them out of Their Homes" (ca. 1660) 174

Isaac Bashevis Singer, *Love and Exile* (1986) 177

Andre Aciman, *Out of Egypt* (1995) 179

Dina Elenbogen, "Exile: Losing the Motherland" (1999) 181

EXILE OF THE OTHER

Sophia Parnok, "Hagar" (ca. 1920)............................ 183

Lea Goldberg, "Fragment" (ca. 1970)........................... 184

Edward W. Said, "Palestine, Then and Now: An Exile's Journey through Israel and the Occupied Territories" (1992) 186

9. Language as the Locus of Exile 188

BABEL AND AFTERWARD

Genesis 11:1–9 189

Anton Shammas, "On Exile and Literature" (1985).............. 190

Eva Hoffman, *Lost in Translation* (1989) 195

Haviva Pedaya, "A Man Walks" (1992)......................... 197

Salman Masalha, "I Write Hebrew" (1997) 200

Giora Leshem, "My Mother's Tongue Is Not My Mother Tongue" (2000)....................................... 201

10. Negation, Ambivalence, and Affirmation of Exile 203

NEGATION

Daniel al-Kumisi, "Appeal to the Karaites of the Dispersion to Come and Settle in Jerusalem" (10th century)... 204

Judah Halevi, "My Heart Is in the East" (12th century) 206

Heinrich Heine, "Jehuda ben Halevy" (1851).................. 207

Theodor Herzl, *Der Judenstaat* (1896)......................... 210

Moses Leib Lilienblum, "Derekh Teshuvah" (1899)............. 213

Ahad Ha'am, "The Negation of the Diaspora" (1909).............215

Rina Shani, "I Am in the East and My Heart Is in the East" (1970) .. 218

A. B. Yehoshua, "Exile as a Neurotic Solution" (1986)...........219

AMBIVALENCE

Eva Hoffman, "Out of Exile: Some Thoughts on
Exile as a Dynamic Condition" (2013)......................... 221

AFFIRMATION

Moses ben Nahman, "Disputation of Barcelona" (1263)........ 222

Dov Baer (the Maggid of Mezritch), "Harḥek
mish'khen raᶜ" (ca. 1760–80)................................... 223

Simon Dubnow, "The Affirmation of the Diaspora" (1909)..... 224

Judah Magnes, "Like All the Nations?" (1930) 227

Coda.. 229

Marjorie Agosin, *A Cross and a Star* (1995).................... 229

Marjorie Agosin, "I Invented a Country" (1994)................ 229

Source Acknowledgments.. 231

Notes... 239

Bibliography.. 257

Index... 265

Acknowledgments

This book, so long in process, accumulated debts to many. We begin with our thanks to the William T. Kemper Foundation, which awarded us the grant for the course that was the genesis of this book; to Washington University in St. Louis, for the opportunity to team-teach the course; and to all of our students, especially those who took the course the first time we offered it. Their questions, insights, and challenges helped us deepen and broaden our understanding of Jewish exile.

We are indebted to The Jewish Publication Society's Rabbi Barry Schwartz for his enthusiastic endorsement since our initial proposal; to Dr. Elias Sacks for his continuing support; and especially to Joy Weinberg, whose meticulous reading, informed queries, and near-immediate responses have significantly improved this anthology from draft to book. She has been a rare partner in this venture. We also thank the readers, whose comments and questions helped us articulate our ideas and explanations; Leif Milliken and other wonderful staff members at JPS's copublisher, the University of Nebraska Press; and David Hornik for his careful and skillful copyediting.

Thank you to the writers and translators who allowed us use of their texts, especially Anton Shammas, who translated his essay "On Exile and Language" anew for this volume. Prof. Van Bekkum graciously provided us with his transcription of the manuscript Hebrew text "O Seville! Ah Castille!" Rabbi Danny Rich generously allowed us access to the Mattuck manuscript. Nehama Aschkenasy and Robert Bonfil each led us to more nuanced readings of respective texts.

We remain grateful to our colleagues, friends, and family, and above all, to Stan and Tamar, to whom we dedicate this book.

Notes about the Cover

The 1991 painting *Refugees* by Nora Kronstein-Rosen speaks to her own life in exile. She was born in 1925 in Vienna. In 1938 she fled with her mother and her older sister to Liechtenstein. Starting in 1939 she lived in Switzerland, studying art in Lausanne and at the Kunstgewerbeschule Zuerich (Zurich Art School). After her mother's death she went to New York and London, where she studied at the Pratt Institute and Central School of Art, respectively. Later she settled in Israel, teaching at both the Shenkar College of Fashion and Textile (Ramat Gan) and the Ort Seminar in Tel Aviv. Initially a designer of textiles, Kronstein-Rosen became better known for her painting. She died in 2013.

Introduction

The word "exile" has unmistakably negative connotations in the English language, most traditionally meaning separation or uprootedness from the Land of Israel. The Hebrew equivalent of exile, *galut*—or, in the Ashkenazic and Yiddish pronunciations, *golus*—is even bleaker, evoking geographical, psychological, and theological associations with a dismal reality devoid of redeeming characteristics: uprooting and continued displacement, subjugation and oppression, shame and humiliation. If all that wasn't enough, the idea of the exilic condition takes on even more negative connotations as *"galutiyut."* Jews become tainted by exile: the failure of most of the exiles to return from Babylonia is the beginning of the long ruin. *Galutiyut* causes or reflects an abnormal condition—one of corrosion and decay or contamination, of dependence and subjugation.

Yet the core events in the collective memory of Israelite origins—the Exodus from Egypt and the Revelation at Mount Sinai—took place outside the Land of Israel, as did most of the history of the Jewish people in the past 1,900 years. So, too, many of the greatest expressions of Jewish cultural creativity—the Babylonian Talmud and its classical commentators, medieval Jewish philosophy, the poetry of the Golden Age in Spain, modern Jewish literature in European and in Eastern languages—are the product of Jews in "exile" encountering and engaging their host environments.

The Jewish holiday cycle also seems to convey multidimensional interpretations regarding the nature of exile. Passover, Shavuot, and Sukkot commemorate and recreate the narrative of the Israelites going into, and coming forth from, exile. Two holidays in particular are themselves

INTRODUCTION

exilic. The fast of Tisha b'Av mourns both the destruction of the First Temple by the Babylonians and the Second Temple by the Romans. Considered the saddest day of the year, it is also the anniversary of other tragic events and forced departures, such as the expulsions from England (1290), France (1306), and Spain (1492). In contrast, Purim is the most celebratory of holidays, and yet, notably, its entire story takes place in exile—not only outside of the Land of Israel, but with nary a mention of the land.

Philosophical and theological analyses and literary expressions of exile have added still more layers of meaning, nuance, and complexity. Running from religious to national, from communal to individual, from univalent to ambiguous, these texts—like the Jewish experience itself—often redefine the nature of exile.

In essence, the history of the Jews can also be seen as the history of a people in tension between contending evaluations of Jewish life in dispersion.

Exile Is Suffering

Jews have spent much more of the past two thousand years outside of the Land of Israel than in it, and the experience of exile could not but have its effect on the people.

For the Rabbis and other Jewish thinkers, exile is equated to suffering on behalf of the Jews. Exile is both the consequence of behaving badly and the opportunity for penance. For Rabbi Hermann Adler, the mission of suffering on the part of Jews atones for all. Voluntary exile emulates the *Shekhinah*, God's presence that accompanies the Jews outside of Zion. Theological discussions attest to the Divine Presence in exile, at times in the form of the *Shekhinah*, as providential protection.

The establishment of the State of Israel is rooted in large part in the negation of exile (*shelilat hagalut*) and the erasure of *galutiyut*. According to the dominant tradition, only in the land of Zion can Jews become fully realized.

Yet Jews have experienced exile not only from Israel, but from other places they have called home. The Jews persecuted by the Inquisition, and ultimately expelled from Spain and Portugal, were just as uprooted as the Babylonian captives. Some Jews experienced the rupture of exile when forced to depart Muslim-ruled Spain for the areas controlled by Christians, only later to face expulsion from the Iberian Peninsula. Jews were uprooted from England, France, and other European cities and states; so too they were expelled from places in the Byzantine, Persian, and Austrian Empires. Even where they were allowed to stay, they were subject to various degrees of discrimination, tyranny, and torment.

To focus on one important medieval figure, Moses ben Nahman (Nachmanides) speaks of exile, *galut*, as a basis of Jewish suffering, with Jews mocked and scorned by their neighbors and often pushed to abandon their religious identity and accept the religious beliefs of the majority. At best Jews could hope for sympathetic kings to guarantee their physical safety, and many medieval kings did protect their Jews. Yet, like many other medieval Jewish figures, Nachmanides accepted exile, with all its oppression, as a key to spiritual immortality: a future life under a messianic king who will inspire all Jews to observe the commandments.

Exile Is Positive

Alternatively, for other Jews, exile is a positive development—for its cleansing potential, for the possibility to make a good life for oneself among non-Jews, for the opportunity it affords to bring good to others and serve as a light unto other nations.

Saul Morteira, a seventeenth-century rabbi in Amsterdam, believed that Jews' compassion for those in desperate need was an outstanding Jewish quality. He sermonized that although the Jews are in exile and do not have their own city or state, their charitableness in comparison with their position exceeds that of all other nations, and that exile is advantageous to Jews specifically because of their geographic dispersal. A proponent of positive thinking, he also asserted that God planted hatred in the hearts of gentiles in order to prevent Jews from assimilating.

Sometimes life in exile was an opportunity for Jews to improve their own profile and, thereby, their larger communities. As court physician, for example, Maimonides was held in high regard, and his coreligionists likely benefited from the halo effect. Elite Jews contributed intellectually and culturally; others benefited the lands in which they lived as merchants, artisans, and viticulturists.

The prophet Jeremiah famously urged the exiled to make a life for themselves in Babylonia. In fact, when King Cyrus of Persia issued an edict allowing the Babylonian exiles to return a few generations after the initial expulsion, the exiles were slow to do so. Many remained and established the longest continuous Jewish community until its demise in the last century. Many Jews exiled in Persia, or Italy, Spain, France, Germany, Poland, and other countries, often made comfortable lives for themselves and their children. In the Netherlands, Rabbi Morteira admonished his congregation not to forget themselves in exile and to refrain from ostentatious displays of wealth. Clearly he saw evidence of at least some of them flourishing all too well!

Dov Baer, the eighteenth-century Maggid of Mezrich, argued for the spiritual benefit of life in exile (see chapter 10). Others have contended—to this day—that the greater efforts to adhere to Judaism demanded by the exilic condition result in a more profound and meaningful practice.

Exile in the Modern Era

In the modern era, grand or abstract categories of sin, divine retribution, and spiritual redemption give way to personal, and even secular, conceptions of exile. As the definition of home changes, the concept of exile changes as well. Rather than punishment for not following God's law, exile is the "natural consequence" of not following the "laws" of nationalism.

Modern Jews' individual concepts of exile did not always map seamlessly onto that of the Jewish collective. More Jews fleeing Nazi Europe sought new lives in the United States rather than in Palestine. Jews from Arab lands—Egypt, Iraq, etc.—mourned their homes when forced to depart, and, even if settled in Israel, struggled to consider themselves anything other than exiles.

Writers, in particular, found their refuge, their home-in-exile, in language. When separated from their mother tongue, they found their linguistic exile every bit as painful as any other exile.

A Full Spectrum of Perspectives

Thus, Jewish history and literature present a full spectrum of perspectives on exile. For some Jews, the negation of exile is both an ideal of redemption (to end the situation of being in exile) and a rejection of the idea of exile (to discard behaviors and attitudes that developed in exile). Other Jews experience an ambivalent relationship to exile. Still others embrace and revalorize the condition, speaking of its potential and its promise.

Even as our understanding of exile deepens, so too we begin to understand that the state of exile is not fixed, but rather fluid and ever-changing.

Developing This Anthology

This anthology began as a course the editors cotaught a number of years ago in the former Literature and History Program at Washington University in St. Louis. Our starting point was the overall significance of exile—as concept and as experience—in both Jewish studies and for Jews. As we taught, the story of the Jewish experience has been read as one of exile and redemption—the former of greater interest, perhaps, in scholarship and text, the latter for the exiled themselves.

Many of the texts initially included in our coursepack were from *Sefer ha-Aggadah*, a masterful anthology of traditional postbiblical narratives.[1] To prepare the work, poet Hayyim Nahman Bialik (1873–1934) and journalist and editor Yehoshua Ravnitsky (1859–1944) had combed through the Rabbinic literature (often drawing from volumes that were themselves compendia) and organized the entire contents (stories, biblical exegesis, extrabiblical legends, sermons, folklore, theology, explications, aspects of contemporary popular religion) thematically, making the selections much more accessible and useful to the average Hebrew reader. By gathering texts from different works, and by collecting and codifying the "oral" tradition for new generations, the very project of *Sefer ha-Aggadah* was a response to the extended Jewish exile, and mirrors the reconstruction and restoration of the Jewish people.

Circumstances precluded our reprising the course in its original team-taught format, but we each continued to work with the material. We realized that the texts we had brought together already constituted a rich collection worthy of a much larger audience. We decided to create what would be the first anthology to examine the Jewish response to exile from the biblical period to our modern day. This anthology would delve into multiple dimensions—political, philosophical, religious, psychological, and mythic—of the response to exile. In concentrating on the multidimensional nature of exile, in examining the tension between contending evaluations of Jewish life in dispersion, and in offering more extensive and varied primary source texts than preceding volumes on the topic, it would elucidate the shifting ways in which exile has been conceived throughout the entire sweep of Jewish history. Alongside texts that characterized exile as "a kind of death," other texts would explore positive aspects of being dispersed and living as a minority, on the margins, in creative tension with the majority culture, suggesting that exile is necessary for the Jewish people to fulfill its historic mission. It would enable readers to explore how the realities and interpretations of exile have shaped the religion and politics of the Jewish community and individual Jewish identity as well. It would even hint—daringly—that God might be more accessible in exile than in the Temple of Jerusalem.

About This Anthology

Gathering texts from all genres of Jewish literary creativity, *Exile and the Jews: Literature, History, and Identity* explores how the realities and interpretations of exile have shaped Judaism, Jewish politics, and individual Jewish identity for millennia.

Ordered along multiple arcs—from universal to particular, collective to individual, and mythic-symbolic to prosaic everyday experience—each of the ten chapters presents a different facet of exile: "Exile as

INTRODUCTION

Human Condition," "Exile in Ancient History," "Exile and Holidays," "Divine Presence in Exile," "Exile as Penance and Atonement," "Life in Exile," "Internalized Exile," "Exile in Medieval and Modern History," "Language as the Locus of Exile," and "Negation, Ambivalence, and Affirmation of Exile." Each chapter's texts are also arranged chronologically, enabling readers to compare and contrast exile throughout history as experience, memory, and metaphor. We conclude, in the "Coda," with two short excerpts by the writer Marjorie Agosin, whose family story contains layers of exile, and who finds herself and her inspiration in the many layers.

We do not claim to have exhausted the sources or even the perspectives on exile. Rather, we hope to have *represented* the multiplicity of Jewish views, contexts, and responses to exile as experience, as memory, and as metaphor. We explore the continuities and ruptures, the similarities and differences, across different categories of exile and the texts that respond to the larger questions. Some selections are well-known, some more familiar in other contexts, and others lesser-known in any context. In all, we cover significant swaths of history, present conventional thought and challenges to it, and tease out the universal and particular aspects of living in exile.

We hope readers will savor the diversity of experiences and reflections, beginning with the original event of exile: the expulsion from Paradise.

EXILE AND THE JEWS

1   Exile as Human Condition

While exile is a central and arguably defining experience for Jews—as the religious studies scholar Arnold Eisen notes, "To write a history of Jewish exile is to write the history of the Jews"[1]—it also encompasses a universal dimension. The foundational text of Jews becoming a nation—the Torah—begins with a universality: the story of Creation, which concludes with the banishment of Adam and Eve from the Garden of Eden. This banishment has been likened metaphorically to birth, the most universal of all experiences.

"Each of us is an exile," asserts long-time BBC foreign correspondent and editor John Simpson, who goes on to apologize for the seeming triteness of the statement, while also arguing that it is still meaningful: "We are exiles from our mother's womb, from our childhood, from private happiness, from peace, even if we are not exiles in the more conventional sense of the word. The feeling of looking back for the last time, of setting our face to a new and possibly hostile world is one we all know. It is the human condition; and the great upheavals of history have merely added physical expression to an inner fact."[2]

Anticipating many of the ideas that follow later in this volume, this chapter gestures to the emotional, political, cultural, and even bodily aspects of exile. Speaking to the human condition—birth, and eventually death—it includes the original account of Adam and Eve's exile as chronicled in the book of Genesis (the first book of the Hebrew Bible): a story invoking both birth and death. The ejection from the garden is likened to a baby's expulsion from the mother's body; yet mortality—the certainty of death—is the most profound consequence of Adam and Eve's transgression. Commentaries from Maimonides and

Don Isaac Abravanel illuminate the story from different angles, from the universal to the particularly Jewish perspective. A modern poem completes the circle, returning to the inherent inevitability of death.

Birth as Exile

Exile can be seen as the most universal of experiences, for it encompasses both birth and death. This first text describes birth as exile—a baby's expulsion from the womb. While the word "exile" does not appear in the passage, the idea of exile is clear. A soul is brought into this world against its will, forcibly removed (in effect, exiled) from the ideal life in the presence of God, and compelled to encounter all the frightening challenges of life that are part of the human condition. According to this view, every human being begins life after having been exiled from a far more attractive realm than the world we know.

The passage contains three references to the theme of "keeping the Torah," but the rest of the narrative seems not to apply specifically to Jews, but to all human beings, and thus is in keeping with the universal nature of birth as exile.

The source of this text, *Midrash Tanḥuma,* is a collection of legends (*aggadot*) and discussions of laws (*halakhot*) named after Rabbi Tanḥuma Bar Abba, a fifth-generation amora (later contributor to the Talmud). The particular commentary concerns Pekudei, the twenty-third parashah (Torah portion) covering Exodus 38:21–40:38, which begins with "These are the accounts of [*pekudei*] the tabernacle." The word *pekudei* connects to both the commandments (*mitzvot*) to be followed and the accounting (*din ve-ḥeshbon*) to be given before the Holy One. The excerpt from the commentary focuses on this accounting rather than on the specifications of the priestly vestments that comprise the Torah portion for which it is commentary. The accounting follows individuals throughout their exile from Eden: life as we know it. The angel in the narrative, our guide, shows that the degree to which these individuals fulfill God's commandments determines their eternal reward.

MIDRASH TANḤUMA, PEKUDEI 3

[Before the embryo is formed in the womb] the Holy One decrees its fate, whether male or female, weak or strong, poor or rich, short or tall, ugly or comely, fat or thin, delicate or coarse, and decrees all that will happen to it. But not whether it is to be righteous or wicked, no, that is a matter placed solely in the hands of the individual, as it is said: "See I have set before you this day life and good and death and evil" (Deut. 30:15).

[The Holy One] calls to the angel appointed over spirits, saying "Bring Me so-and-so's spirit, which is in the Garden of Eden, its name is such and the description is such." All spirits destined to be human beings were created the day the world was created as it is written "Whatever exists has been named" (Eccles. 6:10). The angel immediately goes and brings the spirit before the Holy One. When the spirit arrives, it prostrates itself before the King of Kings. The Holy One tells it, "Enter the drop in so-and-so's hands." The spirit gives voice and says, "Master of the Universe, the world in which I have been living since You created me is enough. Why do You wish to put me in this putrid drop, I am holy and pure, I am hewn from Your honor." The Holy One responds, "The world which I will have you enter is even more beautiful and when I formed you I formed you for this." The Holy One puts it into the drop against its will. Then the angel returns and puts the spirit into the mother's womb....

The angel takes it from there, leading it to the Garden of Eden, showing it the righteous sitting in glory, their heads crowned. The angel asks the spirit, "Do you know who they are?" The spirit: "No, my lord." The angel answers, "Those you see were initially formed like you in their mother's womb; then they emerged into the world and kept the Torah and its commandments. Thus they earned the reward you see. Know that your fate, too, is to go out to the world. If you keep the Holy One's Torah, you will also merit this and will be seated thus. But if not, know that you will merit another kind of place."

In the evening [the angel] leads the spirit to Gehenna, and shows it the wicked, that the angels of destruction strike with sticks of fire. [The] wicked cry out, "Woe, woe!" but to no avail. The angel asks the spirit, "Do you know who these are?" The spirit: "No, my lord." The angel: "Those being burned were formed like you and when they emerged in the world they did not keep the Holy One's Torah and laws thus they came to this disgrace you witness. Know that your fate is to go out to the world to be righteous, not wicked, and thus merit life in the world to come...."

The angel took the spirit everywhere, showing it the righteous and the wicked, and everything. In the evening the angel returned the spirit to its mother's womb, and there the Holy One made a latch and doors....

Finally, it is time to go forth into the world. The same angel appears and says to the spirit, "It is time to go forth into the world." The spirit: "Why do you want to take me out into the world?" The angel: "My son, know that you were formed against your will, now you will be born against your will, you will die against your will and against your will you will give an accounting before the King who is King of Kings, the Holy One." The spirit refuses to leave until [the angel] strikes him with the lit candle on his head and brings it forth into the world against its will. Instantly, the infant forgets all that he had seen and all that he had known. Why does the infant weep at birth? Because he lost a place of comfort and ease—[he weeps] for the world that he was forced to leave....

When it is a person's time to die the same angel appears and asks, "Do you recognize me?" The person answers, "Yes," and asks, "Why did you come today of all days?" The angel: "To take you from this world, your time has come." The person begins to weep and his voice is heard from one end of the world to the other. No one hears his voice except for the rooster. The person asks, "Did you not already take me from two worlds and put me in this one?" The angel: "Did I not tell you that against your will you were formed, against your will you were born and lived, and so you will die, having to give an accounting before the Holy One?"[3]

Exile from Eden

The following passage from Genesis provides the basis for the beginning of exile in Jewish memory. It is of course not a Jewish story: Adam and Eve are the first people and the only living human beings when the snake successfully tempts Eve to violate God's instructions, and to entice Adam to do so in turn. This moving, imaginative explanation of why human life includes difficulties and challenges intimates the universality of exile.

> GENESIS 3
>
> Now the serpent was the shrewdest of all the wild beasts that the Eternal God had made. It said to the woman, "Did God really say: You shall not eat of any tree of the garden?" The woman replied to the serpent, "We may eat of the fruit of the other trees of the garden. It is only about fruit of the tree in the middle of the garden that God said: 'You shall not eat of it or touch it, lest you die.'" And the serpent said to the woman, "You are not going to die, but God knows that as soon as you eat of it your eyes will be opened and you will be like divine beings who know good and bad." When the woman saw that the tree was good for eating and a delight to the eyes, and that the tree was desirable as a source of wisdom, she took of its fruit and ate. She also gave some to her husband, and he ate. Then the eyes of both of them were opened and they perceived that they were naked; and they sewed together fig leaves and made themselves loincloths.
>
> They heard the sound of the Eternal God moving about in the garden at the breezy time of day; and the Human and his wife hid from the Eternal God among the trees of the garden. The Eternal God called out to the Human and said to him, "Where are you?" He replied, "I heard the sound of You in the garden, and I was afraid because I was naked, so I hid."
>
> "Who told you that you were naked? Did you eat of the tree from which I had forbidden you to eat?"
>
> The Human said, "The woman You put at my side—she gave me of the tree, and I ate."

And the Eternal God said to the woman, "What is this you have done!" The woman replied, "The serpent duped me, and I ate."

Then the Eternal God said to the serpent,

> "Because you did this,
> More cursed shall you be
> Than all cattle
> And all the wild beasts:
> On your belly shall you crawl
> And dirt shall you eat
> All the days of your life.
> I will put enmity
> Between you and the woman,
> And between your offspring and hers;
> They shall strike at your head,
> And you shall strike at their heel."

And to the woman [God] said,

> "I will greatly expand
> Your hard labor—and your pregnancies;
> In hardship shall you bear children.
> Yet your urge shall be for your husband,
> And he shall rule over you."

To Adam [God] said, "Because you did as your wife said and ate of the tree about which I commanded you, 'You shall not eat of it,'

> "Cursed be the ground because of you;
> By hard labor shall you eat of it
> All the days of your life:
> Thorns and thistles shall it sprout for you.
> But your food shall be the grasses of the field;
> By the sweat of your brow
> Shall you get bread to eat,
> Until you return to the ground—

For from it you were taken.
For dust you are,
And to dust you shall return."

The Human named his wife Eve, because she was the mother of all the living. And the Eternal God made garments of skins for Adam and his wife, and clothed them.

And the Eternal God said, "Now that humankind has become like any of us, knowing good and bad, what if one should stretch out a hand and take also from the tree of life and eat, and live forever!" So the Eternal God banished them from the garden of Eden, to till the humus from which they were taken: humankind was driven out; and east of the garden of Eden were stationed the cherubim and the fiery ever-turning sword, to guard the way to the tree of life.

Exile as Deprivation

Moses ben Maimon (Maimonides) is certainly one of the best-known Jews of the Middle Ages. Throughout his life he lived in an Islamic environment, first in Spain, then in Morocco, and finally flourishing in Egypt. He combined thorough knowledge of biblical and rabbinic texts with a powerful commitment to philosophy, which entered Jewish thought through the influence of Islamic thinkers. His *Guide of* (or *for*) *the Perplexed*, probably the most influential work of Jewish philosophy, was written in Arabic, but was soon translated into Hebrew and many other languages. The following passage sets the background for the expulsion from Eden, with all its painful ramifications.

> MOSES MAIMONIDES, *GUIDE OF THE PERPLEXED* (CA. 1190)
>
> Adam, as he altered his intention and directed his thoughts to the acquisition of what he was forbidden, was banished from Paradise; this was his punishment, it was measure for measure. At first he had the privilege of tasting pleasure and happiness, and of enjoying repose and security. But as his appetite grew stronger, and he followed his desires and impulses, and partook of the food he was forbidden to taste, he was deprived of everything, was doomed to subsist on the

meanest kind of food, such as he never tasted before, and this only after exertion and labor, as it is said, "Thorns and thistles shall grow up for thee" (Gen. 3:18), "By the sweat of thy brow" (Gen. 3:9), etc., and in explanation of this the text continues, "And the Lord God drove him from the Garden of Eden, to till the ground whence he was taken" (Gen. 3:23). He was now with respect to food and many other requirements brought to the level of the lower animals: "Thou shalt eat the grass of the field" (Gen. 3:18). Reflecting on his condition, the Psalmist says, "Man, unable to dwell in dignity, was brought to the level of the dumb beast" (Ps. 49:13).

May the Almighty be praised, whose design and wisdom cannot be fathomed.[4]

Pain of Exile

Don Isaac Abravanel was one of the most luminous personalities in postbiblical Jewish history. He combined significant political service as a courtier in Portugal, Spain, and Naples with the writing of a small library of books that would have been impressive for a scholar who had no responsibilities other than research and writing.

His commentaries on the Torah, early and later Prophets, and Daniel are so extensive that only relatively brief portions have been translated into English. They provide not only detailed analysis of linguistic elements of the biblical texts but also extensive discussion of conceptual problems that the texts raise. In many cases Abravanel will provide a survey of all the solutions to such problems that have been proposed by earlier commentators before proposing his own solution. These extensive commentaries epitomize the culture of Spanish Jewry that had just reached its catastrophic end and was entering new geographical and cultural environments.

The following passage connects the well-known narrative of the expulsion of Adam and Eve from the Garden of Eden with subsequent Jewish life. Exile was not a onetime event at the beginning of human life; it is characteristic of Jewish historical experience. Some of the examples were in the distant past at the time when Abravanel was writing. But the angels that stood guard to prevent an inappropriate focus on the tree of life reflect the experience of Abravanel himself, along with many other Jews who encountered exile—from Portugal, from Spain, and from Naples—at a time when the Holy Land was not yet ready for a significant Jewish migration.

> DON ISAAC ABRAVANEL, *PERUSH ʿAL HA-TORAH* ON GENESIS 3 (LATE 15TH CENTURY)
>
> Just as the serpent enticed the woman, and she in turn enticed her husband, so the Canaanites living in the land, who were not expelled by the Israelites, incited them to idolatrous worship. And just as Adam and Eve heard the voice of God moving about in the garden, and they hid, and God chastised them because of their sin, so Israel heard the voice of God through the prophets while they were still in the garden of the Holy Land, and they hid and deceived themselves, so God rebuked them many times for their sins. And just as the snake was the first to be cursed, "On your belly you shall crawl, and you shall eat dirt all the days of your life" (Gen. 3:14), so the Canaanites were the first to be expelled from the land, cursed by the other nations, crawling on their bellies outside their land, eating dust because of their poverty, with continuous enmity between them and the People of Israel.
>
> Just as the woman was cursed with painful toil, so the daughters of Israel are cursed with the pain and anxiety of exile, as Isaiah and Amos and the other prophets warned. And just as Adam was condemned, "Cursed be the ground because of you" (Gen. 3:17), so with the curse of Israel, their land was also cursed, with thorns and thistles sprouting (3:18). And just as at the end of the curse upon Adam, it says, "Until you return to the ground, for from it you were taken" (3:19), so at the end of the curses, it is said, "The Lord will send you back to Egypt" (Deut. 28:68), for the people have returned to their exile from which they were liberated. And just as God sent Adam away from the Garden of Eden because of his sin, and expelled him from it, so God sent away and expelled Israel from their land, as said by R. Yose bar Hanina.

And just as "He placed east of the Garden of Eden the cherubim and the fiery ever-turning sword to guard the way to the tree of life" (Gen. 3:24), . . . so at the time of the destruction of Jerusalem the Divine Presence moved away from there, and the ark and the cherubim were hidden in order to guard the path to the tree of life, which means to hope that the Children of Israel will still return and seek the Lord their God, and the cherubim will return to their place, and the flame of the Divine Presence to its original status. This is an appropriate way of homiletically expressing in this story what occurred to Adam as a sign for Israel, his children.[5]

Exile Is a Kind of Dying

Amos Neufeld is a New York writer and journalist; his poems have appeared in several anthologies and Jewish journals. An earlier poem of his, "My Difficult Country," uses exile as a metaphor ("The climb, / like exile, / is always difficult"), suggesting the concept is one the poet continues to ponder. In the poem below Neufeld references both Orpheus—the Greek hero who visits the underworld to retrieve his wife but ultimately fails—and Eden, the paradise from which everyone is banished. Exile is a lonely state, a condition infused with loss, separation, and absence.

> AMOS NEUFELD, "EXILE" (1988)
>
> Exile is a kind of dying:
> one life spinning itself out alone.
> It is Orpheus descending into hell
> to emerge alone,
> knowing that he lives
> always apart—
> his world, known
> and lost.
> It is time and place
> echoing a world gone,
> dissonant sounds

forever seeking a lost chord,
questioning the fate that separates one.
Exile is life torn down
surviving as memory—stones and ruins
of an ancient city we would rebuild.
It is Eden
remembered freshly
in the difficult dark landscape after.[6]

2 Exile in Ancient History

The Jewish people have been significantly shaped by the biblical and early historical exiles rooted in their collective memory. The Egyptian, Babylonian, and Roman exiles were forced separations from the Land of Israel and—once built—from the Temple in Jerusalem. The biblical account of the exile from Egypt is central to the national narrative, the annual holiday cycle (see chapter 3), and the Jewish ethos through today: "for you were slaves in the Land of Egypt" (Deut. 15:15). The Babylonian and Roman exiles followed the destruction of the First and Second Temples respectively, sending away from their homeland a people whose religion, culture, and even peoplehood depended on the central location in Jerusalem. Yet instead of erasing the Jewish people, these experiences strengthened their ability to adapt and to endure.

The chapter begins with the biblical account of what the Israelites faced in Egypt, and an excerpt from an eighteenth-century sermon addressing the unique bitterness of Egyptian persecution. The Bible provides two more excerpts, chronicling the exile at the hands of the Babylonians and the lyrical response of the Psalmist. From there we turn to a Rabbinic elaboration of the exile, an aggadic exploration of Psalm 137 ("By the rivers of Babylon . . ."), and excerpts from an early twentieth-century sermon that present a positive and resonant perspective on the Babylonian exile. Three works by the celebrated Israeli poets Lea Goldberg, Amir Gilboa, and Yehuda Amichai offer updated interpretations of Psalm 137.

Unlike the Egyptian and Babylonian exiles, the Roman exile scattered the Jews. The Rabbinic legends (*aggadot*) of the oral tradition reveal different responses to the tragic event. In the texts that follow we see responses from a fourteenth-century forced convert, an adviser to the court of Queen Isabel and King Ferdinand, a fifteenth-century liturgical poet, a mid-nineteenth-century rabbi, and a comparison of exiles. This last text, from a commentary on the book of Esther, leads into the following chapter, which looks at several ways in which exile has shaped the Jewish calendar and finds expression in the holidays.

Egypt

The biblical verses below present an amazingly rapid historical transformation. Up until this point, the Israelites are depicted as living comfortably under Egyptian rulers who appreciated the royal service of Joseph. Even after Joseph's death, the Israelites are living comfortably, and their population is increasing. Then a new king suddenly characterizes the Israelites as potential dangers and ruthlessly undermines their status, turning them into forced laborers. It is the beginning of a process in which the Israelites come to feel they are living in exile, and need to escape and return to their homeland.

> EXODUS 1:8–14
>
> A new king arose over Egypt who did not know Joseph. And he said to his people, "Look, the Israelite people are much too numerous for us. Let us deal shrewdly with them, so that they may not increase; otherwise in the event of war they may join our enemies in fighting against us and rise from the ground." So they set taskmasters over them to oppress them with forced labor; and they built garrison cities for Pharaoh: Pithom and Raamses. But the more they were oppressed, the more they increased and spread out, so that the [Egyptians] came to dread the Israelites.
>
> The Egyptians ruthlessly imposed upon the Israelites the various labors that they made them perform. Ruthlessly they made life bitter for them with harsh labor at mortar and bricks and with all sorts of tasks in the field.[1]

EXILE IN ANCIENT HISTORY

Exile in Egypt versus Persia

Eighteenth-century Prague was facing the pressures of powerful forces that were just beginning to transform European Jewish society. The Enlightenment movement, the shift toward manufacturing and growing prosperity, colonial expansionism and burgeoning nationalism, the spread of print culture and the rise of the intellectual salon across the continent generally improved the status of Jews as individuals and communities. In Prague the Austrian emperor Joseph II's Toleranzpatent (Edict of Tolerance) seemed to presage a new relationship between Jews, their gentile neighbors, and the state.

At the time the scholar and halakhic authority Ezekiel Landau held one of the prestigious rabbinical posts in Europe—chief rabbi of Prague—and thus the then-ruling Austrian government recognized him as the supreme rabbinical authority in Bohemia. His sermon, delivered on the Sabbath preceding Passover, 1782, reveals the preacher reacting to the Austrian emperor's Edict of Tolerance. The recognition that despite the Jews' horrifying experience under Pharaoh in Egypt, the Bible shows that certain kings (in Persia) did treat the Jews kindly leads to an explicit reference to Joseph II in their own time. His policy toward the Jews is markedly better than that of his mother, Queen Maria Theresa, who expelled the Jews in 1744. As Landau's full text explains: "Now, too, we are in exile, outside our land. . . . It is their own land, while we are only guests. . . . It is enough that His Majesty the emperor has extended his protection over us, so that no one will use force to harm or degrade us. . . . Even if there should be a gracious and compassionate king who abundantly helps us, we should inwardly know that we are in a land not our own, and that we should remain submissive to the peoples of that land."[2]

What a revealing message from the chief rabbi of Prague: be grateful for His Majesty, the emperor, and do not forget that we are only guests.

EZEKIEL LANDAU, "EXILE IN EGYPT
VERSUS EXILE IN PERSIA" (1782)

Pharaoh was by nature an evil king, a cruel man, filled with hate for those who found refuge in his realm. His intention in subjugating the people of Israel was not to improve his own lot, but rather to degrade the Israelites, to cause them sorrow and to embitter their lives. This is what the Bible says: The Egyptians *embittered their lives . . . with all the work that they ruthlessly imposed upon them* (Exod. 1:14). In addition to the taxes and the forced labor, the Israelites were debased and humiliated in Egyptian eyes. Even the servants of Pharaoh lorded it over Israel. This is what Rashi wrote on the verse, *[and every first-born in the land of Egypt shall die, from the first-born of Pharaoh who sits on his throne] to the first-born of the slave girl* (Exod. 11:5): "Why were the slave girls stricken? Because even they made Israel subservient."

That bitter Egyptian exile was unlike the experience in Persia. Although we were in exile there, we were considered important and respected. Cyrus and Darius were compassionate and merciful toward us. This is also the case in our own time, when our Lord His Majesty the emperor has decided to help us and to raise us from our degradation. May God reward him for his good deed and raise his glory ever higher![3]

Babylonia

The recounting of the exile of kings from the second book of Kings (*Sefer Melakhim*) is an extraordinary account of terrifying and disastrous events. In a few verses we learn about Jehoiachin, who becomes king when he is eighteen and reigns for only three months, while the Babylonians besiege Jerusalem, until he surrenders to King Nebuchadnezzar. The result is catastrophic: "all of Jerusalem" are deported to Babylon "in exile [*golah*]," along with the royal family. Only the poorest people in the land remain (24:16).

The Babylonian king appoints Jehoiachin's uncle, Zedekiah, to succeed him. We learn nothing about him until he rebels in the ninth year of his reign, leading a revolt that lasts for a year and a half, until famine devastates the rebels and the Babylonians prevail.

Brought to Babylonia, Zedekiah is humiliated and imprisoned. The conquerors have destroyed every building of significance in Jerusalem and appropriated everything of value. "Thus Judah was exiled from its land" (25:22).

The second book of Kings ends with a new Babylonian king who does not permit the Jews to return to their home, but who apparently shows pity for the blind, imprisoned King Yehoiachin, allowing him to remove his prison garments and receive proper food for the rest of his life. Thus, the book's ending does not offer any explicit hope for the Jews' return to their homeland. And yet, the conclusion of this large section of the Hebrew Bible—placed centrally between the books of the early Prophets and the later Prophets—does provide hope for a peaceful life in exile.

2 KINGS 24:8–25:21

Jehoiachin was eighteen years old when he became king, and he reigned three months in Jerusalem; his mother's name was Nehushta daughter of Elnathan of Jerusalem. He did what was displeasing to God, just as his father had done. At that time, the troops of King Nebuchadnezzar of Babylon marched against Jerusalem, and the city came under siege. King Nebuchadnezzar of Babylon advanced against the city while his troops were besieging it. Thereupon King Jehoiachin of Judah, along with his mother, and his courtiers, commanders, and officers, surrendered to the king of Babylon. The king of Babylon took him captive in the eighth year of his reign. He carried off from Jerusalem all the treasures of the House of God and the treasures of the royal palace; he stripped off all the golden decorations in the Temple of God—which King Solomon of Israel had made—as God had warned. He exiled all of Jerusalem: all the commanders and all the warriors—ten thousand exiles—as well as all the artisans and smiths; only the poorest people in the land were left. He deported Jehoiachin to Babylon; and the king's mother and wives and officers and the notables of the land were brought as exiles from Jerusalem to Babylon. All the able men, to the number of seven thousand—all of them warriors, trained for battle—and a thousand artisans and smiths were brought to Babylon as exiles by the king of Babylon. And the king of Babylon appointed Mattaniah, Jehoiachin's uncle, king in his place, changing his name to Zedekiah.

Zedekiah was twenty-one years old when he became king, and he reigned eleven years in Jerusalem; his mother's name was Hamutal daughter of Jeremiah of Libnah. He did what was displeasing to God, just as Jehoiakim had done. Indeed, Jerusalem and Judah were a cause of anger for God, so that they were cast out of the divine presence.

Zedekiah rebelled against the king of Babylon.

And in the ninth year of his reign, on the tenth day of the tenth month, Nebuchadnezzar moved against Jerusalem with his whole army. He besieged it; and they built towers against it all around. The city continued in a state of siege until the eleventh year of King Zedekiah. By the ninth day [of the fourth month] the famine had become acute in the city; there was no food left for the common people.

Then [the wall of] the city was breached. All the soldiers [left the city] by night through the gate between the double walls, which is near the king's garden—the Chaldeans were all around the city; and [the king] set out for the Arabah. But the Chaldean troops pursued the king, and they overtook him in the steppes of Jericho as his entire force left him and scattered. They captured the king and brought him before the king of Babylon at Riblah; and they put him on trial. They slaughtered Zedekiah's sons before his eyes; then Zedekiah's eyes were put out. He was chained in bronze fetters and he was brought to Babylon.

On the seventh day of the fifth month—that was the nineteenth year of King Nebuchadnezzar of Babylon—Nebuzaradan, the chief of the guards, an officer of the king of Babylon, came to Jerusalem. He burned the House of God, the king's palace, and all the houses of Jerusalem; he burned down the house of every notable person. The entire Chaldean force that was with the chief of the guard tore down the walls of Jerusalem on every side. The remnant of the people that was left in the city, the defectors who had gone over to the king of Babylon—and the remnant of the population—were taken into exile by Nebuzaradan, the chief of the guards. But some of the poorest in the land were left by the chief of the guards, to be vinedressers and field hands.

The Chaldeans broke up the bronze columns of the House of God, the stands, and the bronze tank that was in the House of God; and they carried the bronze away to Babylon. They also took all the pails, scrapers, snuffers, ladles, and all the other bronze vessels used in the service. The chief of the guards took whatever was of gold and whatever was of silver: firepans and sprinkling bowls. The two columns, the one tank, and the stands that Solomon provided for the House of God—all these objects contained bronze beyond weighing. The one column was eighteen cubits high. It had a bronze capital above it; the height of the capital was three cubits, and there was a meshwork [decorated] with pomegranates about the capital, all made of bronze. And the like was true of the other column with its meshwork.

The chief of the guards also took Seraiah, the chief priest, Zephaniah, the deputy priest, and the three guardians of the threshold. And from the city he took a eunuch who was in command of the soldiers; five of the royal privy councillors who were present in the city; the scribe of the army commander, who was in charge of mustering the people of the land; and sixty of the common people who were inside the city. Nebuzaradan, the chief of the guards, took them and brought them to the king of Babylon at Riblah. The king of Babylon had them struck down and put to death at Riblah, in the region of Hamath.[4]

A Communal Lament of a People in Exile

Composed in the voice of those exiled from the Kingdom of Judah early in the sixth century BCE, Psalm 137 ("By the rivers of Babylon..."), a communal lament of a people in exile, asks, how can the people of Judah sing songs of Zion when they no longer live there? That is, how can they continue to worship God and celebrate who they are when they are so far from the home that defines them?

Recited on Tisha b'Av (the fast day commemorating the destruction of the Temple) and before the Grace after Meals on weekdays, Psalm 137 has been further immortalized in classical, pop, and reggae music, as well as in the short story "By the Waters of Babylon" by Stephen Vincent Benet. The rivers are the Tigris and the Euphrates, the defining waterways of present-day Iraq.

The often-forgotten last stanza is one of the most perplexing and disturbing passages in the Bible. Answering the sorrow of the beginning, the psalm concludes with the wish for raw vengeance against the exiles' former neighbors as well as their present captors, depicted with horrific, unsettling images of murdered infants and happy avengers.

PSALM 137

> By the rivers of Babylon,
> there we sat,
> sat and wept,
> as we thought of Zion.
> There on the poplars
> we hung up our lyres,
> for our captors asked us there for songs,
> our tormentors, for amusement,
> "Sing us one of the songs of Zion."
> How can we sing a song of the Lord
> on alien soil?
> If I forget you, O Jerusalem,
> let my right hand wither;
> let my tongue stick to my palate
> if I cease to think of you,
> if I do not keep Jerusalem in memory
> even at my happiest hour.

> Remember, O Lord, against the Edomites
> the day of Jerusalem's fall;
> how they cried, "Strip her, strip her
> to her very foundations!"
> Fair Babylon, you predator,
> a blessing on him who repays you in kind
> what you have inflicted on us;
> a blessing on him who seizes your babies
> and dashes them against the rocks!

The Rabbis' Addition to the Biblical Account

The Rabbis' additions to the biblical account of Babylonian exile appear in various compilations of the Talmud, among them the following selection, from the Tanḥuma collection of legends (named after the first Rabbi referenced) commenting on the weekly portion Yitro. Here the Ishmaelite captors are understood as kinsmen, descendants of Abraham's firstborn son Ishmael who have played an important role in the life of Joseph (see Gen. 37:25–28, 38:1). The Jews, having felt close to the Ishmaelites, assume that the captors will take pity on their humiliated kinsmen and at least provide them with something to eat and drink—but the Ishmaelites make things even worse.

The use of the term Ishmaelites to apply to Muslims comes much later, and was probably not intended this way. The idea seems simply to be that in times of war, you cannot rely even on relatives who seem to be friendly.

> *TANḤUMA*, YITRO 5 (8TH–9TH CENTURY)
>
> *I called upon those who were supposed to love me, but they deceived me* (Lam. 1:19). R. Joshua ben Levi said: When the wicked Nebuchadnezzar exiled the children of Israel to Babylon their hands were tied behind their backs, they were chained together with iron shackles, and led naked like beasts. They asked those in charge of them, "Show us compassion and pity, and take us by way of our kinsmen, the children of Ishmael." This they did. The children of Ishmael came out to

them with salted bread and broth. They also brought empty hides stained with water and hung these at the entrances of their tents. When the Israelites saw this, their minds rested, for they thought the hides were filled with water. [The Ishmaelites] said, "First eat some bread, and then we will bring you water." After the Israelites had eaten the bread, [the Ishmaelites] came and said, "We could not find any water." The Israelites tore the hides with their teeth, and died from the rush of hot air filling their insides.[5]

Imagining the Exiler

Sometimes the Rabbis wrote startling narrative. In the following passages, two biblical verses from Psalms (137:1 and 4) and one verse from Deutero-Isaiah (43:14) become the basis for powerful and painful imagination. In *Yalkut Shimoni* (a later compilation—eleventh-century or after—of older interpretations of biblical passages) the image of the Babylonian king Nebuchadnezzar traveling back to Babylon by ship with an orchestra while large numbers of captive Jews are forced to walk in a humiliating manner, "naked along the edge of the river," reveals the outlook of Jews living during the Crusader period, many of whom had been forced to leave their homes in the Holy Land. The idea in *Pesikta Rabbati* (an earlier, 845 CE compilation of similar rabbinic commentaries) that Nebuchadnezzar, about to leave the Holy Land for home, is now afraid that the Jews will repent and God will put him to death is of course fantasy. And, similarly, the claim that upon reaching Babylonian territory, Nebuchadnezzar asks the Levites to play their harps as they did in the Temple, and the Levites respond by mangling their own hands (or, in some accounts, tongues) so they are unable to play an instrument or even sing a song, reveals the impressively painful imagination of later Jewish writers.

> ### PESIKTA RABBATI 31:4 (CA. 845 CE)
> When Nebuchadnezzar came and burned the Temple and exiled Israel, taking them captive, he allowed no rest stops throughout all the Land of Israel, for they were pursued. As it is said, *To our necks*

we are pursued (Lam. 5:5). Why did they pursue them? They feared for their own lives, saying, "The God of this nation expects them to repent. They may repent while still in their own Land, and [their God] will then do to us as He did to Sennacherib."[6] Thus they did not allow any rest in all the Land of Israel. Only when they came to the rivers of Babylon, [and the Babylonians] saw [the Israelites] in their hands in their land, they allowed a stop. [The Babylonians] turned to eating and drinking; [the Israelites] turned to weeping and mourning.

Nebuchadnezzar asked, "Why are you sitting weeping?" And he called to the tribe of Levi and said to them, "Prepare yourselves! While we eat and drink, I want you to stand and play your harps before me as you played them in your Temple before your God." [The Levites] looked at each another and said, "Is it not enough that we destroyed His Temple with our sins? Must we now play our harps for this dwarf?"[7] They all stood up, hung their harps upon the willows by the river, and then, with great dignity, put their thumbs in their mouths and bit them off.

David elucidates saying: *"How shall we sing the Lord's song?"* (Ps. 137:4). They did not say, "We shall not sing," but "How shall we sing?," showing [the Babylonians] their hands and said, "You know the iron shackles were tight around our hands and cut our fingers. Look! How shall we sing?"[8]

YALKUT SHIMONI, PSALMS, REMEZ (SECTION) 883, NO. 16 ON PS. 137 (11TH–14TH CENTURY)

By the rivers of Babylon, there we sat, sat and wept (Ps. 137:1). What made Israel sit and weep by the rivers of Babylon? R. Yohanan explained: It was the Euphrates, which killed more of them than had the wicked Nebuchadnezzar. While they lived in the Land of Israel, they drank only rainwater, running water, or spring water. But when they were exiled to Babylon, they drank water from the Euphrates, and died. So the exiles wept—for those killed by their enemies, those who died on the way, and those killed by the Euphrates water.

Not only that but Nebuchadnezzar sat in a ship—he and his nobles and his officers. They had all kinds of [musical] instruments, as is said, *The Chaldeans, in the ships of their singing* (Isa. 43:14). At the same time, all the members of the royal house of Judah were walking naked and shackled along the river's edge. The wicked Nebuchadnezzar looked up and saw them. He said to his servants, "Why are they walking with such bearing and without burdens? Have you no burdens to load on their necks?" Instantly the servants brought Torah scrolls, made them into sacks that they filled with sand and loaded on their necks until they were bent over. They said of themselves, *To our very necks we are pursued* (Lam. 5:5). And in that hour all Israel were overcome with weeping until their cries reached the heavens.[9]

Singing in Exile

Israel Mattuck was born in Lithuania in 1883 and—like many other important American rabbis of the first half of the twentieth century—came to America with his family as a child. He studied Semitics at Harvard and was ordained at the Hebrew Union College in Cincinnati in 1910. The following June he was invited to apply to become the first ordained rabbi of the Liberal Jewish Synagogue in London; the following address was delivered at LJS in June 1911 as part of his interview. Beginning his new position in January 1912, he would go on to serve as the synagogue's rabbi for forty years.[10]

Starting with the theme of exile in Psalm 137, Mattuck emphasizes the transformation in Jewish life: at first, exile seems to make proper Jewish life impossible, but Babylonia eventually became a thriving center of Jewish life. He then applies these circumstances to present ones: the challenge of continuing to sing "the song of the Lord" despite the allurements of relative ease in early twentieth-century Europe. Of course the challenges Mattuck and his congregants faced would significantly intensify during the two world wars, but in 1911, the memory of exile seemed rather distant.

> ISRAEL MATTUCK, "HOW SHALL WE SING"
>
> A writer of Psalms has in the few words of the one hundred and thirty seventh psalm noted the feelings of the Jews exiled from their

native Palestine to the shores of the Euphrates. The disaster that had befallen their nation covered their lives with ashes as with a pall. The sun had vanished from their heavens and the stars had fallen from their firmament. And their souls poured out their bitterness in mournful strains. Joy was at an end—Cheer was gone—and their religion, they thought, had lost its life. Despairingly, imploringly they ask—"How shall we sing the song of the Lord on a foreign soil?" Little did they think of the great truth that was to be revealed to their descendants but a few decades later, the truth that is that which the Rabbis have put so happily—"In the days that the Temple was destroyed the messiah was born"—and their question of despair was later answered in Babylon by proclaiming their Judaism as a triumph.—The songs of the Lord *were* sung in a foreign land. And in Babylonia and out of Babylonia came a new Judaism, a strong Judaism, a hopeful Judaism, a universal Judaism.

The question of the first exiles is now being asked again—not in despair or grief, but in happiness and eagerness. The lands wherein we live are not foreign lands—none of them—and they are our fathers' lands. But they are not Judaea, they are not in the Orient [Babylonia]. Jews have travelled far from their original home—and wherever they have gone they have carried with them their Judaism. As the children of Israel in the wilderness carried the ark of the Lord in all their journeys, so in later years the Jews carried within their hearts tables of testimony. And our gratitude will never lessen to those who, despite oppressions and persecutions, who despite the allurements of ease and the siren call sent along, tenaciously clung to the father's faith and to us delivered the message of Judaism. It is now ours to keep and preserve. And so we ask again the question "How shall we sing the song of the Lord?"—but we ask it eagerly with our hopes in our harps attuned to the strains that will issue from the depths of our hearts. Upon our answer depends our Judaism and the Judaism of the future.[11]

Child's Play

Amir Gilboa (1917–84), né Berl Feldmann, was one of Israel's foremost poets. As in the poem below, his writing is replete with biblical allusions. It often plays with binary oppositions, combining the traditional with the contemporary, and the personal with the national.

"By the Waters of Babylon," originally published in 1953 in Hebrew, makes a direct reference to Psalm 137, but this time the voice is that of a child. The lyrical "I" distinguishes between the captives and captors, but within the former are the adults and the child/ren, while within the latter are those rejoicing over their victory with dancing, and the guards cruelly mocking their hostages.

Even while commemorating a tragic event, the boy finds a way to make music however briefly, and the text celebrates the language of the psalm and the poem: "There is no language like ours for color and sound, for depth and distance."

> AMIR GILBOA, "BY THE WATERS OF BABYLON" (1953)
>
> On the willows we hung our harps. I mean the grownups.
> As for me, I had a little harp and I hid it in under my cloak.
> On the far side of the river the victors lit fires and wild with joy
>   they reveled.
> Evening fell and fell. The grownups sat crying. A big fire over there.
>
> And the guards assigned to us, not taking part in the dancing,
> Reviling us with impatience, raucously,
> Aping our language in grotesque ways.
>
> The grownups listened, and looked at their harps. The waters
>   filled with tears.
> And I out of sorrow dared to cry: Who is grotesque here,[12]
> You wild beasts, and how can you mock us with gibberish?
> For there is no language like ours for color and sound, for
>   depth and distance.

> And they laughed louder, their mouths gaped at me.
> They began chasing me, getting entangled in darkness.
> I would stop to rest a brief moment briefly to pluck my harp,
> They would swell like sacks, glow like copper.[13]

Paradox

The poet, essayist, and translator Lea Goldberg (1911–70) wrote for adults and children. Born in Kovno, Lithuania, she moved in 1935 to Palestine, where she would come to found the Department of Comparative Literature at the Hebrew University of Jerusalem and become one of the foremost voices in modern Hebrew literature. Her poem "Night," the second of three included here referring to Psalm 137 and the first of four in her "Songs of Zion" cycle, asks a series of questions that gesture toward the complexity of the immigrant's relationship to Israel, and to the paradox of the feeling of *galut*, exile, in the land of Zion by aligning with the Babylonian captives.[14]

> LEA GOLDBERG, "NIGHT" (1955–56)
>
> Does a gold clapper move in the upper heavens?
> Does a droplet of dew drip onto the crown of the cypress?
> Sing to us from the songs of Zion!
> How can we sing a song of Zion in the land of Zion
> And we have not yet begun to hear?[15]
>
> > ©All rights to Lea Goldberg's poems reserved to Hakibbutz Hameuchad Publishers Ltd.

Forgetting and Remembering

Yehuda Amichai (1924–2000), né Ludwig Pfeuffer, was best known for his focus on the quotidian, his gentle irony and clever wordplay, as well as the originality of his images.

His poem (here in Aliza Auerbach's translation) begins from the medial verses of Psalm 137 traditionally recited by the bridegroom before breaking the glass during the wedding ceremony: to remember the loss of Jerusalem and the destruction of the Temple at even the happiest moment. Originally published in Hebrew in 1968, shortly after Israel's victory in the Six-Day War and the reunification of Jerusalem, the poem seems to temper the general jubilation with remembering earlier loss and envisaging future setbacks.

The first stanza slowly builds from the biblical verses that are repeated, countering the right hand with the left, forgetting with remembering, closing with opening. The communal exile is superseded by the speaker's personal feelings, and history by immediacy. Already unable to make music, the prisoners in the psalm are threatened by losing their abilities to create ("may my right hand lose its cunning") and to communicate ("may my tongue cleave to the roof of my mouth"); the poet's speaker is threatened by the loss of his memory ("I shall forget"), of his being remembered ("my blood be forgotten"), and most importantly, of his voice ("or silence").

YEHUDA AMICHAI, "IF I FORGET THEE, JERUSALEM" (1968)

Then let my right be forgotten.
Let my right be forgotten, and my left remember.
Let my left remember, and your right close
And your mouth open near the gate.
I shall remember Jerusalem
And forget the forest—my love will remember,
Will open her hair, will close my window,
will forget my right,
Will forget my left.
If the west wind does not come
I'll never forgive the walls,
Or the sea, or myself.
Should my right forget
My left shall forgive,
I shall forget all water,
I shall forget my mother.

> If I forget thee, Jerusalem,
> Let my blood be forgotten.
> I shall touch your forehead,
> Forget my own,
> My voice change
> For the second and last time
> To the most terrible of voices—
> Or silence.[16]

Rome and the Long Exile

A number of early midrashim—talmudic stories—compare the different exiles of the Jewish people. The first such passage here, from *Yalkut Shimoni*, is rather straightforward: unlike the Babylonian exile, in which all of the exiled Jews were brought to a relatively small region to the east, the current exile (beginning with the destruction of the Second Temple in 70 CE) meant that Jews were being scattered, like the exiles of the Northern Kingdom who were dispersed throughout the Assyrian Empire. This was frightening, but clearly understandable.

The second paragraph, also from *Yalkut Shimoni* but here presented in a nineteenth-century translation by Edward G. King, reviews the past and current history of Jewish exile, as divided into four kingdoms: Babylon, Persia, Greece, and Rome. In each kingdom, the text informs us, Jews experienced a different mode of humiliation—an idea grounded in the prophet Zechariah's vision of four horses, each of a different color. In the biblical text, the four kingdoms are all present at the same time; the Rabbinic text applies them to four different periods of exile.

The third excerpt is taken from *Shir ha-Shirim Rabbah*, a seventh- to-eighth-century midrashic compilation that provides verse-by-verse commentary on the Song of Songs. Reviewing the different exiles of the Jewish people, the text points out that despite the Jews' suffering under foreign empires, in each case they could return to a normal life under their own government—except in the case of the latest exile, which seems different in that it is lasting indefinitely. This reflects historical reality: the exile imposed by Roman rule did last longer than any of the preceding exiles named (although not longer than the exile of the Northern Kingdom).

The fourth passage from *Eikhah Rabbah* (also known as *Midrash Kinnot*, a commentary on the book of Lamentations dated to 500 CE) is perhaps the most interesting in that it moves the furthest away from any biblical basis. A single verse from Psalms 69:13, which in context appears to be the complaint of one suffering individual, is expanded and transformed into the situation of the Jewish nation, suffering not so much because of overt oppression, but because of the strangely imagined mockery of their captors. It is as if the Romans have nothing better to do than to make fun of the Jews and their customs, even if it means bringing a camel into their theaters (!).

YALKUT SHIMONI (CA. 13TH CENTURY)

"And you I will scatter among the nations" (Lev. 26:33). This is an especially harsh measure against Israel. When a people from one place are banished together, they see each other, and thus find comfort. Here it is said, "And I will scatter you among the nations"—I will disperse you among the world's nations so that not one of you is near another, as it is said, "I will scatter you among the nations and disperse you through the lands" (Ezek. 23:15). As it is said, "I will scatter them with a pitchfork through the gates of the earth" (Jer. 15:7), the way a man does who scatters barley with a pitchfork, so that one [grain] will not stick to another. . . .[17]

"And I lifted my eyes, and I saw, and lo four chariots" (Zech. 6:1)—these are the four kingdoms: "*Red horses*" (Zech. 6:2)—This is the kingdom of Babylon, which shed much blood of Israel. "You are the head of Gold" (Dan. 2:38) "*Black horses*"—This is the kingdom of *Persia and Media*;—"The second is like to a bear" (Dan. 7:5) since they *darkened* the face of Israel by the decrees of Haman. "*White horses*"—This is the kingdom of *Greece*, since they *made white* the face of Israel with the reproaches and blasphemies. "*Horses spotted and powerful*"—This is the fourth kingdom [Rome]; since they decreed decrees *of ever so many* colours, different from one another.[18]

SHIR HA-SHIRIM RABBAH (CA. 7TH–8TH CENTURY)

"At nights on my bed" (Song 3:1). The congregation of Israel said to the Holy One: "Master of the universe, in the past You gave me light between one night and another—between the night of Egypt and the night of Babylon, between the night of Babylon and the night of Media, between the night of Media and the night of Greece, and between the night of Greece and the night of Edom. But now night follows night!"[19]

EIKHAH RABBAH (CA. 500 CE)

"I have become a laughingstock to all my people" (Lam. 3:14). R. Abbahu opened, "Those sitting by the gate discuss me" (Ps. 69:13), "those" being the nations of the world who sit in theaters and circuses. "And [I am] the song of the drunks" (ibid.)—after they eat and drink and get drunk, they would sit and discuss me and mock me, saying, "We do not need carobs like the Jews." Again they say to each other, "How many years do you wish to live?" "Like the Sabbath robes of the Jews." Then they bring a camel into their theaters, with his robes on him, and say to each other, "Why is he mourning?" "These Jews are observing the shmitta, and since they have no greens, they ate his thorns—and so he mourns."

They bring a mime into their theaters, his head shaven, and ask each other, "Why is his head shaven?" and they say, "Those Jews observe their Sabbath, and all that they work for they eat on the Sabbath; If they don't have wood, they break up their [wooden] beds and cook with them. Then they have to sleep on the ground, and get covered in dust, and [need to] anoint themselves with oil, [using so much] that oil becomes expensive."[20]

Still Jewish

Profiet Duran is a stirring example of a Jew whom the Church considered to have converted to Christianity and who apparently followed the necessary Christian practices in public, but who continued to think of himself as a Jew and was able to write powerful Jewish texts in Hebrew.

Born in Catalan, Duran studied Talmud in a traditional school in Germany and philosophy outside of it. He officially converted to Christianity, appearing in the Church's records as Honoratus de Bonafide, during the anti-Jewish riots that swept through the Iberian Peninsula in 1391. For Iberian Jews who were spared, a critical issue was how to relate to those who had accepted baptism in order to save their lives. Christian doctrine considered baptism to be permanent, and expected all baptized Jews to observe Christian doctrines and traditions. Jews who did convert against their will, such as Duran, lived a liminal existence, facing suspicion from both Christians and Jews. Duran reportedly returned to Jewish practice after fleeing Spain, and wrote polemics against Christianity.

Obviously none of Duran's texts were published during his lifetime, but among the texts that have been preserved are *Al Tehi ka-Aboteka* (Be not like thy fathers), with an ironic title (1396); *K'limat ha-Goyim* (Shame of the gentiles), an openly anti-Christian polemic (1397); and *Ma'aseh Ephod* (The making of the ephod), finished in 1403, from which the current passage and his sobriquet are taken.

> PROFIET DURAN (THE EPHODI), "EPISTLE OF
> LAMENTATION, GRIEF AND CONSOLATION" (1393)
>
> I say that this [statement in B. T. *Menaḥot* 53b] alludes to that part of the seed of Abraham who were forced publicly to deny their faith, upon whom the decree of apostasy fell in this great region. . . .[21] Some of them have been lax with regard to repentance. . . . It is therefore thought that this group has left the category of the Jewish people, which God has chosen as His legacy. . . . The answer that comes . . . means that the salvation and redemption that we await encompass the seed of Abraham, both those upon whom the decree of apostasy has fallen, who were "broken, trapped, and taken captive" (Isa. 8:15) and those "who subscribe by hand to the Lord, and are called by the name of Israel" (Isa. 44:5).[22]
>
> This matter in the present exile is just like that in previous ones. In the Egyptian exile, the people stumbled in idolatry, willingly . . . ,

yet this did not remove them from the category of the seed of Abraham. In the Babylonian exile, all of them stumbled in idolatry under duress except for a few individuals such as Hananiah and his companions, yet this did not remove them from the category of the seed of Abraham; no, in love and compassion God redeemed them. So it should be in this great exile of the present: if a part of the people has stumbled in a similar manner under absolute duress,[23] because of fear for their lives, this has not removed them from the category of God's people and the seed of Abraham who loved Him [see Isa. 41:8], for God knows the secrets of their hearts, and He will redeem them with the rest of their brothers.[24]

Bitter Exile

Judah ben David ibn Yahya was a communal leader of Spanish Jewry whose family suffered from the spiritual upheavals of the first third of the fifteenth century, including waves of conversions in the wake of compulsory public disputations and popular evangelical preaching. He composed many liturgical poems that have survived in manuscript.

The technical genre of the following poem, "Me'orah" (Light), serves to introduce a liturgical passage praising God as the "Creator of Light." But the refrain poignantly contrasts the darkness of contemporary Jewish experience with the Creator, who seems quite distant and beyond hearing the exiles' bitter cries. Even the heavenly bodies God created plead with God to act—apparently they have no astrological power of their own to determine the Jewish people's fate as they do with the gentiles[25]— but in vain. The poet emphasizes the length of the exile—1,360 years, apparently dating from the destruction of the Temple, during which God has allowed the Jews to suffer, and indeed helped their enemies—in juxtaposition with the even longer period when Christian sanctuaries appear to have been under divine protection.

Immediately following the supplication in the fifth strophe or verse, the sixth strophe reaffirms traditional Jewish beliefs about the Messiah and the future restoration of the Jewish people to its former greatness. One would expect the poem to conclude with this affirmation, but instead, the final two stanzas return to the scandal of the present when, as stated earlier, "we are in exile, and there are no redeemers." Rhetorical questions, introduced by a fourfold recurrence of the word *eichah* ("How?," the opening word of the book of Lamentations), express confusion and consternation over the incompatibility of the suffering and humiliation of the Jewish people in exile and God's justice and power. In these questions, the contempt for Jews in the minds of their "enemies" (a word appearing three times in the short poem) is paramount. Jews are called "a defiling and unclean people"—the antithesis of the Jewish aspiration to be a "holy people" (Exod. 19:6). As a result, God's Torah is "turned into mockery," as Christians deride the humiliated Jews who continue to observe it without any vindication from God. The final question appears to repudiate the Christian belief in the advent of a redeemer as incompatible with the ongoing suffering of the Jews, yet the literary form leaves the poet in a stance of anguished and discouraged amazement.

JUDAH BEN DAVID IBN YAHYA, "ME'ORAH" (CA. 1428)

Bitterly do the people of exiles cry
to Him who made great lights (Ps. 136:7).

Judah with all my people,
weep my day and my night,[26]
because God supports my foe,
and my community is in the hands of conspirators
bitterly do the people of exiles cry
to Him who made great lights.

O, this exile has taken so long,
the summer is over, the harvest is gone,[27]
already for 1360 years
we are in exile and there are no redeemers,[28]
bitterly do the people of exiles cry
to Him who made great lights.

My sanctuary has been destroyed twice,
two times, yes, two!
Yet, the numerous houses of my enemy
have been rescued in 1390 years,[29]
bitterly do the people of exiles cry
to Him who made great lights.

High heavens and signs of the zodiac,
stars, constellations and hosts,
plead with loud voices,
that He may rescue His circumcised people,
bitterly do the people of exiles cry
to Him who made great lights.

My people Judah and its tribes
suffer from the yoke and punishments of the enemy,
return it to His places of refuge.
O Lord, living God, who heals the sick,
bitterly do the people of exiles cry
to Him who made great lights.

The son of David will revive the people who hope for him,
he will teach them to return from their sins,
he will redeem them from amidst their enemies,
he will build the sanctuary in greatness,
bitterly do the people of exiles cry
to Him who made great lights.

How can God stand this and how
is the crown of His people trodden!
Amidst the people it is said that
the Torah of Sinai has turned into mockery,
bitterly do the people of exiles cry
to Him who made great lights.

How can people who believe in God
be called a defiling and unclean people?

> How can they say that a redeemer has come,
> and that he left the sanctuary in waste,
> *bitterly do the people of exiles cry*
> *to Him who made great lights.*[30]

Neither Peace nor Respite

Don Isaac Abravanel's life vividly reflects the paradoxes and tensions of the Jewish experience in exile. He held high-level positions as financial and political adviser in the courts of three different realms: Alfonso V of Portugal, the "Catholic monarchs" Ferdinand and Isabella of Aragon and Castile, and Ferrante I and Ferrante II of Naples. In these capacities he attained considerable personal wealth and power. He also represented, in an informal manner, the interests of the Jewish inhabitants of the realms to the respective Crowns. Yet his life was interrupted by dramatic reversals, including three instances of devastating personal exile: from his native land of Portugal in 1483 because of political upheavals; from Spain together with all his coreligionists in the expulsion of 1492; and from Naples, together with the king and the royal entourage in the wake of a French invasion in 1495, which resulted in the destruction of much of his personal library, including the unique manuscript of another of his books.

Undoubtedly one of the cruelest disappointments of his life was his failure, working in tandem with other Jewish and sympathetic Christian courtiers, to effectuate a reversal of the royal decision to expel the Spanish Jews from the territories of the Crown. He expresses his ambivalent evaluation of the years of royal service in the introduction to his commentary on the biblical books of 1 and 2 Kings, written in Naples:

> When I wanted to begin my commentary on the Book of Kings, I was summoned to come to the royal palace of the King of Spain, supreme among the world's monarchs, who rules over the kingdoms of Castile and Aragon and Catalonia and Sicily and various other islands. I then came to the court of the king and his consort and I

was close to them for an extended period.³¹ God gave me favor in their sight and in the sight of the leading ministers of the realm. I was engaged in their service for eight years. The wealth and honor that men attain for their living I acquired for myself in their courts and their palaces. Therefore the work of Torah diminished and came to an end. Because of my service of Gentile monarchs, not descended from Israel, I abandoned my estate, the realm of Judah and Israel and the exegesis of their history.³²

Yet despite the intense demands of royal service and the physical and psychological upheavals of his life, he succeeded in writing massive commentaries on most of the books of the Hebrew Bible and a variety of works in other genres, producing an oeuvre that would in its quantity daunt most scholars who had no other obligations than to study and write. His works may be seen as an encyclopedic summary of Jewish culture in Christian Spain.

The brief passages selected here express the attitudes of this cultural giant toward exile. The first text, from a letter to an Italian Jewish colleague, preceded the earliest major disruption of his life: when he was compelled to flee his native land. The second passage, from *Ma'yenei ha-Yeshu'ah* (The wells of salvation), a vast commentary on Daniel serving as the first work in a trilogy devoted to messianic themes, outlines three central deficiencies of exilic life, which also speak to the contemporary Jewish self-image. The third excerpt, from his commentary on the Passover Haggadah, looks back at the exile from Egypt with an element of self-criticism from the imagined perspective of the future redemption.

DON ISAAC ABRAVANEL, "LETTER TO YEHIEL OF PISA" (OCTOBER 4, 1482)

From the day that our City was laid in ruins, our Temple destroyed and our people exiled, we have known neither peace nor respite. The nations amongst whom we live do not stop taking council and devising means for assailing and harming us; and if we do enjoy peace for a brief moment, we are soon terrified by frightful news of savage persecution against the remnants of Israel coming from all the corners of the earth. What man subjected throughout life to the fear of enemies and the strain of distress would grieve when his last hour arrives? It is all the more so with the noble sons of Zion who repeatedly witness how, with the rise of evil, their honor is besmirched and their name disgraced. How can they attach any value to their life of sorrow and not rejoice over the prospect of the grave? Weep not for the dying among Israel and do not bemoan them![33] Weep for those who are cast from one misfortune to another, and for whom God has blocked all avenues of relief. *For honor has departed from Israel* (1 Sam. 4:21), and I wish we were all dead and no more given to scorn and derision, to contempt and humiliation.[34]

DON ISAAC ABRAVANEL, *MA'YENEI HA-YESHU'AH* (1496)

Dominion, glory, and kingship were given to him; all peoples [and nations of every language] must serve him. His dominion is an everlasting dominion that shall not pass away, and his kingship, one that shall not be destroyed (Dan. 7:14).

This means that at that time [of messianic redemption], Israel will be worthy of having everything that was lacking to them in their exile. As is well-known, they experienced three kinds of misfortune. The first is that in exile they had no fortitude or bravery, but rather weakness and great cowardice came over them, in accordance with the biblical curses, *As for those of you who survive, I will cast a faintness into their hearts* (Lev. 26:36). And in the final chastisement it is said, *Yet even among those nations you shall find no peace, nor shall your foot find a place to rest. [The Lord will give you there an anguished heart and eyes that pine and a despondent spirit.]* (Deut. 28:61).

The second category of misfortunes is that instead of their being *the precious children of Zion, valued as gold,* now once they are in exile, *they are accounted as earthen pots* (Lam. 4:2), their glory and honor gone. This is like the statement of the prophet, *He is despised, shunned by men, a man of suffering, familiar with disease,* and so forth (Isa. 53:3). And this is as it should be, for God's glory and honor was in the Holy Land, and the Divine Presence that was in their midst; once this was taken away from them, the glory of honor departed, *Israel was given over to despoilment, Israel to plunderers* (Isa. 42:24). As [the High Priest] Eli's daughter-in-law wisely said, *"The glory is gone from Israel,"* referring to the capture of the Ark of God (1 Sam. 4:21).

The third category of misfortune is that instead of having autonomy and sovereignty on the Holy Land, and *the ruler's staff between his feet* (Gen. 49:10), when they went into exile among the nations, their king and their leaders *have gone into captivity before the enemy* (Lam. 1:5). They no longer have a king or political official. This is the meaning of *The Eternal will drive you, and the king you have set over you, to a nation unknown to your fathers . . . ; you shall be a consternation, a proverb [and a byword among all the peoples to which the Eternal will drive you]* (Deut. 28:36–37). And the prophet said, *For the Israelites shall go a long time without king and without officials* (Hos. 3:4). For in every place they came to, they have been servants of all the various sovereignties. Even though they had a kind of scepter from the Babylonian exilarchs,[35] sovereignty was always lacking for them.[36]

DON ISAAC ABRAVANEL, *ZEVAḤ PESAḤ* (1496)

Because of the length of the exile, many despair of salvation, saying, *Our bones are dried up, our hope is gone; we are doomed* (Ezek. 37:11). Therefore the poet said, in the name of the nation, *I believe that I will speak, I have suffered greatly* (Ps. 116:10), meaning, I believe with enduring faith that just as now on this Passover night we speak and narrate the Exodus from Egypt and tell of the enslavement and the oppression we endured there, so in the time of redemption, I believe that I shall speak and tell how in this exile I was impoverished and destitute. That is the meaning of *that I will speak, I have suffered greatly*: that I will speak and tell of the exile and oppression that we endured. Furthermore, I will speak of how *I said things rashly* (Ps. 116:11), for it was due to the anguish and distress of the exile. This word *rashly* (בחפזי) is the same as ופחזים in the phrase *worthless and reckless* (Judg. 9:4)—an extremely strong expression of humiliation and anguish.

Then in the time of redemption, when I will be free, I will speak and tell of how I said in those days, *All men are false* (Ps. 116:11). This means, I said that all the prophets who prophesied about my redemption and salvation were all lying, for *the harvest is past, the summer is ended, but we have not been saved* (Jer. 8:20). I said that Moses lied in his promises about the future, Isaiah lied in his comforts, Jeremiah and Ezekiel lied in their prophecies, and so with all the rest of the prophets: *All men are false*. When the time of the future redemption comes, the nation will remember and speak of all the despairing things they said during the time of the exile.[37]

Comparing Exiles

The comparison of the degree of oppression in different exiles, or different manifestations of the same exile, has a long pedigree. Medieval and early modern Jews were aware that despite the generic characteristics outlined by Abravanel, local conditions varied, and some Jewish communities were more fortunate than others.[38]

The most important comparison was between the experience of Jews living in Christian Europe and those in Islamic lands (or, to use the standard typology: the lands of Edom and the lands of Ishmael). The general consensus among Jews in both realms—somewhat surprisingly in that it counters the common consensus of historical memory today—followed a statement cited from the thirteenth century and attributed to the talmudic sages, "Better under Edom than under Ishmael."[39] Before this, Maimonides had famously asserted that the exile under Islamic rule was the worst of all. Speaking of "the nation of Ishmael," he writes:

> No nation has ever done more harm to Israel. None has matched it in debasing and humiliating us. None has been able to reduce us as they have. . . . We have borne their imposed degradation, their lies, and absurdities, which are beyond human power to bear. . . . We listen, but remain silent. . . . In spite of all this, we are not spared from the ferocity of their wickedness and their outbursts at any time. On the contrary, the more we suffer and choose to conciliate them, the more they choose to act belligerently toward us.[40]

EXILE IN ANCIENT HISTORY

Yet this view was not universal. After the expulsion from Spain and the mass forced conversions in Portugal during the 1490s, at least one highly respected Ottoman rabbi (Joshua Soncino) held in a legal opinion that after these experiences, all Jews should know that no Christian country was safe for Jews, and any Jew who left the Iberian peninsula and settled in another Christian land rather than under Ottoman protection should be considered in the legal category of a suicide, for whom there is no obligation to mourn one's death.[41]

The following text is taken from a commentary on the book of Esther, but the actual passage is presented as a homily on the first verses of Psalm 120. Its author, Abraham Saba, a Jewish thinker expelled from Spain who settled in Portugal, experienced the mass forced conversions of 1497, and finally settled in Muslim North Africa, presents the issue of comparative exiles in dramatic form: as a debate between two Jews, one from each realm, and each applying verses from the psalm to his own experience. Surprisingly, the inhabitant of Christian Europe asserts that Christian oppression is not primarily physical but verbal: oppression is manifest in Christian intellectual arguments that the Jewish condition in exile is proof of Jews' reprobate status as spurned and rejected by God. By contrast, the inhabitant of Islamic lands states that Muslim oppression is expressed through physical violence, which is far worse. Both debaters agree that little in contemporary exile merits approval. As the medievalist Barry Dov Walfish has put it, the two characters "may each wish to live in the exile of the other, but when all is said and done, there is not much to choose between them. No matter where in exile one lives, the heavy hand of the oppressor is sure to be felt in one way or another."[42]

> ABRAHAM SABA, "A DEBATE OVER
> WHICH EXILE IS WORSE" (CA. 1500)
>
> [It is] as if two Jews in exile met each other and each one tells what befell him in his particular exile. One tells of the evil deeds that the Edomites committed against him and the other tells what the

Ishmaelites did to him. Each one thinks his troubles are so great that he desires to be in the exile of the other and suffer what the other suffered. The man living under the exile of Edom says: *o Lord, save me from treacherous lips, from a deceitful tongue* (Ps. 120:2). This is an allusion to Edom who has power in his tongue to debase and scorn every living thing with his well-ordered speech and smooth talk ... so that in their wisdom they commit every imaginable evil to Israel except kill them or do them bodily harm as the Ishmaelites do.[43]

His counterpart who came from the Ishmaelite exile replies to him, *What are you complaining about? What can you profit, what can you gain, o deceitful tongue?* (Ps. 120:3), i.e., what harm can they do to you with a deceitful tongue? If they do not hit you or kill you, what do you care about words aimed at you, even if they be like *a warrior's sharp arrows, with hot coals of broom-wood* (Ps. 120:4). None of this is as bad as the exile of Ishmael. I have a right to complain since I have been under Ishmaelite exile. I have a right to mourn and cry "Woe, woe." This is referred to in the verse *Woe is me, that I live with Meshech* (Ps. 120:5).

Another way of interpreting *a warrior's sharp arrows* is to explain it as the reply of the Jew under Edomite exile who says, "You say, *what can you profit, what can You gain, O deceitful tongue?* (Ps. 120:3). You should know that a sword wound heals more quickly than a tongue-lashing which is like a warrior's sharp arrows."[44]

His counterpart replies to him: "Despite this, I deserve to be cried for because I sojourned in Meshech among *a nation far and remote* (Isa. 18:2,7) who smites on the cheek and plucks out the hairs of one's beard and hand. *I dwell among the clans of Kedar* (Ps. 120:5) who blacken and darken one's face with blows without speech, since no one understands their language.[45] If this were for a short time I could endure it, but *too long have I dwelt among those who hate peace* (Ps. 120:6), those who do not wish to be greeted, saying that it is not proper for a Jew to greet them nor for them to greet a Jew. Therefore, *I am all peace* (Ps. 120:7), i.e., even though I speak of peace *they are for war* (ibid.): to make war with me and smite me."[46]

Consolation

Abraham P. Mendes (1825–93) was the scion of two of the oldest Sephardic families. Born in Jamaica and trained in England, he served as rabbi of Jewish communities in both places, completing his career at the historic Touro Synagogue in Rhode Island.

The following passage is taken from "The Sorrows and Consolation of Jerusalem," an 1855 sermon delivered to the Birmingham Hebrew Congregation (which he served from 1851 to 1858). The occasion, Shabbat Naḥamu, the Sabbath of Comfort, follows the Ninth Day of Av, the traditional day of mourning for the great historical disasters in Jewish national experience. That this was an important occasion for Jewish preaching is attested by many other such sermons published in contemporaneous periodicals.

While the theme of this Sabbath, derived from the opening verses of Isaiah 40 which are read in a liturgical setting, requires an emphasis on hope, much of the first part of the sermon speaks to the disaster commemorated a few days earlier. Continuing a strong tradition of Jewish historiography extending through the nineteenth century, Mendes portrays Jewish experience in exile as unremittingly bleak. He is unsparing in depicting the Jews' suffering as the Romans entered the Holy City of Jerusalem and set fire to the Temple. The bravery of the overwhelmed Jewish fighters is set in counterpoint with the pathos of the slaughter. And then, at a climactic point, Jerusalem "saw her children go into captivity."

The second part of his sermon derives lessons from the experience of exile. Despite the granting of full political rights to Jews in his home country of Jamaica (in 1831) followed by a number of firsts that marked increasing acceptance of Jews in England—the first Jew knighted (Moses Montefiore, 1837), the first to receive a hereditary title (Isaac Goldsmid, 1841), the first to become Lord Mayor of London (Sir David Salomons, 1855)—Mendes continues to emphasize the precarity of Jewish existence in exile.

The sermon's third and final section is devoted to the "promised comfort of Jerusalem" that will bring solace to the ever-persecuted Jews: the reestablishment of home and altar, and the end of exile.

ABRAHAM P. MENDES, "THE SORROWS AND CONSOLATION
OF JERUSALEM: A SERMON FOR SHABBAT NAḤAMU" (1855)

But alas! My brethren, this brightness [of the Second Commonwealth with its rebuilt Temple] is ephemeral. Prosperity begets its common consequences; internal warfare and disunion convulse the land, and crime takes up its abode in the priestly city. At last, as the result of intestine[47] contest for supremacy, we see Judea under the yoke of Rome, a yoke whose severity continues to gall the self-enslaved people, until infuriated by the tyranny and oppression of the procurator Florus,[48] they take up arms and drive the Romans from Jerusalem. Now commences that fearful struggle whose issue is so pregnant with evil for Jacob's race and land. The people, flushed with their victory over Cestius, dream no more of subjection beneath a hated yoke, but deem themselves able to contend successfully against the giant hosts of Rome.[49] And nobly they do contend, in spite of every disadvantage. Against the greatest warriors of the age they are in arms; but undisciplined though they be, their hearts burn with an ardor for the cause of liberty, which renders every man a legion in himself.[50]

Yet is their heroism unavailing. Internal dissension weakens them daily more and more, while slowly but surely the invaders onward press, until once more Jerusalem is besieged. Around her walls are marshalled mighty legions with all the engines of war, burning for vengeance; while within her gates, her children are suffering miseries unparalleled in the history of the world. Her streets are strewn with dead, for famine stalks in her midst and lays her defenders low by thousands. They cry aloud for food: they slay each other in contest for a morsel, and pray for death to terminate their agonies. Mothers slay their children, and, nature dead within them, they feast upon the flesh.[51] Meanwhile, the conflict rages fiercely, and nearer approach the invader's hosts. Titus enters the city, and yet the people struggle with superhuman energy, defending step by step, their homes and altars. Rivers of blood course along the streets, the avenues are strewn with the dead and the dying, and still the din of battle is heard, the people yield not.

But now, the fatal ninth of Ab recurs—that day, already dark with the memory of Babylon's conquest—and on that morn, despair is spread into the heart of Jerusalem, not by the success of her assailants, for that she is prepared to bear heroically, but by the sight of her temple in flames.[52] All now is consternation. The shouts of barbaric triumph mingle with the roar of the conflagration; the shrieks of the old and defenceless as they are stricken down pitilessly, and the groans of the patriots as they cast their dying glance at the burning sanctuary, all unite to swell the horrors of that day of misery, when Jerusalem suffered for her sins and saw her children go forth to captivity.

Nearly eighteen hundred years have elapsed, my brethren, since the period to which we have reverted; and through all these weary centuries, we can describe the history of our people in the words: sorrow and suffering, woe and tribulation.[53] From clime to clime we have been driven, never finding rest for the soles of our feet. In every age persecuted, in every land despised, we have lived on, in spite of all the ills that have attended us, sustained by one hope, the hope of future restoration. This hope was in our hearts, as the blade of oppression thrust its way through it; it was before our eyes amid the burning brands of the stake which bigotry kindled for us: neither the fire nor the sword could suppress it.[54] We suffered all patiently, assured that our present sorrows would yet be forgotten, in the glories of that future promised by Divine love and mercy, when Zion should see her paths restored and her children ransomed. But to approximate [in the older meaning of "to bring close or near"] that epoch, my brethren, we must direct our thoughts to the lessons taught by our captive state.[55]

3 Exile and Holidays

The Jewish calendar—the annual cycle of holidays—is largely governed by the idea of exile. The three harvest holidays (*shalosh regalim*) connect intimately with this theme. Passover commemorates the great Exodus from Egypt; Shavuot and Sukkot both recall the Children of Israel's forty years' wandering in the wilderness. Ironically, the people initially celebrated these holidays by pilgrimage to the Temple in Jerusalem, a practice that could not be followed in exile. The pilgrimage, an act of coming to a specific place, needed to be translated into alternative observance when Jews were exiled from the Land of Israel.

While other holidays are referenced elsewhere in this volume, this chapter focuses on the contrasting days of Tisha b'Av (the ninth of Av) and Purim, a fast and a feast. Through a day of mourning, deprivation, and prayer Tisha b'Av commemorates the historic events that sent Jews into exile: the destruction of the First Temple by the Babylonians, of the Second Temple by the Romans, and the Expulsion from Spain. Torah study—considered a source of joy—is suspended for the day; instead, recitation of Megillat Eikha (the book of Lamentations) ensues during evening and morning services. In this chapter, the fast day is signified by an excerpt from the megillah (literally: scroll), a prayer written for the day, a *piska* (talmudic passage) on the topic, a sermon, and a literary representation of the Tisha b'Av observance that has become a classic.

Purim, in contrast, is a holiday of joyous indulgence. Celebrations include costumes, noisemakers, merrymaking, and drink. The story of Purim is told in Megillat Esther. Not only is the book significant for its unique style—reading more as a tale from the *Arabian Nights* than ancient Israel—and for the absence of any mention of God (true of only one other book of the Hebrew Bible), it is also the only narrative that takes place entirely outside of the Land of Israel without any reference to it. It is the most inherently exilic of all biblical texts.

The megillah tells the story of the Jews in Shushan (present-day Shush, Iran), who are living a precarious existence as a minority. They are assimilated: the heroine, Hadassah, is known by her vernacular name Esther (presumably derived from the name of the goddess Ishtar/Astarte) and keeps her identity hidden. Only through her finding favor with the king—and her heroism in risking her own life by revealing herself as Jewish—are the Jews, descendants of the original Babylonian exiles, saved from annihilation. And not (necessarily) by the hand of God—here the Jews are allowed to defend themselves from the decree to "destroy, massacre, and terminate" the Jewish people. Instead of fasting and mourning, Jews are instructed to indulge and celebrate.

The holiday and the megillah continue to resonate with Jews in the Diaspora today.

Tisha b'Av

The fast day of Tisha b'Av (the Ninth of Av) commemorates the destruction of the First and Second Temples, and thus the beginning of two distinct periods of exile. The Mishnah (*Ta'anit* 4:6) adds the return of the twelve spies from Canaan and the end of Bar Kokhba's revolt to the disasters befalling the Israelites on the very day. Historians have also noted a number of tragic events that have occurred on (or near) Tisha b'Av, including expulsions of Jews from England (1290), France (1306), and Spain (1492), as well as Germany's entrance into WWI (1914), the Nazis' adoption of the Final Solution (1941), and the mass deportation from the Warsaw Ghetto (1942).

The book of Lamentations is part of the Tisha b'Av liturgy. The fifth—and last—chapter begins with a communal lament, becomes a prayer for repentance, and ends with the possibility of God's rejection.

LAMENTATIONS 5

Remember, O Eternal One, what has befallen us;
Behold, and see our disgrace!
Our heritage has passed to aliens,
Our homes to strangers.
We have become orphans, fatherless;
Our mothers are like widows.
We must pay to drink our own water,
Obtain our own kindling at a price.
We are hotly pursued;
Exhausted, we are given no rest.
We hold out a hand to Egypt;
To Assyria, for our fill of bread.
Our ancestors sinned and are no more;
And we must bear their guilt.
Slaves are ruling over us,
With none to rescue us from them.
We get our bread at the peril of our lives,
Because of the sword of the wilderness.
Our skin glows like an oven,
With the fever of famine.
Those slaves have abused women in Zion,
Maidens in the towns of Judah.
Princes have been hanged by them;
No respect has been shown to elders.
Young men must carry millstones,
And youths stagger under loads of wood.
The elders are gone from the gate,
The youngsters from their music.
Gone is the joy of our hearts;
Our dancing is turned into mourning.
The crown has fallen from our head;
Woe to us that we have sinned!

> Because of this our hearts are sick,
> Because of these our eyes are dimmed:
> Because of Mount Zion, which lies desolate;
> Jackals prowl over it.
>
> But You, O Eternal One, are enthroned forever,
> Your throne endures through the ages.
> Why have You forgotten us utterly,
> Forsaken us for all time?
> Take us back, O Eternal One, to Yourself,
> And let us come back;
> Renew our days as of old!
> For truly, You have rejected us,
> Bitterly raged against us.
> Take us back, O Eternal One, to Yourself,
> And let us come back;
> Renew our days as of old!![1]

Finding Comfort

This *piska* was apparently intended for the "Sabbath of Comfort" immediately following the Ninth Day of Av, as it is introduced with the verse *Comfort, comfort My people, says your God* (Isa. 40:1), the beginning of the prophetic reading for this day. Parables of kings are one of the most common tropes of Rabbinic discourse; the king represents God, the queen (or, in other cases, the king's son) represents the Jewish people. What makes this romantic version unusual is the assertion that there was no wrongdoing by the queen, that the couple's barrenness was due to the king, and that the separation was for the queen's benefit. The details about the king's inebriation are apparently not intended to have significance for the meaning of the parable other than to explain how he could have been moved without his knowing. Note the assumption of the resurrection of the dead projected back by the Rabbis to a time when there is no evidence for this belief among Jews.

PESIKTA RABBATI 30:2 (CA. 845 CE)

When the Children of Israel were banished from their land [by the Babylonians], the Holy One, blessed be He, asked, "Who do you want of the Patriarchs that I will raise from the grave to lead you? Whether it be Abraham, Isaac, or Jacob, whether Moses or Aaron, I will raise him from the grave to lead you. Or David or Solomon, I will raise from his grave to lead you." Israel said: "Master of the universe, we want no one but You, as it is said, *For You are our Father; for Abraham does not know us, and Israel does not recognize us; You are our Father, our Redeemer, everlasting is Your Name*" (Isa. 63:16).

The Holy One replied, Since you said this, I will go up with you to Babylon, as it is said, *For your sake I have been sent to Babylon* (Isa. 43:14);[2] and also, *I will set My throne in Elam* (Jer. 49:38).

[A parable:] A king took a wife who lived with him for many years without bearing children. He said to her, "Go forth and marry another man so that you will have children by him. When you go take with you everything from here you desire."

She told him, "If it is to be then I will make you a feast, and we will eat and drink, before I take leave of you, so that they do not say: See the king's wife, because he despised her he sent her away."

The king agreed. Thereupon she made the feast. The king ate and drank until he was drunk. She summoned her servants at midnight, and they took him in his bed to her father's house.

When he awoke he asked: "Where is this place?"

She answered: "My father's house."

He asked: "Why am I in your father's house?"

She replied: "Thus you told me 'When you go forth take with you everything you desire.' There is nothing I want more nor that makes me happier than you."

So too the congregation of Israel. When the Holy One asked: "Who do you want Me to raise from the grave to lead you to Babylon?" they replied: "We want none except You, as it is said, *For You are our Father*" (Isa. 63:16). Thereupon the Holy One said, "I will be your companion, and I will go up with you, as it is said, *For your sake I have been sent to Babylon*" (Isa. 43:14).[3]

On Account of the Fruits

A number of sermons and homilies have been found among extant texts in Judeo-Persian, a language written in Hebrew script and spoken by Jews throughout the former Persian Empire, one of the oldest continuous diasporic communities. The author of the sermon excerpted here is unknown, but scholar Vera Moreen notes both his erudition and adherence to the classic homiletic structure: theme verse (*nose'*), seemingly unrelated midrash (*ma'amar*), and eventual resolution of the two.

Written for the occasion of Tisha b'Av, the sermon begins with a verse from Jeremiah and jumps to an *aggadah* (legend) that after the Golden Calf incident (Exod. 32), Moses pleads with God to forgive his brother Aaron for the sake of Aaron's sons, much as the vine is left unscathed because of the sweetness of its grapes. The sermon further generalizes to parents being given mercy on their children's behalf. How much more so in exile: "Even in this state [of dispersion leading to 'sorrows and humiliations'] we . . . have raised our children according to Your *Torah*."[4]

> ANONYMOUS, "A DERASHAH ON THE HAFTARAH FOR THE NINTH OF AB" (CA. 1700–1900)
>
> I will make an end of them—declares the Lord:
> No grapes left on the vine,
> No figs on the fig tree
> [The leaves all withered;
> Whatever I have given them is gone.] Jer. 8:13 . . .
>
> Moreover, we have a *law* that if the wood of the vine or of the fig . . . is *prohibited even* in these days when we have no *Temple*, then no one can cut down . . . these woods; but the wood of the vine and fig which produce no fruits are *permissible* to cut down . . . , the principal reason being that we have no *Temple*. Therefore, it is well known that during the time that the *Temple stood*, it was not permissible to cut down the wood of the grape and of the fig. They did not cut them down or burn them . . . although there was no

prohibition against it. Therefore we should understand that for the sake of good offspring, fathers and mothers are released from all *laws*, calamities, and [evil] *decrees*.

When the *Holy One, Blessed be He*, wished to destroy Israel, the prophet Jeremiah petitioned at the court of the *Holy One, Blessed be He*, and said, "*Lord of the Universe, You have apportioned honor to woods*, that is, on account of the fruits of the trees You forgave and had mercy on the trees that were their fathers and commanded that they should not be cut down. . . . And now that You wish to finish off all Israel, why have you no regard for their offspring, for *priestly offerings* will come from them. . . . You have no mercy on them although they will be righteous? Have mercy on them and do not destroy them!" *The Holy One, blessed be He*, said, "*I will make an end of them,*" that is, I wish to destroy them utterly. Concerning them Jeremiah said, "Why did He say, '*No grapes left on the vine, / No figs on the fig tree*'?" That is, these Israelites that you see today . . . all walk in the midst of *dregs*,[5] and the *other side*[6] mired them into its pitch; whatever they produce is the property of the *other side*. They did not produce and will not produce any *righteous man*, because they commit *evil and sin* and are not worthy of My mercy for the sake of their offspring, as in the case . . . of the vine and the fig. Rather, they are like trees that bear no fruit, which it is *permissible* to cut down . . . ; that is why Jeremiah said, "*I will make an end of them — declared the Lord / No grapes left on the vine, / No figs on the fig tree."* . . . God proclaimed concerning them, "I will destroy them utterly." If you say that they will produce good offspring, well and good. [But] "*No grapes left on the vine, / No figs on the fig tree. / The leaves all withered*" means that the leaves they will also be destroyed.[7]

"Changeth Mourning into Rejoicing"

David Einhorn, one of the most influential spokesmen in American Reform Judaism in the nineteenth century, emigrated to the United States in 1855 in the wake of a controversial career in Central Europe. Born in Dispeck, Bavaria, in 1809, he engaged in philosophical study at the Universities of Würzburg and Munich following his rabbinical ordination in Fürth, and proceeded to play an important role in the German rabbinical conferences of the 1840s on questions relating to reform in Judaism. While opposing some of the more radical tendencies in Reform, he championed such innovations as using a vernacular liturgy and eliminating prayers for the restoration of the Jewish state and the Temple. His liberal positions raised problems with governmental authorities, and following the Austrian government's closure of the Budapest synagogue he was serving, he left Europe to accept a position at Har Sinai Congregation of Baltimore. Soon after his arrival in the United States, he inaugurated a German-language monthly magazine called *Sinai* and saw the publication of his new prayer book, *Olat Tamid*. First published in Hebrew and German in 1858, and then in Hebrew and English in 1872 (a subsequent translation by his son-in-law, Emil G. Hirsch, used below, followed in 1896),[8] Einhorn's *Olat Tamid*, begun in Europe, "bears some structural resemblance to both the Hamburg Temple prayerbook and the liturgy of the Reform Congregation in Berlin," notes historian of Reform Judaism Michael Meyer. "It also draws upon the scientific research of Leopold Zunz. But *Olat Tamid* is no merely eclectic work. It consistently expresses the religious ideology of its editor."[9]

The ideologically charged character of the following prayer for the observance of Tisha b'Av and its implications for a revised understanding of Jewish history are on display here. The prayer's beginning—an evocation of the glory of the ancient Temple, the tragedy of its destruction, and the bitter experience of a prolonged exile ("With bleeding hearts they wandered forth to seek strange lands void of love, like sons disowned by their father, everywhere meeting the fury of hostile nations, everywhere made to drain the cup of suffering, forced to wear the garb and walk the gait of servitude, stricken and stung to death")—seems quite traditional, similar to Abraham Mendes's sermon in chapter 2. But then—without warning—in the middle of the prayer, the tone changes dramatically, and the valorization of the experience in exile is transformed. Exile is not just about Israel's fulfilling a providential role as God's "suffering servant," as seen in Hermann Adler's sermon, although this too is present ("The flames which consumed Zion, lit up the birth-hour of Israel as the suffering Messiah of all mankind"). Exile has become something more—not a burden, and certainly not a punishment, but an opportunity to fulfill a sacred mission: "Verily, not as a disinherited son, Thy first-born went out into strange lands, but as Thy messenger to all the families of man." The mood of the occasion seems to have changed from a day of mourning to a time of rejoicing.

DAVID EINHORN, "FOR THE ANNIVERSARY OF THE DESTRUCTION OF JERUSALEM" (1896)

THE MINISTER: With profound emotion, O Lord, we remember in this hour the dire day of desolation on which the enemy entered Thy stronghold, giving over Thy sanctuary a prey to devouring flames. Then was left disconsolate the populous city, the beauty of all the lands, like a sorrowing widow. Then was laid low the pride and crown of Israel, the magnificent temple on Moriah's proud height, in which the scions of Abraham used to praise the glory of Thy name at a time when none of the nations knew Thee; then fell the home of light, with the ark of the divine testimony, the Cherubim with wings turned heavenward, the altar of atoning sacrifices, the candlestick with the seven flaming tongues. Then was hushed in silence the lovely song of the Levites which had during so many years risen to heaven in choruses thousand-voiced, only the woeful lament of priests, robbed of their office and ornaments, resounded, and the wails and groans of the homeless children of Thy people awakened a doleful echo.

O, heavy and bitter was the fate which befell the house of Jacob on that day. With bleeding hearts they wandered forth to seek strange lands void of love, like sons disowned by their father, everywhere meeting the fury of hostile nations, everywhere made to drain the cup of suffering, forced to wear the garb and walk the gait of servitude, stricken and stung to death, so that, in their deep distress, they often cried out unto Thee: Thou hast thrust me into a deep pit, into a dark abyss; Thy wrath is upon me, and all Thy waves afflict me; Thou hast driven from me all my friends, and rendered me an abomination unto them; I am imprisoned, and cannot move; my eye is grown dim from weeping; I cry unto Thee every day, O God, and stretch my hands towards Thee; wilt Thou work miracles for the dead? shall shades arise and praise Thee? why, O Lord, castest Thou off my soul, and hidest Thou Thy face from me? Lover and friend hast Thou taken from me; and darkness is my sole confidant.[10]

Truly, indescribable are the sufferings Israel hath endured in the weary years of his wandering. He, once the bearer of the royal purple, became the pitiful butt of pitiless assaults; his eye, once beaming with the light of happiness, was changed into an ever-flowing fountain of tears. Whithersoever his fugitive foot carried him, he found but the yoke of oppression, the curse of hatred, the poisoned arrow of calumny; and thousands and thousands of his sons and daughters had to lay down their life and possessions in the combat for Thee and Thy holy law. They were swifter than eagles, stronger than lions,[11] in the fulfilment of Thy sublime will; inseparable, in life and in death, from their loyalty to Thee, O Inscrutable One. For they knew that Thou wilt bring forth light out of darkness, and wilt also lead Thy people from the deepest depths of humiliation to a most glorious triumph.

This uplifting thought is also the source of our consolation, the stay of our courage, and the wing of our hope; it changeth our mourning into rejoicing, our lamenting into dancing. However deeply and painfully our soul is moved by the recollection of the unutterable grief with which our ancestors went forth from their beloved Zion, their house, to go into the vast wilderness of heathen nations; doomed to tread the thorny path of martyrdom, in all these sore trials we recognize Thy guiding, fatherly hand, means for the fulfilment of Thy inviolable promises and the glorification of Thy name and Thy law before the eyes of all nations. Verily, not as a disinherited son, Thy first-born went out into strange lands, but as Thy messenger to all the families of man.[12] Israel was no longer to dwell in separation from all the rest of Thy children, who were languishing in darkness and folly; he was to spread abroad the stream of his salvation, and become himself the carrier of the refreshing waters of healing powers.

The one temple in Jerusalem sank into the dust, in order that countless temples might arise to Thy honor and glory all over the wide surface of the globe.[13] The old priestly dignity was taken away and the old sacrificial worship ceased, but in their stead the whole community, in accordance with its original distinction, became a priest and was called upon to offer up those sacrifices which are more acceptable in Thy sight than thousands of rivers of oil,[14] the sacrifices of active love to God and man, the sacrifices of pure and pious conduct, which, even in extremity and death will not deviate from the path of truth, the sacrifices of an unparalleled allegiance to God with which the centuries have become vocal. The true and real sanctuary, Thy imperishable testimony, remained ours, untouched and undimmed. It assumed a new glory and emerged purer and in increased splendor from the flames. It was freed from the encircling walls which had shut it in and hidden its glory from the eyes of the millions of beings created in Thy image. These to lift up to the recognition of their dignity as men and to bring them into the fold of Thy spiritual people united in love and righteousness, Thy priest, Israel, had to go out among them, and speak before them Thy message of duty and righteousness.

The flames which consumed Zion, lit up the birth-hour of Israel as the suffering Messiah of all mankind. Freed from the bonds of his childhood, in martyr heroism, Israel had to pilgrim through the whole earth, a man of sorrows, without form or comeliness, despised and rejected of men, to deliver by his very fetters his own tormentors, by his wounds to bring healing to those who inflicted them.[15] When at last his great sacrifice of atonement is completely wrought, he will find his reward in seeing all men gather into one brotherhood, doing God's service in love to man. In this our hope, this day of mourning and of fasting, hath, according to the word of Thy prophet, been turned into a solemn day of rejoicing in view of the glorious destiny of Thy law and our high messianic mission which had its beginning with the historic events which we recall today.[16] Though this sublime mission hath entailed on us bitter sacrifices, and long be the way we still have to traverse—our heart is full of profoundest gratitude for Thine infinite grace which hath found us worthy to be sacrificing priests for all mankind. Our trust remaineth firm in Thy promise that one day all who are endowed with Thy breath will bow down before Thee. Vouchsafe, O God, that all Israel may recognize this, the goal of its wanderings, and pursue it with united strength and cheerful courage. Let his mourning end wherever he is still languishing beneath the oppression of hatred, and to the better thought open the eyes of those who deem Thy messenger still cast out from before Thy countenance, and would have him return to the narrow home where his cradle once stood,[17] without his true aim as a prince of God and depriving him of his world-blessing duty.

O, strengthen us all for Thy service, invigorate us for our mission. Let the time speedily draw near when all the earth will become one atoning altar, from which all hearts and spirits shall flame up to Thee in burning love. Let Thy message of truth and Thy word of righteousness like protecting cherubim, spread their wings over the sanctuary of mankind united in and with Thee. Let this brotherhood of man, like yon candlestick of pure gold, shine in seven-fold luster in the higher temple, and from the ruins of desolation, rise this new temple wide as the earth, and unwalled as its fresh air, the temple which will be a house of prayer and inspiration unto all the nations—the Sinai and Zion of all the world, the new Jerusalem on this earth, rebuilt in righteousness universal, and saved by justice flowing like a stream through all the lands.

THE CONGREGATION: Amen.[18]

Whither?

Mordecai Ze'ev Feierberg was born in 1874 in the northwestern Ukrainian province of Volhynia. His father was a pious Lubavitcher Hasid, and he studied traditional texts in a Hasidic school. Gradually, he began to expand his reading beyond talmudic literature to include medieval philosophy, ethics, and mysticism, and then the literature of the Haskalah (Jewish Enlightenment movement), which led to intense conflict with his father and severe condemnation by the community. Traveling to Warsaw for treatment of his tuberculosis, he met and received encouragement for his writing from several leading Jewish literary figures: Nahum Sokolow, Y. L. Peretz, Ahad Ha'am (q.v.). He died in 1899, at age twenty-five, having produced six short stories, several journalistic articles and reviews, and an autobiographical novella, *Le'An?* (Whither?), a poignant account of the excruciating yet irreparable break with a tradition to which the young protagonist had once been wholeheartedly, even passionately, committed.[19]

The depiction of exile in this novella is expressed through one of the most powerful descriptions of the observance of Tisha b'Av in Hebrew literature. The scene is hauntingly narrated in counterpoint with the cantor's rendering of the verses from Lamentations; knowledgeable readers would have heard in their minds the mournful melody to which these verses were chanted on this day. An entire community spending a day fasting, sitting on the synagogue floor, lamenting the loss of Temple, sovereignty, and land: what could better encapsulate the negative qualities of exile?

But for the narrator, the anguish is intensified by a secret that separates him from the others: he has lost his faith in the God of his fathers. Pretending to be part of a community in mourning, he is really alone. At one moment, triggered by the memory of an old folktale, he realizes there is something fundamentally wrong with the scene he is observing—the ritualistic enactment of exile is paralyzing and must be abandoned. Yet in repudiating the past and present, he is left without any clear direction for the future.

MORDECAI ZE'EV FEIERBERG, "WHITHER?" (1900)

It was the eve of the fast of the Ninth of Av, the day of mourning for the destruction of the Temple. Despair and sorrow were written on his father's face. The old man walked back and forth in the house with a preoccupied air, his shoulders stooped and his eyes on the ground. The books that were allowed to be read on the fast day had already been set out on the table: Job and Jeremiah, the midrash on the Book of Lamentations, the tractate *Mo'ed Katan*, and others. A spirit of special sadness had settled over the silent house. The women prepared the pre-fast meal and argued with each other over what foods were permissible for the occasion. People passed somberly in and out of the house as though visiting a mourner, without pausing to say hello or good-bye. The street outside the window had a different look too. Children roamed about in it with play wooden swords.[20] The women hurried from house to house, busy with the meal and with getting out their hour books[21] in which they would follow the chanting of the Scroll of Lamentations in the synagogue and read about the destruction of God's house.[22] The children would have liked to be carefree and flourish their wooden swords on this day that they had off from school, but they knew it was forbidden. "What makes you so merry today?" their mothers had demanded. "Is it because our Temple was destroyed? This is no day for fun and games!" . . .

Yet Nachman felt remote from it all. He was no longer the person he should be or that others still thought that he was. He had become someone else.[23] All was lost. Everyone seemed a stranger. If only his father knew that for the first time today phylacteries had not touched his son's head! If only he knew that this son was a heretic, an unbeliever! If he knew that he would be mourning tonight not for the destruction of the house of God, but for the ruin of his own house, his life and dreams. . . . Why couldn't he look his father in the face? Why couldn't he look at anyone? He wanted to confess everything, he must! Why did everyone still pay him such deference? Why did they treat him so kindly? Their every word pierced him like a knife. He was a liar, a hypocrite, a swindler. If only there was one living soul to whom he could bare his inner life, who would know and understand what he was going through. How happy it would make him to be able to believe that God above was looking down on his sorrow and comprehending his pain.

It was dusk when he reached the synagogue. The building was packed with men as though on a holiday, yet all wore their workaday clothes. The benches had been turned upside down. The lecterns lay on the ground. The holy ark stood bare, stripped of its embroidered drape.[24] A tallow candle burning on the cantor's podium cast its dim light over the crowd of men seated barefoot on the floor. The cantor chanted the evening prayer to the melody of the Book of Lamentations, which bleakly filled the half-lit building with a melancholy woe. Everyone but himself was absorbed in the evening prayer.

From now on, he had made up his mind the night before, he would pray no more. The entire worshipful congregation was one heart and he another. He was cut off from the House of Israel, banished from among his own people. How terribly he would have liked to rejoin them! He would have given his life to do it. But how was it possible? He had sundered the bonds of his own free will and could never mend them again.

The prayer was over. The large congregation remained on the ground, each man with a candle in his hand and the Book of Lamentations before him. The cantor sat on a stone before the podium and read from the scroll in a low, drear voice. Nachman glanced about the building. All were intently following the words of the chant in their books. Now and again a faint sigh could be heard. His father sat near him, staring in his book with unseeing eyes. Tear after tear dropped from his cheeks to the old lamentary, which was stained with tears and tallow already. The cantor sang on. A great sea of trials, a sea of tears, burst from the throat of this simple man. Every word was a wave of suffering and pain, a stormy breaker that crashed upon the shore. Wave called to wave and trough to trough. *O wall of the daughter of Zion, let tears run down like a river day and night; give thyself no respite; let not the apple of thine eye cease. Arise, cry out in the night, at the beginning of the watches; pour out thy heart like water before the face of the Lord; lift up thy hands toward Him for the life of thy young children, that faint for hunger at the head of every street* (Lam. 2:18–19).

The cantor read on. *I am the man that hath seen affliction by the rod of His wrath. . . . My flesh and my skin hath He worn out; He hath broken my bones. . . . He hath made me to dwell in dark places, as those that have long been dead. He hath hedged me about, that I cannot go forth; He hath made my chain heavy. . . . He is unto me as a bear lying in wait, as a lion in secret places* (Lam. 3:1,6–7,10) . . .

Then his soul grew bitter within him.—Ah, he demanded, why have they robbed me of the Lord who is good unto them that wait, to the soul that seeketh Him? Why have they robbed me of the brave, the mighty and terrible Lord who breaketh the cedars of Lebanon and maketh them dance like sheep, the merciful Lord who restoreth the humbled in spirit, who knoweth what lieth in darkness while his people dwelleth in light? Give me back my God, the God of the Jews! The God of Aristotle can do nothing for me. He is a figurehead, a king without a kingdom, not a God who lives. Give me a God who rules, who *loveth the stranger, in giving him food and raiment* (Deut. 10:18). Give me back the God who is near to me and I to Him! The God of Abraham, Isaac, and Jacob, the God of Moses and the prophets.[25] The God of all this holy congregation that is melting in its tears for the destruction of Jerusalem while its heart trusts and hopes that God will rebuild Zion and gather the scattered remnants of Israel from the far corners of the earth.... Take what you want from me—heaven and hell, my share in the world to come—but give me back my light, my heart, my soul, my people, my God! Why should anyone care if there is a God in heaven or not? It's enough to know Him in one's own heart, to feel Him there every second. Ah, the heart, the heart! Judge for yourselves, you philosophers: here is the heart that you have labored to produce—and here is the heart that is the labor of Moses and the Prophets.

The cantor was done with the chant. One by one the congregation drifted home. His father sat on the floor in a corner by the east wall surrounded by the village elders, to whom he read aloud from a passage in the *Midrash Rabba*. A terrible stillness engulfed the building, which was steeped in murk. His father's low voice mingling with the sighs that burst from the elders blanketed all with a horrible woe. Nachman sat on the ground, forgetful of all he had been thinking, his head in his hands, his eyes upon his father, his mind a perfect void.... Suddenly he stirred and cast an uncertain glance over the synagogue. The sight seemed strange and new to him; his scattered thoughts began to regroup. One by one his memories of the past twenty-four hours flew home to roost, joining to form a large and dismal likeness. How he wanted to forget them, to erase them from his mind with one stroke, to be reborn a wholly different, wholly other person!...

"Nachman, Nachman," his father admonished, the flicker of a smile on his lips, "is it Jerusalem you're mourning for? *Thus saith the Lord of hosts: My cities shall again overflow with prosperity; and the Lord shall yet comfort Zion, and shall yet choose Jerusalem* [Zech. 1:17]. Son, son, the land of Israel is nothing but earth and dust. Jerusalem is just a city of houses, markets, and towers. The Temple itself was only a large building, with great slabs of marble and much silver and gold. What more was there? Here too, praise God, we have large buildings and synagogues. Once our synagogue burnt down with all its Torah scrolls — you were just a small boy at the time — and I didn't even weep or mourn. But once I overheard an ignorant Jew swear vulgarly at a scholar, and I tore my clothes and fasted all day. . . . Do you understand, son, do you understand?"

"But for what are you mourning tonight, then, papa?"

"For what? I'm mourning because at the same time that Titus ravaged the Jerusalem of earth, the spirit of Rome, as it were, ravaged the Jerusalem of heaven. Yes, when we were driven into exile, so was . . . but you know what else was exiled with us. I don't want to have to put it in plain words . . . everything is in exile . . . holiness itself is in exile . . . all the spiritual powers of our people are in exile, bound in the clutches of Samael and his crew. The Holy One Blessed Be He never requites Himself on a nation unless He requites Himself on its guiding spirit first, and though our own guide is the *Shekhinah*, since we have no other god beside Him, He still chose to deal with us in this manner, which we mustn't question. And so our hands are tied and there is nothing we can do for ourselves, because our powers are enslaved to Samael and aren't ours to command. Our very existence depends entirely on prayer and the commandments, through which we must try to recapture the divine flow of grace from the days when the Temple still stood and the *Shekhinah* was not in captivity.

"To what can I compare it for you? It's like a rich man who has lost his whole fortune yet hopes to make it all back. What does he do with himself now that he has been ruined? Every minute of the day he seeks to keep alive the memory of the comforts and refinements that were his when he still had his wealth. So we too are ruined in the Exile, because Samael has stopped all the channels that lead to holiness, so that we would have died a spiritual death, God forbid, or nourished ourselves from the *klipa* [evil spirit] (for the spirit must nourish itself just like the body), if it weren't that by recalling the divine flow from the days when our Temple still stood, we can manage to survive the Exile until the Redemption has been wakened. Yet until then we are helpless, because our spiritual powers are in exile and in thrall to Samael, which is what the rabbis meant when they said that 'The prisoner cannot free himself from his own cell'" (b. *Ber.* 5b). . . .

His father believed that the Redemption could be brought only by a mystic awakening, and he had spent his life seeking "to weed out the brambles and thorns that surround the supernal rose."[26] Now that he had aged, he wished to pass on the standard to him, Nachman, and make him swear to continue the fight. He would always remember the morning when his father had first told him to be a soldier.[27] . . . But in taking up the flag, he could not take his father's weapons too: these had grown rusty, they would no longer do. If his people had been able to live for thousands of years in the moldy air of the cloister, rebuilding thousands of times what had been built already so as to keep from perishing from sheer idleness and ennui—why could it not also live a new life for new things under God's glorious skies? Had it not stood long enough before its ruins? It was time to move on.

To move on! But whither?[28]

Purim

Megillat Esther (the book of Esther), which tells the story of Purim, is not only one of the two biblical books in which the name of God is not mentioned; it is also the most diasporic, portraying the life of assimilated Jews living outside the Land of Israel. Of dubious historicity, the story features the characters of Mordecai and his cousin Esther, who are known by their distinctly non-Hebraic names: Mordecai most probably a variation on Marduk, the Babylonian god; and Esther, on Ishtar (Astarte). That Mordecai instructs Esther not to disclose her Jewish identity suggests she "passes" as gentile. Neither is imbued with the consciousness of the Land of Israel as home. The passage below details Esther's entry into the king's household.

BOOK OF ESTHER 2:5–22

In the fortress Shushan lived a Jew by the name of Mordecai, son of Jair son of Shimei son of Kish, a Benjaminite. [Kish] had been exiled from Jerusalem in the group that was carried into exile along with King Jeconiah of Judah, who had been driven into exile by King Nebuchadnezzar of Babylon. He was foster father to Hadassah—that is, Esther—his uncle's daughter, for she had neither father nor mother. The maiden was shapely and beautiful; and when her father and mother died, Mordecai adopted her as his own daughter.

When the king's order and edict was proclaimed, and when many maidens were assembled in the fortress Shushan under the supervision of Hegai, Esther too was taken into the king's palace under the supervision of Hegai, guardian of the women. The maiden pleased him and won his favor, and he hastened to furnish her with her cosmetics and her rations, as well as with the seven maids who were her due from the king's palace; and he treated her and her maids with special kindness in the harem. Esther did not reveal her people or her kindred, for Mordecai had told her not to reveal it. Every single day Mordecai would walk about in front of the court of the harem, to learn how Esther was faring and what was happening to her.

When each maiden's turn came to go to King Ahasuerus at the end of the twelve months' treatment prescribed for women (for that was the period spent on beautifying them: six months with oil of myrrh and six months with perfumes and women's cosmetics, and it was after that that the maiden would go to the king), whatever she asked for would be given her to take with her from the harem to the king's palace. She would go in the evening and leave in the morning for a second harem in charge of Shaashgaz, the king's eunuch, guardian of the concubines. She would not go again to the king unless the king wanted her, when she would be summoned by name.

When the turn came for Esther daughter of Abihail—the uncle of Mordecai, who had adopted her as his own daughter—to go to the king, she did not ask for anything but what Hegai, the king's eunuch, guardian of the women, advised. Yet Esther won the admiration of all who saw her.

Esther was taken to King Ahasuerus, in his royal palace, in the tenth month, which is the month of Tebeth, in the seventh year of his reign. The king loved Esther more than all the other women, and she won his grace and favor more than all the virgins. So he set a royal diadem on her head and made her queen instead of Vashti. The king gave a great banquet for all his officials and courtiers, "the banquet of Esther." He proclaimed a remission of taxes for the provinces and distributed gifts as befits a king.

When the virgins were assembled a second time, Mordecai sat in the palace gate. But Esther still did not reveal her kindred or her people, as Mordecai had instructed her; for Esther obeyed Mordecai's bidding, as she had done when she was under his tutelage.

At that time, when Mordecai was sitting in the palace gate, Bigthan and Teresh, two of the king's eunuchs who guarded the threshold, became angry, and plotted to do away with King Ahasuerus. Mordecai learned of it and told it to Queen Esther, and Esther reported it to the king in Mordecai's name. The matter was investigated and found to be so, and the two were impaled on stakes. This was recorded in the book of annals at the king's behest.[29]

A Vernacular Retelling

According to Judeo-Persian scholar Vera Moreen, Amīnā was the pen name of Binyamin ben Misha'el (1672–after 1732), an important Jewish poet from the central region of Isfahan. The poet's following commentary on Megillat Esther does not explicitly refer to exile, but the connections are implicit, the story of Esther being the basis for Purim, a holiday that both celebrates and lays bare the difficulties of life in exile.

Esther, heroine of the biblical story, saves her people from persecution by the evil Haman. While King Ahasuerus cannot undo his decree allowing his evil vizier to attack the Jews, the king can and does allow the Jews to defend themselves. The original story portrays the tenuousness of life in exile, and the necessity for Jews in exile to be self-reliant. The poet's commentary ends in praise of Mordecai, who becomes the "chosen" (1:175), the grand vizier and leader of the Jews, who are no longer subject to discrimination or abuse.

EXILE AND HOLIDAYS

The Purim story takes place in Shushan (Shushtar in the poem, Shush in modern Iran). This poem is especially resonant given its composition within the former Persia and during a period in which Jews were alternatively subjected to discriminatory practices, expulsion, and forced conversion. Although the date of its composition—and thus the specific circumstances of Jews at the time—remain unknown, it is not a stretch to read the text as consolation and hope for the future.

> AMĪNĀ (BINYAMIN BEN MISHA'EL), *COMMENTARY ON THE BOOK OF ESTHER* (EARLY 18TH CENTURY)
>
> Then Mordekai donned royal garments,
> Upon his head a royal cap and crown;
> And all the Jews were merry and rejoiced,
> With hearts serene and much relieved.
> There was rejoicing not only in Shushtar
> But throughout Bahman's realm.
> Many infidels, Christians, and Hindus,
> Turned Jew in dread of Mordekai;
> All the shah's khans showed great esteem
> And much respect to all the Jews,
> For Mordekai was chosen and preferred;
> His fame was spread throughout the world. . . .
>
> Ahasueros reigned with equity and justice.
> He no longer took from Jews, near or far,
> Neither poll tax nor customary tribute.
> All his royal decrees were in accordance
> With the ancient customs of Kay Khosrow;[30]
> They were recorded in the book of annals
> As was the way and custom of the princes.
> Mordekai the Jew was the shah's Asaf,[31]
> The grand vizier of the palace elite.
> He was the head and leader of the community
> Of Jews, the world's most benevolent man:

A seeker of peace, a source of learning,
An adviser in all its trials

O Lord, Who have performed miracles,
You are the Jews' refuge, patron,
And intimate companion. Favor us
Once again; command the Messiah to come.
Let *Redemption* take place in our time;
Let us read this *scroll* with happy hearts.
Amīnā makes this pact with God:
If he lives to see the Messiah's coming
He will be the panegyrist of the Mahdi.[32]
By God's grace, might, and favor,
If you are a Jew, say quickly Amen.[33]

Today's Esther

Abba Hillel Silver, born in Lithuania to a family of Orthodox rabbis, came to the United States as a child. The first in his family line to identify with Reform Judaism, Silver completed his BA at the University of Cincinnati and his rabbinic ordination at the Hebrew Union College in 1915, when he was only twenty-two. After a two-year service in a congregation in Wheeling, West Virginia, he was accepted as rabbi of Tifereth Israel, a prestigious Reform temple in Cleveland, where he served for the rest of his career. He was especially known for his oratorical skills, delivering strong sermons from the pulpit and, later, addresses championing Zionism.

The date of this Purim sermon—March 8, 1936—is telling. The Nazis' systematic murder of European Jewry would begin in 1941. Five years earlier, Silver makes a striking connection between Haman and Hitler, the danger facing the Jews in ancient Shushan and those in contemporary Germany. As Silver writes, "everything connected with the story" of Purim "is typical of the Jewish experience in exile from those days to these . . . a story of the uncertainty and impermanence characteristic of Jewish life in the Diaspora."

ABBA HILLEL SILVER, "BUT MORDECAI BOWED NOT DOWN" (1936)

Purim is our one festival whose locale is in the exile, outside of Palestine, and everything connected with the story is typical of the Jewish experience in exile from those days to these.

First of all, the story of Esther is a story of the uncertainty and impermanence characteristic of Jewish life in the Diaspora. For years people had lived at peace in the vast empire of Persia. Suddenly out of the clear sky came this desperate fact into their lives: that a man close to the king had been angered by a Jew, and because of his anger he had persuaded this king to destroy not merely this man and his family but the entire Jewish people. The tragic insecurity of the Jews in the Diaspora is brought out most dramatically in the Megillah: "And thy life shall hang in doubt before thee" (Deut. 28:66). You will have no assurance in your life. That has been the mark of the exile. . . .

Haman became angry at Mordecai. Hurt pride led him to turn against Mordecai and his people. Haman was not satisfied to put his hand out toward Mordecai alone; he turned against Mordecai's [people]. How characteristic this is of Jewish experience in exile! The anti-Semite starts with a personal grudge against some individual Jew, and ends up as an enemy of the entire people. . . .

There can be no peace for sixteen million Jews in the world if the program and the policies of the Nazis spread throughout the world. It is not going to spread if the Nazis are destroyed. Even if we get two or three million Jews out of the countries in Europe and settle them in Palestine, that does not solve the problem for the rest of the Jews who are going to remain in the Diaspora. So, our problem is to fight for an order of society which will allow us to live any place, anywhere on the face of the earth.

It is not enough to raise money for relief. It is important to raise money for relief, but it is more important to raise money for war against the enemies of civilization.[34]

4 Divine Presence in Exile

The question of whether God accompanied the Children of Israel into exile or whether the condition of exile included being separated from God occupies Jewish literature from its beginning. Some commentators view exile as punitive removal from God's presence (see chapter 5) while others recognize the divine as universal and universally accessible. The greatest expression of God's love is said to be the *Shekhinah* joining the exiles. Generally translated as Divine Presence and often interpreted as the feminine aspect of God, the *Shekhinah* speaks to the idea of the Temple as God's abode or dwelling place. In exile, the *Shekhinah*'s presence is understood to serve both as consolation and protection.

Yet, as we will also see, persecution, national catastrophe, and personal suffering provoke challenges to these traditional beliefs regarding the Divine Presence in exile.

Shekhinah

The word *shekhinah* does not appear in the Hebrew Bible, but other forms of the root reflect the meaning, as in Exodus 25:8: "Let them make Me a sanctuary, that I may dwell (*ve-shakhanti*) among them." Here the teaching concerns the constant presence of God in a unique holy site on earth, in addition to God's existence in the heavens. Later, God's presence would be recognized not only in specific locations where the Jewish people gathered outside of Jerusalem (Egypt, Babylonia), but wherever Jews lived.

B. *MEGILLAH* 29A

It has been taught: R. Simon b. Yohai said: Come and see how beloved are the People of Israel before the Holy One, to every place they were exiled—the *Shekhinah* is with them. They were exiled to Egypt—the *Shekhinah* was with them, as it is said, "I revealed Myself to the house of your father when they were in Egypt" (1 Sam. 2:27). They were exiled to Babylon—the *Shekhinah* was with them, as it is said, "For your sake I was sent to Babylon" (Isa. 43:14). And when they will be redeemed in the future—the *Shekhinah* will be with them, as it is said, "The Lord thy God returns [with] your captivity" (Deut. 30:3). It does not say here *ve-heshiv* [and will bring back] but *ve-shav* [and He will return]. This teaches us that the Holy One will return with them from the places of exile.

The Divine Presence amid Gentiles

The following passage from the Zohar, a foundational text of Jewish mysticism (Kabbalah), begins and ends with reference to the biblical Jonah's attempt to flee from the Land of Israel, indeed to flee from God. But the main point in the text relates to the People of Israel as a whole. There is a division between two different eras: the first when the Israelites worshiped God appropriately, and the second "when Israel sinned and defiled the land," with dramatic results. The passage alludes to the Greeks and Romans, the Christians and Muslims, who consequently exerted political control over the Holy Land.

Yet, the crucial figure in this narrative is the *Shekhinah*. First we are told that the *Shekhinah* was expelled from her home in the Jerusalem Temple, so that the *Shekhinah* herself was in exile. But, strikingly, we are then told that the other nations were able to draw the *Shekhinah* to themselves when they ruled in the Holy Land—an apparent reference to Christian and then Muslim worship of God in Jerusalem. And, finally, the exile of the *Shekhinah* is applied to her presence among the Jews scattered among other peoples with their own guardian angel. Jonah's attempt to flee from God thus leads to a devastating ordeal for the Divine Presence along with that of the Jewish people.

DIVINE PRESENCE IN EXILE

ZOHAR I, 84B–85A

Rabbi Abba began by quoting: *But Jonah arose to flee to Tarshish from the presence of the Lord* (Jonah 1:3). Woe to the man who tries to hide himself from the Holy One, blessed be He, of whom it is written *Do I not fill heaven and earth, says the Lord?* (Jer. 23:24). And yet he tried to flee from Him! . . .

Come and see. When Israel dwelt in the Holy Land, everything was ordered as it should be, and the throne was in perfection over them, and they engaged in worship [in the Temple]. . . . The worship ascended above, to its place, because Israel, alone in the earth, was prepared for worship. Consequently, the other peoples, the idolaters, were kept at a distance, for they had no power over [Israel] as they have now, because they were nourished only by the last drops.[1]

You might object, and say that we know that there were several kings ruling in the world when the Temple was still standing. But come and see. During the era of the First Temple, before Israel defiled the land, the other peoples, the idolaters did not rule, but they were nourished only by the last drops, and this gave them their power, which was not very great. When Israel sinned and defiled the land, they immediately forced the *Shekhinah*, as it were, to leave her place, and she drew near to another place,[2] and then the other peoples began to rule, and permission to rule was granted them.

Come and see. No other ruler[3] has been appointed for the land of Israel except the Holy One, blessed be He, alone. But when Israel sinned, and fell to offering incense to other gods in the midst of the land, then the *Shekhinah* was expelled, as it were, from her place, and they continued to offer incense and to link other gods with the *Shekhinah*, and then the power to rule was given to them, for incense helps to forge a link.[4] Then the other peoples began to rule, and the prophets ceased, and none of the supernal levels[5] ruled over the land. And the rule of the other peoples was not taken away, because they had drawn the *Shekhinah* toward them. Consequently, while the Second Temple stood, power was not taken away from the other peoples, and this is all the more true in the time when the *Shekhinah* was exiled among the other peoples, to a place where the other guardian angels have authority; for all of them draw nourishment from the *Shekhinah* who has come near to them.⁶

Therefore, when the people of Israel dwelt in their land, and were engaged in the worship of God, the *Shekhinah* acted chastely among them, and did not leave the house and show herself outside. Consequently, all the prophets who lived at that time received their prophecy only in her place, as we have said.⁷ It was for his reason that Jonah wanted to flee outside the Holy Land, so that prophecy might not be revealed to him, and so that he would not have to go on the mission of the Holy One, blessed be He.⁸

The Lost Princess

Rabbi Nachman of Bratzlav (Breslau, 1772–1810), the direct descendent of the Baal Shem Tov (founder of Hasidism) and the leader of the Breslover sect, combined the esoteric tradition of the Kabbalah with Torah study. He is closely associated with the concept of *hitbodedut*, an individual's seclusion for unstructured prayer and meditation in order to become closer to God. Beloved by his followers, he told stories in the form of thirteen fairy tales that concealed kabbalistic tales. His burial place in Uman (now Ukraine) has become a pilgrimage destination.

The following selection, the first of Rabbi Nachman's tales, can be read in multiple ways, including as an allegory of the Jewish experience of exile: the expulsion from the Garden of Eden; the Children of Israel's wandering in the desert; the *Shekhinah*'s banishment following the Temple's destruction. In his book *Reimagining the Bible*, the writer and folklorist Howard Schwartz suggests that the princess and her brothers stand in for the days of the week, the apple refers to the story of Adam and Eve, and the water turning into wine recalls the Flood as well as Noah's sin of drunkenness. The three giants are the patriarchs Abraham, Isaac, and Jacob; the palace is the Holy Land; the scarf represents scripture. While the allegory can be read on the collective level, it also lends itself to a personal interpretation in which each one of us experiences our own search. The ending is simultaneously open and closed; the audience is informed that the minister—possibly standing in for the Messiah—has succeeded in liberating the princess, although the assurance comes in the form of a postscript and not in the actual story itself. So the happy end is just out of reach, but assuredly in the future; the way to the happy end lies beyond the actual text or its telling.

R. NACHMAN OF BRATZLAV, "THE LOST PRINCESS" (1816)

There once was a king who had six sons and one daughter. His daughter was especially dear to him, but one day he became angry with her and said, "Go to the Devil" and the next day she was gone.

The heartbroken king then sent his most loyal minister on a quest to find her, giving him all that he might need to accomplish the quest, including a servant. The minister searched everywhere in the world but failed to find the princess. At last he came to a remote palace where he discovered her, and he managed to talk to her. She told him that she was being held captive in the palace of the Evil One, who took her when the king sent her to him, and that in order to set her free, the minister must long for her release for a year, and at the end of the year, fast for one day, neither eating nor drinking, and then she would be able to return to her father, the king.

The minister remained there for a year, longing for her freedom, but on the last day, when he was supposed to be fasting, he saw an apple on a tree that was so appealing that he picked it and ate it. After this he fell asleep and slept for seventy years. When at last he awoke, his servant told him of his long sleep. Then, heartbroken, he returned to the lost princess, who told him to repeat the year of longing, but this time he was permitted to eat—but not to drink—on the last day. He repeated the year-long vigil, but on the last day he saw the waters of a familiar spring had turned red, and he could not resist tasting them. They turned out to be a delicious wine, and he drank his fill and again fell asleep.

This time, while he was sleeping, the princess left the palace of the Evil One and rode past him in a carriage. She got out of the carriage and tried to wake him, but when she could not, she wept into her scarf and left it with him. When he finally awoke seventy years later, his loyal servant told him all that had taken place and showed him the scarf. He held it up to the sun and discovered that the tears of the lost princess had written a message on the scarf, in which she told him that henceforth she could be found in a palace of pearls on a golden mountain.

So it was that the heartbroken minister set out on a second quest, which turned out to be far more arduous than the first, because no one he met had ever heard of a palace of pearls on a golden mountain. He searched for many years, and his quest brought him at last to a great desert where he encountered three giants—one in charge of all the animals, one in charge of the birds, and one in charge of the wind—all of whom were brothers. Each of the giants carried a giant tree as a staff. These giants called together the animals, the birds, and the winds, but none had heard of the palace of pearls. At last, a late wind arrived, and when rebuked by the giant for being late, it explained that it had been carrying a princess to that very palace of pearls.

The giant then gave the minister an enchanted bag with an endless supply of gold and ordered the wind to bring him to the foot of the golden mountain. There the story ends, with Rabbi Nachman's assurance that eventually the minister did free the princess, although he does not reveal how this took place.[9]

Providential Protection in Exile

Isaac ben Yedaiah, a thirteenth-century scholar from southern France, wrote massive commentaries on the aggadic (nonlegal) passages of the Talmud and *Midrash Rabbah*. Below he emphasizes God's providential concern through a biblical commandment that he believes provides the basis for Jewish economic life in Christian Europe during the High Middle Ages: Jews may (or must) lend money at interest to non-Jews. The "this" in his opening sentence, "Divine wisdom decreed that this be commanded to the people for their own benefit," refers to Deuteronomy 23:21, *le-nokhri tashikh*, meaning you may (or, according to some authorities, "you must") lend at interest to an alien. Ben Yedaiah, following Maimonides, understands this as a mandate or a commandment of the Torah. Following the philosophical tradition, he explains that this commandment, like all the others, is for the benefit of the Jewish people. His innovation is that the benefit applies specifically to the period of the long exile.

> ISAAC BEN YEDAIAH, "COMMENTARY ON THE AGGADOT OF THE TALMUD" (LATE 13TH CENTURY)
>
> Divine wisdom decreed that this be commanded to the people for their own benefit. Just as the other commandments come for the benefit of the entire people, so is this beneficial. For it was clearly known to God that the people would have to be punished by exile and that He would uproot them from their land because of their sin, and they would go to a different land, from nation to nation. And if, among the other peoples, they worked in crafts, the Torah would quickly be forgotten from Israel, for they would not have sufficient time to follow the proper ways of the Torah.[10] They would thus be swallowed up in the midst [of their gentile neighbors], and they would lose their way like [the gentiles] because of the great toil necessary to provide sustenance and food for their households. But God gave them provisions for the road and good advice: that they could lend their money among the Gentiles for directly stipulated interest, so that the best among them would be free to teach the people knowledge and to show them the way to go. Thus they would be able to endure among [the nations], and the Torah would not be forgotten from their offspring to eternity.[11]

Benefits of Dispersal

Saul Levi Morteira was born ca. 1596 in Venice, where one of his teachers was the colorful and highly respected rabbi Judah Aryeh (Leon) Modena. In 1616 circumstances brought him to the new Jewish community of Amsterdam, where he would remain until his death in 1660. His congregation was composed entirely of recent immigrants from Portugal and their children. Morteira wrote his weekly sermons in Hebrew and then delivered them in Portuguese.

Excerpts from 2 of the approximately 550 preserved sermons follow.

In the first, composed for an ordinary Sabbath (Parashah Va-yetse'), Morteira explains the advantages of geographical dispersion during the period of the long exile. The second, later, extensive sermon for the Sabbath of Repentance (the Sabbath between Rosh Hashanah and Yom Kippur) explores the various ways in which God providentially protected the Jewish people in order to sustain their unique identity in the centuries of exile. Most intriguing is the claim that hatred of the Jews is unnatural, antithetical to the emotions that Jews naturally would arouse among their neighbors, implanted miraculously by God in the hearts of gentiles in order to safeguard against total assimilation through intermarriage. Yet in order to protect against this hatred becoming lethal and hence posing a different danger to Jewish survival, God providentially scattered Jews throughout the world, so that no local outburst of hostility could threaten the people as a whole.

SAUL LEVI MORTEIRA, "DUST OF THE EARTH" (CA. 1623)

Your descendants shall be as the dust of the earth; you shall spread out to the west and to the east, to the north and to the south. All the families of the earth shall bless themselves by you and your descendants (Gen. 28:14).

Genesis Rabbah, chapter 41. *I will make your descendants as the dust of the earth* (Gen. 13:16). Just as the dust of the earth is found from one end of the world to the other, so shall your children be scattered from one end of the world to the other. Just as the dust of the earth can be blessed only through water, so will Israel be blessed only for the sake of Torah, which is likened to water. And just as the dust of the earth wears out even metal utensils yet itself endures forever, so will Israel exist while the nations of the world will cease to be. And just as the dust is downtrodden, so will your children be downtrodden under the heel of foreign kingdoms. . . .

Among the various good tidings promised, God informed Jacob how, if his descendants should sin against Him, He would chastise them *with the rod of men and the affliction of mortals* (2 Sam. 7:14). This would however in the end be to their own advantage, and from the punishments themselves they would derive great benefit. All this is hinted in His statement, *Your offspring shall be as the dust of the earth* (Gen. 28:14). All the various analogies stated by the Sages are hinted in the verses that follow this.

They said first, "Just as the dust of the earth is found from one end of the world to the other, so shall your children be scattered from one end of the world to the other." This means, when they sin against Me, one aspect of their punishment is that they will be as the dust of the earth that is found everywhere. Yet from this punishment, great benefit will ensue for them in what God said immediately afterward, *You shall spread out to the west and to the east, to the north and to the south* (Gen. 28:14). This indicates that four great benefits come to us from this general scattering in our exile. . . .

1. The first benefit is that if God were to put us in one place in this exile of ours, because of the great multitude of our people and our nation in the world—for whoever reads *The Travels of Rabbi Benjamin* just on the places he visited will find the number of Jews astonishing, not to mention the places he did not visit[12]—if *a people plundered and despoiled* (Isa. 42:22) like us were to increase in population to this extent openly, so that the Gentiles would be aware of our aggregate numbers, they would certainly try any means possible to reduce our size. . . . Therefore, in order to conceal us from their evil eye, God scattered us a few here and a few there, so that our large population would not be apparent . . . and the Gentiles would not attempt to diminish it. In this way, a great benefit comes to you from this dispersion.

2. The second benefit is that in this dispersion the sins of Israel are erased more easily. If we were all in one place, our witness would be before only one nation. But our duty is to confess God's greatness before all the peoples of the earth, and before the citizens of all the nations. . . . Instead of being stubborn in your efforts to abandon Me, you shall be stubborn in your efforts to make Me known. In this way, wherever you may be—west and east, north and south—you shall plead the case that your faith is true and that your God is the true God. In this way, from your punishment, your exile, your scattering, great merit will come to you, which would

not be the case were you not like the dust scattered from one end of the world to the other.

3. The third benefit is that if we were together under one government, they might decide to wipe us all out together, as indeed occurred in several kingdoms to some of us—for example in the time of Ahasuerus—*were it not for the Eternal, who was on our side* (Ps. 124:1–2). . . . But since we are dispersed, they cannot annihilate us, for one abandons us and another takes us in. In this we are saved from them, and God *has not let us be ripped apart* (Ps. 124:6). . . .[13]

4. The fourth benefit is that God has decreed upon the Jewish people in this exile that in the land of our enemies we would not own *so much as a foot can tread on* (Deut. 2:5), so that we would recognize that we are exiled from our land and constantly raise our hearts to God to beseech food for our sustenance, and benefit from our own physical labor. . . . If we were all in the same land, the competition between Jews would be lethal. But being scattered, each one can engage in matters appropriate to his own country—some as sellers of clothing and others as merchants on the sea, some as moneylenders at interest, and others as craftsmen, some as purchasers of livestock and others as brokers for merchandise—so that everyone can find what he needs for a livelihood. . . .

In this way, God made Jacob a great promise in saying that when his offspring would be *as the dust of the earth*, they would not increase in population in a manner noticeable to their enemies, they would bear witness in every location to their faith in God, they would annul the plan of those who wanted to wipe them out, and all would be able to find what they needed for sustenance.[14]

5. The Sages further said, "Just as the dust of the earth can be blessed only through water, so will Israel be blessed only for the sake of Torah, which is likened to water." Their intention in this was to express another benefit that would accrue to us as a result of God's punishing us through dispersal. This is that many times the world has deserved destruction because of its evil deeds. God has scattered us among them as one who sprinkles salt over meat, so that our presence everywhere enables us to preserve the world from destruction.[15] This is because of the Torah, which is studied

wherever we are found.... And all this the Torah expressed in the phrase, *All the families of the earth shall be blessed through you and through your offspring* (Gen. 28:14), for because of you they will be blessed. It is connected to what preceded it: *Your offspring shall be as the dust of the earth, and all the families of the earth shall be blessed through you and through your offspring.*

6. They said further, "Just as the dust of the earth wears out even metal utensils yet itself endures forever, so will Israel exist while the nations of the world will cease to be." In this they revealed to us another great benefit in God's scattering us among the peoples. In this exile, Israel endures under pressure and pain, toiling to eke out a livelihood, experiencing afflictions and terrible diseases that come upon them. Now on many occasions it has become necessary to change their country, to travel *from nation to nation, from one kingdom to another* (1 Chron. 16:20), to change climate whether for reasons of health or sustenance. If the Jewish people were in one place, when a Jew wanted to move from his home and depart for a different land, [the inhabitants of the new land] would drive him away, for not knowing him they would be astonished at him. That is why God scattered His people to the four corners of the earth: so that wherever one Jew goes to change his residence, he will find his fellow Jews established. This will make his journey easier, for all will help each other, thereby facilitating their survival in their exile.... This too the Scripture taught by saying, *Your offspring shall be as the dust of the earth*, referring to perpetuity and endurance, for it goes on to say there, *I will bring you back to this land* (Gen. 28:15), meaning, "I will bring you back to this land after the exile: whether lowly or in honor you shall return here, for you shall not be destroyed."

7. Finally, the Sages said, "Just as the dust is downtrodden, so will your children be downtrodden under the heel of foreign kingdoms." In this they wanted to communicate a seventh benefit that comes to us out of our dispersion among the Gentiles. If we were all together, upon seeing our great numbers and the length of our exile, we might conceivably select a leader and rise up against the people in whose midst we lived, thereby seeking to speed up the end [of the exile].... But that is against God's plan.... God will go before us; He will

redeem us! That is why God scattered us, a few here, a few there: so that we would not set our minds to such a course. Yet with all this, God will not withhold from them His promise, for *I, I who am the savior* (cf. Deut. 32:39) *will not leave you until I have done what I have promised you* through My servants the prophets. Therefore, *The Eternal will battle for you; you hold your peace* (Exod. 14:14).[16]

SAUL LEVI MORTEIRA, "GUARDED HIM AS THE PUPIL OF HIS EYE" (DELIVERED 1631, PUBLISHED 1645)

Divine wisdom foresaw yet another well-known danger that would imperil Israel in this current exile according to the natural order, to which the experts will testify, attaining the full truth. From this too, God saved Israel through His marvelous providential care. This is that, as we learn from the other exiles, when the Jews are aliens in a land not theirs, the nations of those lands will seek to marry with them, because of their noble lineage. Even kings will be honored by them. . . .

According to proper investigation of the natural order, Jews should be highly honored by all peoples, both physically and spiritually.[17] These people should want the Jews to be nobles, to draw close to them, saying, "Bring us your abundant gifts of purity, marry with us, give us your daughters and we will give our daughters to you."[18] Thus Israel would assimilate among the nations, God forbid![19] . . .

And if this was so in the other exiles, in the present exile it would naturally be even more so, for Jews have noble lineage not only of a physical nature, but also spiritually, since they claim that their God and savior came from the Jews. Thus by law and custom, Jews should be considered by the Christians to be the most important and the noblest people conceivable, and they [Christians] should therefore want to cleave to them and marry with them. However, foreseeing this natural danger, God removed it from us, and generated in the hearts of these nations a great unnatural hatred, unprecedented before, so that they would despise us and set us at a distance from them. Lest they seduce us with their honors, God ensured that they would set us aside like a menstruous woman in her impurity—all for our own benefit and to ensure our survival up to this day. . . .[20]

Now if God has implanted hatred in the hearts of the nations so that they will not seek to draw near to us, we are certainly obligated to distance ourselves from intermarrying with them (heaven forbid!), for this is a criminal act. This is what exiled Israel from their land, and confounded their tranquility in the lands of their dispersion. In this way alone, the enemies found it possible to conquer God's people and to make strife between them and their God. For the closer they draw to the other peoples, the farther God draws away from them. . . .

It sometimes occurs that when a physician gives a dose of medicine or a drug to a sick person for a specific purpose, the constitution and nature of the sick person is so compatible with that of the medication that its effect is stronger than anticipated; consequently, the result of the medication is not benefit but harm. Similarly, when God implanted hatred in the hearts of the Gentile nations for the reason we mentioned, He found their nature to be so well disposed to it that it spoiled the pattern and crossed the boundary line. . . .[21] Therefore, it was necessary for God to correct this perversion and defend against this depredation through His wondrous individual providence, so that we would not be annihilated from the earth. For were it not for God's arising on our behalf, they would have swallowed us up alive.

Now the antidote and defense against this danger that is prepared and lurking around us was implemented by scattering us among the nations. God did not want us to be under one king in this exile. . . . Thus God has providentially watched over us in scattering us among the nations as a great remedy for their hatred so that they would not annihilate us. He placed us under many rulers, so that they would not all agree on a single plan.[22]

Providence and Potential

In 1655 the Amsterdam rabbi Menasseh ben Israel appealed to Oliver Cromwell to accept a Jewish presence back in England, from which Jews had been expelled in 1290. Arguing on mercantilist grounds for the economic benefit Jews brought to any country, Menasseh further claimed that Jews' empirically verifiable talent in commerce reflected God's providence in granting them the precise skills that would benefit them most in their exile. Menasseh's claim differs from the previous one in that the core economic activity has changed from moneylending to commerce, and that the benefit is not only for the Jews but for the nations that provide them a temporary home. While the conference discussing the petition did not immediately grant Jews citizenship and other rights, in fact, their presence became openly tolerated and their religious practices allowed.

> MENASSEH BEN ISRAEL, "TO HIS HIGHNESSE THE LORD PROTECTOR OF THE COMMONWEALTH OF ENGLAND, SCOTLAND, AND IRELAND" (1655)
>
> It is a thing confirmed, that merchandizing is, as it were, the proper profession of the Nation of the Jews. I attribute this in the first place, to the particular Providence and mercy of God towards his people. For having banished them from their own Country, yet not from his Protection, he hath given them, as it were, a natural instinct, by which they might not only gain what is necessary for their need, but that they should also thrive in riches and possessions; whereby they should not only become gracious to their Princes and lords, but that they should be invited by others to come and dwell in their Lands.
>
> Moreover, it cannot be denied [sic], but that necessity stirs up a man's ability and industry; and that it gives him great incitement, by all means to try the favour of Providence.[23]
>
> Besides, seeing it is no wisedome [sic] for them to endeavour the gaining of Lands and other immovable goods, and so to imprison their possessions here, where their persons are subject to so many casualties, banishments, and peregrinations, they are forced to use merchandizing until that time, when they shall returne to their own Country, that then as God hath promised by the Prophet Zachary, *There shall be found no more any merchant amongst them in the House of the Lord* [Zech. 14:21].[24]
>
> From that very thing we have said, there riseth an infallible Profit, commodity and gain to all those Princes in whose Lands they dwell above all other strange Nations whatsoever, as experience by divers Reasons doth confirme.[25]

DIVINE PRESENCE IN EXILE

Preliminary Redemption

In 1791 the French National Assembly resolved to annul all existing discriminatory legislation that still applied to French Jews (or, as the assembly formulated it, "Frenchmen of the Jewish persuasion")—a decision often viewed as ushering in the legal Emancipation of French Jewry, and thereby inaugurating a new era in Jewish history.[26]

The passage below is an immediate response to the heady news. Berr Isaac Berr, a merchant and manufacturer from Nancy in the province of Lorraine, had helped to present the case for the Emancipation of French Jews before the assembly, yet his "Letter of a Citizen to His Fellow Jews" says nothing about his own role in the process that led to this long-delayed decision, or about the Christian supporters of the Jewish cause in the assembly. Rather, Berr gives full credit to God, reasserting a traditional belief in God's providential control of historical events and special concern for the Jewish people.

Berr expresses an intriguing position on the relationship between Emancipation and exile. Exile, represented by the Jewish status in the Old Regime, is extremely negative: Jews were "vile slaves, mere serfs, a species of men merely tolerated and suffered . . . liable to heavy and arbitrary taxes." Despite exulting in the transforming significance of their sudden change in status, Berr insists that this is not the full redemption for which the Jews continue to pray. It is, rather, an intermediate stage, bestowed upon the French Jews by a gracious God—not because the Jews deserve it, but because God recognizes that for them, continued discrimination against them is a source of far greater humiliation and pain than the widespread discrimination against many groups under the Old Regime, and French Jewry is incapable of enduring the psychic trauma of "these new torments." Here Berr is referring to the French National Assembly's 1789 passage of the "Declaration of the Rights of Man and of the Citizen" stating that "All men are born and remain free and equal in rights" and that "No person shall be molested for his opinions, even such as are religious, provided that the manifestation of these opinions does not disturb the public order established by the law." Jews were capable of submitting to the burdens of exile under the old system, but not under this new arrangement where all other groups were included as equals and Jews alone were subjected to discrimination. Therefore, God, seeing that Jews could not endure this new situation, provided the remedy in the September 28 declaration—ending this most negative characteristic of the exile, but without yet bringing the ultimate redemption.

> BERR ISAAC BERR, "LETTER OF A CITIZEN
> TO HIS FELLOW JEWS" (1791)
>
> We are now, thanks to the Supreme Being and to the sovereignty of the nation, not only Men and Citizens, but we are Frenchmen! What a happy change Thou hast worked in us, merciful God! . . .
>
> Let it be acknowledged, dearest brethren, that we have not deserved this wonderful change by our repentance, or by the reformation of our manners; we can attribute it to nothing but to the everlasting goodness of God. He never forsook us entirely, but—finding that we were not yet worthy of seeing the accomplishment of his promises of a perfect and lasting redemption—He has not, however, thought proper still to aggravate our sufferings. Surely our chains had become the more galling from the contemplation of the rights of man, so sublimely held forth to public view.[27] Therefore, our God, who reads the heart of man, seeing that all our resignation would have proved unequal to the task, and that supernatural strength was wanting to enable us to support these new torments, has thought of applying the remedy: He has chosen the generous French nation to reinstate us in our rights, and to effect our regeneration, as, in other times, he had chosen Antiochus, Pompey, and others, to humiliate and enslave us. . . .[28]
>
> What bounds can there be to our gratitude. . . . We are, of a sudden, become the children of the country, to bear its common charges, and share in its common rights.[29]

Abandonment by the Divine Presence in Exile

Hayyim Nahman Bialik (1873–1934), known as the father of modern Hebrew poetry, was quick to share his wrath. Sent by the Jewish

DIVINE PRESENCE IN EXILE

historical commission in Odessa to report on the survivors of the 1903 Kishinev pogrom, he produced the epic poem "Ba-Ir ha-Haregah" ("In the City of Slaughter") condemning the passivity of the Jews in exile. The excerpt here records the reaction—or lack thereof—on God's part, as well as the shameful impotence of the *Shekhinah*.

HAYYIM NAHMAN BIALIK, "IN THE CITY OF SLAUGHTER" (1904)

What says the Shekinah? In the clouds it hides
In shame, in agony alone abides;
I, too, at night, will venture on the tombs,
Regard the dead and weigh their secret shame,
But never shed a tear, I swear it in My name.
For great is the anguish, great the shame on the brow;
But which of these is greater, son of man, say thou—
Or liefer [willingly] keep thy silence, bear witness in My name
To the hour of My sorrow, the moment of My shame.
And when thou dost return
Bring thou the blot of My disgrace upon thy people's head,
And from My suffering do not part,
But set it like a stone within their heart!
Turn, then, to leave the cemetery ground,
And for a moment thy swift eye will pass
Upon the verdant carpet of the grass— . . .

Take thou a fistful, fling it on the plain

Saying,
"The people is plucked grass; can plucked grass grow again?"
Turn, then, thy gaze from the dead, and I will lead
Thee from the graveyard to thy living brothers,
And thou wilt come, with those of thine own breed,
Into the synagogue, and on a day of fasting,
To hear the cry of their agony,
Their weeping everlasting. . . .

Look in their hearts—behold a dreary waste,
Where even vengeance can revive no growth,
And yet upon their lips no mighty malediction
Rises, no blasphemous oath. . . .

Leave now this place at twilight to return
And to behold these creatures who arose
In terror at dawn, at dusk now, drowsing, worn
With weeping, broken in spirit, in darkness shut.
Their lips still move with words unspoken.
Their hearts are broken.
No lustre in the eye, no hoping in the mind,
They grope to seek support they shall not find:
Thus when the oil is gone,
The wick still sends its smoke;
Thus does the beast of burden,
Broken and old, still bear his yoke.
Would that misfortune had left them some small solace
Sustaining the soul, consoling their gray hairs!
Behold the fast is ended; the final prayers are said.
But why do they tarry now, these mournful congregations?
Shall it be also read,
The Book of Lamentations?
It is a preacher mounts the pulpit now.
He opens his mouth, he stutters, stammers.
Hark
The empty verses from his speaking flow.
And not a single mighty word is heard
To kindle in the hearts a single spark.
The old attend his doctrine, and they nod.
The young ones hearken to his speech; they yawn.
The mark of death is on their brows; their God
Has utterly forsaken everyone. . . .[30]

5 Exile as Penance and Atonement

Exile is traditionally seen as punishment for wrongdoing. Where good deeds are amply rewarded, the Hebrew Bible is rife with warnings not to disobey commandments because of the dire consequences. In both Leviticus and Deuteronomy the comprehensive list of blessings to be bestowed upon those who follow the commandments is followed by a longer list of curses to befall those who sin. As the transgressions become progressively more acute, the repercussions increase in severity as well, with exile being last and the harshest of all. Exile is seen as the natural consequence for murder: Cain's fratricide condemns him to wandering the earth. Readers are also reminded how Adam and Eve's fall from grace is capped by their banishment from the Garden of Eden, and the builders of the Tower of Babel are punished for their hubris by being scattered to the four corners of the earth.

Yet exile is also seen as potentially penitential and an opportunity to achieve atonement. The severity of the sentence is matched by its power to render atonement: "Exile atones for all."[1] Because exile is such a harsh consequence for transgressing, the experience of exile may shock the offender into awareness of the transgression. Enduring the condition of exile is then purifying.

More positive readings of exile allow it to be redemptive, whether for the nation or the individual. And the longer the period of exile, the greater the hope of redemption.

National Exile

The following two passages from the third and fifth books of the Bible respectively enumerate a series of curses that shall befall the Israelites should they not live according to the commandments. In both cases the specter of exile—bring uprooted and scattered throughout foreign lands—looms as the harshest of consequences.

LEVITICUS 26:31–45

I will lay your cities in ruin and make your sanctuaries desolate, and I will not savor your pleasing odors. I will make the land desolate, so that your enemies who settle in it shall be appalled by it. And you I will scatter among the nations, and I will unsheath the sword against you. Your land shall become a desolation and your cities a ruin.

Then shall the land make up for its sabbath years throughout the time that it is desolate and you are in the land of your enemies; then shall the land rest and make up for its sabbath years. Throughout the time that it is desolate, it shall observe the rest that it did not observe in your sabbath years while you were dwelling upon it. As for those of you who survive, I will cast a faintness into their hearts in the land of their enemies. The sound of a driven leaf shall put them to flight. Fleeing as though from the sword, they shall fall though none pursues. With no one pursuing, they shall stumble over one another as before the sword. You shall not be able to stand your ground before your enemies, but shall perish among the nations; and the land of your enemies shall consume you.

Those of you who survive shall be heartsick over their iniquity in the land of your enemies; more, they shall be heartsick over the iniquities of their forebears; and they shall confess their iniquity and the iniquity of their forebears, in that they trespassed against Me, yea, were hostile to Me. When I, in turn, have been hostile to them and have removed them into the land of their enemies, then at last shall their obdurate heart humble itself, and they shall atone for their iniquity. Then will I remember My covenant with Jacob; I will remember also My covenant with Isaac, and also My covenant with Abraham; and I will remember the land.

For the land shall be forsaken of them, making up for its sabbath years by being desolate of them, while they atone for their iniquity; for the abundant reason that they rejected My rules and spurned

My laws. Yet, even then, when they are in the land of their enemies, I will not reject them or spurn them so as to destroy them, annulling My covenant with them: for I the Eternal am their God. I will remember in their favor the covenant with the ancients, whom I freed from the land of Egypt in the sight of the nations to be their God: I, the Eternal.

DEUTERONOMY 28:64–69

God will scatter you among all the peoples from one end of the earth to the other, and there you shall serve other gods, wood and stone, whom neither you nor your ancestors have experienced. Yet even among those nations you shall find no peace, nor shall your foot find a place to rest. God will give you there an anguished heart and eyes that pine and a despondent spirit. The life you face shall be precarious; you shall be in terror, night and day, with no assurance of survival. In the morning you shall say, "If only it were evening!" and in the evening you shall say, "If only it were morning!"—because of what your heart shall dread and your eyes shall see. God will send you back to Egypt in galleys, by a route that I told you should not see again. There you shall offer yourselves for sale to your enemies as male and female slaves, but none will buy.

These are the terms of the covenant that God commanded Moses to conclude with the Israelites in the land of Moab, in addition to the covenant that was made with them at Horeb.

The Atoning Power of Exile

This next passage presents exile in a more positive light: it can atone for sins. The specific examples based on the biblical passages may not seem very compelling, but the idea that—presumably in addition to the sinner's sorrow—the experience of exile itself can wipe the slate clean is a source of comfort and reassurance.

SANHEDRIN 37B (4TH–6TH CENTURY)

And Rav Yehuda, son of Rabbi Ḥiyya, says: Exile atones for half of a sin. As initially it is written in the verse concerning Cain that he said: "And I shall be a fugitive [*na*] and a wanderer [*vanad*] in the earth" (Gen. 4:14), and ultimately it is written: "And Cain went out from the presence of the Lord, and dwelt in the land of Nod" (Gen. 4:16). Rav Yehuda, son of Rabbi Ḥiyya, equates "Nod" with "*nad*," and understands that Cain was given only the punishment of being a wanderer. Exile atoned for half his sin, thereby negating the punishment of being a fugitive.

Rav Yehuda says: Exile atones for three matters, i.e., three types of death, as it is stated: "So says the Lord: Behold, I set before you the way of life and the way of death. He that abides in this city shall die by the sword, and by the famine, and by the pestilence; but he that goes out, and falls away to the Chaldeans that besiege you, he shall survive, and his life shall be for him for a prey" (Jer. 21:8–9), indicating that exile from Jerusalem will save one from those three deaths.

Rabbi Yoḥanan says: Exile atones for all transgressions and renders a sinner like a new person, as it is stated concerning the king Jeconiah, a descendant of King David: "So says the Lord: Write you this man childless, a man that shall not prosper in his days; for no man of his seed shall prosper, sitting upon the throne of David, and ruling anymore in Judah" (Jer. 22:30). And after Jeconiah was exiled it is written: "And the sons of Jeconiah, the same is Assir, Shealtiel his son" (1 Chron. 3:17). The verse employs the plural "sons of" although he had only one son, Shealtiel. "Assir," literally, prisoner, teaches that his mother conceived him in prison. "Shealtiel," literally, planted by God, teaches that God planted him in a way atypical of most plants [*hanishtalin*], i.e., people.[2]

The Street of the Tanners

This passage from the Zohar, in the form of a midrashic comment on several verses from Leviticus 26 (quoted above), is one of the most striking statements of God's decision to accompany God's people into the exile that is the necessary punishment for their sin. God makes the decision for two reasons: concern lest the people be totally destroyed if they are abandoned to the hazards of exile, and an unconditional love that impels God to venture into the most unsavory locale to be with the Divine's beloved.

The parable of the tanners is noteworthy. Tanners, whose work with dyes and animal skins produced a repulsive smell that clung to their bodies, were near the bottom of the social scale, and the street of the tanners was one that people tended to avoid if at all possible. The Zohar uses this image for gentile society. According to the parable, nothing could induce God to be present in that environment except for the presence of God's beloved: the People of Israel, depicted here not as a queen who returns to her father's house, but as an ordinary woman who lives in the worst part of town.

The novel homiletical interpretation seems to be that "*I will not reject them, nor will I abhor them*" refers not to the Jewish people but to the gentile *enemies* (represented by the tanners) in whose midst the bride lives. This is syntactically and conceptually possible for the first part of the verse, although applying it to the rest of the verse ("*annulling My covenant with them, for I the Eternal am their God*") would be quite radical.

ZOHAR III, 115A–B (13TH CENTURY)

The Blessed Holy One said as follows: "Israel, what should I do with you? I have already punished you, and you have not heeded Me. I have brought fearsome warriors and flaming forces to strike at you and you have not obeyed. If I expel you from the land alone, I fear that packs of wolves and bears will attack you and you will be no more. But what can I do with you? The only solution is that you and I together will leave the land and both of us go into exile. Thus it is written, *I will discipline you*—forcing you into exile, but if you think that I will abandon you—*Myself* (Lev. 26:28) too, along with you. . . ."

Rabbi Hiyya said: I have heard a new interpretation that Rabbi Eleazar said: "*I will not reject them, nor will I abhor them, so as to destroy them utterly*" (Lev. 26:44). Should it not have said, "I will not smite them, nor will I slay them, so as to destroy them utterly"? Yet [it says] *I will not reject them, nor will I abhor them*. What it means is this. Usually one who is hated by another person is repulsive and abhorrent to him. But in this case, "*I will not reject them, nor will I abhor them.*" Why is this? Because My soul's beloved is among them, and for her sake they are all beloved to Me. It is written *lekhalotam* ("to destroy them"), without the letter *vav* [which could therefore be read *lekhalatam*: "for their bride"]: because of her *I will not reject them, nor will I abhor them*, for she is the love of my life; my love is with her.

It is like a man who was in love with a woman who lived in the street of the tanners. If she had not been there, he would never have set foot in the place; but because she was there it seemed to him like the street of the spice merchants, where all the finest perfumes in the world could be found. So here *Yet for all that, when they are in the land of their enemies* (Lev. 26:44), which is the street of the tanners, *I will not reject them, nor will I abhor them*. Why? *Lekhalatam*, because of their bride, whom I love; for it is My soul's beloved who dwells there, and to Me it is like all the finest perfumes in the world, because of the bride that is with them.[3]

The Interminable Exile

The fifteenth-century philosopher-financier-statesman Don Isaac Abravanel drew on his knowledge of history and his contemporary context in his Bible commentary (see chapters 1 and 2). So, too, in commenting on two biblical sources (first Lev. 26:38–39 and then the entire book of Deuteronomy) in the two excerpts below, Abravanel draws on his own personal experience of exile—that of his family's when they were forced to flee Castille, and that of English (1290), French (1394), and Provençal ("the entire country of France," 1498/1501) Jews.

DON ISAAC ABRAVANEL, *PERUSH ʿAL HA-TORAH* ON
LEVITICUS 26:38–39 (LATE 15TH CENTURY)

In order to connect their sins with the sins of their ancestors, another exile was required, not like the Babylonian exile, but more difficult and much longer. . . .

In order to indicate that this exile would be extremely long, not short like the Babylonian exile, God said, "You will perish among the nations, and the land of your enemies shall consume you" (Lev. 26:38). This is among the strange maladies, together with the length of time of the exile. Then He said, "Those of you who survive shall be heartsick over their iniquities" (Lev. 26:39). This was in order to inform them that they would not return to Jerusalem as in the first exile. In this divine visitation they could never imagine that in a relatively short time God would make another visitation to their land because of their heathenism. For there all of the exiles will be "heartsick over their iniquities," they and their children and grandchildren, not because of their bankruptcy [?] [*shemitut/shemitot?*], for the land has already rested [*shavtah*] because of them, but "they will be heartsick over their iniquities" that have seized them even in the lands of their enemies. "More, they shall be heartsick over the iniquities of their fathers" (Lev. 26:39), meaning that they will be heartsick because of the sins that their ancestors committed when they were in the land, before the destruction of the First Temple, worshipping the stars . . . and the other sins that they committed. It is because of these sins—both early and the recent—that this bitter and lengthy exile will continue. "They will be heartsick" refers to the punishment of the body.[4]

DON ISAAC ABRAVANEL, *PERUSH ʿAL HA-TORAH*
ON DEUTERONOMY 28 (LATE 15TH CENTURY)

The interpretation of "You shall perish among the nations, and the land of your enemies shall consume you" (Lev. 36:38) applies to the calamities and the murders that have afflicted Israel in the [current] exile. Many of the Jews have perished from famine, and pestilence and bloodshed [or "the sword"], among them in the massacre of sacred communities, and the expulsion of the Jews from the land of England and other countries of the west, especially the expulsions from the entire country of France, in which the number of the dead was twice as many as those who left Egypt. And what can be said now about the expulsion of "the Exile of Jerusalem that is in Spain" [see Obad. 1:20], which applied to a number greater than all previous expulsions! Our souls have grieved from what we have heard![5]

The Suffering Servant

Hermann Adler was born in Hanover, Germany, in 1839 of a distinguished rabbinic family. His grandfather, Marcus Baer Adler, was chief rabbi of Hanover. His father, Nathan Marcus Adler, succeeded Marcus Adler in this post, and then, in 1845, was elected chief rabbi in London, a position in which he served until his death in 1890. His mother was the niece of Nathan Mayer Rothschild. (His older brother, Marcus, and his younger brother, Elkan, also had illustrious careers in public life.)

Educated at University College London (where he received a Prize and a First Certificate in English Language and Literature), Hermann Adler studied Talmud and received rabbinical ordination in a renowned yeshiva in Prague, then earned a PhD at Leipzig with a thesis on Druidism. Returning to England, he became temporary principal of Jews' College, the seminary established by his father to train Modern Orthodox clergymen. In 1864 he began to serve as preacher of the newly established Bayswater Synagogue of London, where he delivered the sermon excerpted here. Later, he would become deputy to his father ("Delegate Chief Rabbi" in 1879), and was elected to succeed his father in 1891. His policy called for moderate innovation on the part of mainstream Orthodox congregations as a necessary accommodation to modernity and citizenship. His first published book of sermons, *Naftulei Elohim* (Gen. 30:8: "Struggles over God"): *A Course of Sermons on the Biblical Passages Adduced by Christian Theologians*, was an apologetical and polemical defense of Judaism felt to be under attack by Christian conversionary organizations.[6]

The following passage discusses exile in the context of the so-called "suffering servant" passages in Deutero-Isaiah (Isa. 52:13–53:12). Early Christian believers applied these verses to explain the "scandal of the cross"—how the Messiah could be put to an excruciating death in the most humiliating manner known in antiquity—and the passages became one of the staples of Christian conversionist argumentation: "Can't you see that these verses are prophecies of Jesus, fulfilled in his passion?" Jews, in response, noted that the passages said nothing about the Messiah, but they had to provide another explanation of what the verses did refer to. The most common explanation was that God's servant was a personification of the Jewish people. Applying this to the Jewish experience in exile allowed Jews to present the oppression at the hands of the gentile world in all its horror, and also to claim that it was not (as the Christians maintained) a punishment for the Jews' sin of refusing to accept the Messiah; not a sign of God's anger and rejection; not (as Abraham Mendes, chapter 2, would have it) a prolonged punishment for other failures to fulfill their covenantal obligations; and not (as Judah ibn Yaḥya, also chapter 2, professed) simply a painful enigma. Rather, it was a fulfillment of a divine role, a "mission," teaching all humanity by example the truth of their belief by living as "the exemplar of unflinching obedience to the One God."

HERMANN ADLER, *A COURSE OF SERMONS ON THE BIBLICAL PASSAGES ADDUCED BY CHRISTIAN THEOLOGIANS* (1869)

Our expositors agree in saying that the servant, here spoken of, is the nation, Israel. Just one page before, the prophet, speaking in the name of the Lord, says *Avdi atah Yisrael asher be-kha etpa'er, Thou art my servant, Israel, in whom I will be glorified* (Isa. 49:3) All the preceding chapters have spoken of the glorious exaltation that awaits Israel. The prophet now proceeds to speak in more explicit terms of this future greatness. *Behold my servant shall prosper, he shall be exalted and extolled, and be very high* (Isa. 52:13). He shall be exalted in the same degree as he had been degraded during his exile. On beholding this, all the nations and the kings of the earth will be astonished; they will call to mind that state of abasement which had formerly been the lot of the Israelites.

Then follows that wondrous record of our nation's sufferings, depicted by a master hand, on which each page in our history during the middle ages is a life-breathing, vivid commentary. "Israel was *despised and rejected, acquainted with grief, and we* (the nations of the earth) *esteemed him not*" (cf. Isa. 53:3). Now, why was Israel dispersed to all quarters of the globe? Why had he to suffer all these afflictions? That he might fulfil his mission and wean mankind from error and irreligion. When at last the nations of the earth shall reflect upon the martyrdom Israel endured for so many centuries, how he was cut off from the land of the living, how his grave was made with the wicked and his death compassed by the mighty of the earth, and how he bore it all that healing might be effected; redemption from error and sin, healing from false belief—for Israel was to be the teacher of mankind, the exemplar of unflinching obedience to the One God. . . .

The prophet continues, *Yet it pleased the Lord to bruise him; he has put him to grief: when his soul shall make an offering for sin, he shall see his seed, he shall prolong his days, and the pleasure of the Lord shall prosper in his hand* (Isa. 53:10). Israel shall be gloriously rewarded for the sufferings he has borne. *Through his knowledge*—through practising and teaching the sacred lessons of his faith—*shall my righteous servant justify many* (i.e., bring them to virtue), *for he shall endure their iniquities* (Isa. 53:11). *Therefore will I divide him a portion with the great, and he shall divide the spoil with the strong* (in other words, he will be the equal of the mightiest of the earth in honour and glory), *because he has poured out his soul unto death: and he was numbered with the transgressors, and he endured the sin of many, and made intercession with the transgressors* (Isa. 53:12). How sublime is this view of the prophet! He stands here, looking, as it were, from the summit of his prophetic intelligence upon the history of the world, and divines the future development and ultimate perfection of man—the golden age that awaits mankind when they will acknowledge the errors of which they have been guilty, tender the hand of brotherhood to redeemed Israel and acknowledge Israel's God.[7]

From Suffering Alone

Born in Hungary, the son of Rabbi Adolf Altmann of Trier, Rabbi Alexander Altmann studied at the Pressburg Yeshiva, the Hildesheimer Rabbinical Seminary in Berlin, and Berlin University. While still in Europe, he acquired a reputation as a preacher, talmudic scholar, and expert in Jewish philosophy. In 1938 he became communal rabbi in Manchester, England; ten years later he was a leading contender for the position of chief rabbi. He was offered but declined a position in Jewish philosophy at the Hebrew University; in 1959 he moved to the United States and had a highly successful career as professor of Jewish philosophy at Brandeis University. Extremely prolific in his academic publications, he is probably best known for his nine-hundred-page book *Moses Mendelssohn: A Biographical Study*.

> ALEXANDER ALTMANN, "SERMON FOR
> ROSH HASHANAH 5695" (1934)
>
> *If a shofar is blown in a city, will the people not be afraid?* (Amos 3:6.) Woe to us, if we do not become afraid! The God of history Himself calls to us the words, *Ve-shavtem ish el aḥuzato ve-ish el mishpaḥto*: "You shall return, every one of you to your property and every one of you to your family" (Lev. 25:10). Return to Judaism is the sign of our times. . . .
>
> The Jew of the *golus* [exile] must let people say, "You lack creative energy, your existence is worthless." He sees life around him growing, spreading. He stands in the midst of the world like a stranger. Should he deceive himself to think that he is a people like the others, an equal link set in the chain of the peoples of the world? Surely, he roams through the life of this world with the others; he does not shut himself off, yes, he even renders a contribution to the production of goods on this planet that is not insignificant. But is he not in reality not a *ḥativah aḥat ba'olam*, a unique entity in the world (b. Ber. 6a), a type whose character somehow doesn't fit into the environment—and therefore is subject to misunderstandings? Can anyone deny that ever since [our march through the *golus*], we have

ceased to own a right to our existence, like all other peoples, from the very basis of our being? The period of Emancipation wanted to convince us: see, Jewry fits wonderfully into this world! But today we know: so long as we are in *golus*, we do not fit into this world. And yet we bear the *golus*. That is the greatness of the Jew: to know of his fate and yet—feeling the rift in his soul—not to sink. That means bearing the Jewish fate. Such is Jewish pride. To feel the tragedy of our being and yet stand with dignity. Not to affirm the *golus*—for in reality one negates it inwardly though spiritual assimilation—but rather to be willing to bear the *golus as golus*, as God's servant. Not begrudgingly, and—like Hannah—with the full strength of a love that cannot be suffocated, even when there is no one to receive it. . . .

But at the same time, Rosh Hashanah ignites the torch of hope. The final act of the drama of Hannah reveals the heroine as the happy one. In Hannah's prayer of thanksgiving, the power of joy derived from suffering is exultant. This conclusion is not a cheap "All's well that ends well," but rather the great preliminary draft, the great symbol of Jewish eschatological hope.

Kol maqom she-ne'emar ein lah, havah lah. "Wherever you believe that nothing is granted, it is already granted" (Gen. Rabbah 38:21; *Yalkut Shimoni* on 1 Sam. 1:2, and elsewhere). From suffering alone can redemption be born. Even now in our days the glimmer of future redemption already shines. This curse of the *golus* is beginning to depart from us. If the signs do not all deceive, the Jewish people seems not only to be about to put an end to the epoch of the aberrations of blind assimilation, but even more, to overcome, through God's mercy, the millennia of its "Wandering Jew" existence, the long night of *Tokhecha*, the great punishment. The land of our ancestors is changing from the desert back to the Promised Land. . . . Creative powers are arising. The suffering of our times is—already today—overshadowed by the blessing of what is to be.[8]

To be sure, *golus* is not by any means yet overcome. No one believes that we have already been redeemed. We still do not yet stand at the messianic "end of days." . . . But this we know: *He raises up the poor from the dust, lifts up the needy from the ash heap . . . ; for the pillars of the earth are the Lord's, He has set the world up on them* (1 Sam. 2:8).[9]

Individual Exile

Cain and Abel represent a new generation, fundamentally different from that of their parents. Adam and Eve were both unique as the only human beings on earth, and at the same time they represented all human life; Cain and Abel are distinct individuals. God is said to favor Abel, the shepherd, over Cain, the farmer.

Cain kills his brother. As punishment, God condemns Cain to wander forever on the earth (and fail as a farmer), but God also reassures Cain that no one will murder him—the first hint that there are other people on the earth. This seems as if Cain has been sentenced to painful exile, far away from his parents, but then we are told that Cain found a wife and established a city. It seems as if, despite his sin of fratricide, he is able to live a fairly respectable life.

> **GENESIS 4**
>
> Now the Human knew his wife Eve, and she conceived and bore Cain, saying, "I have gained someone new with the help of God." She then bore his brother Abel. Abel became a keeper of sheep, and Cain became a tiller of the soil. In the course of time, Cain brought an offering to God from the fruit of the soil; and Abel, for his part, brought the choicest of the firstlings of his flock. God paid heed to Abel and his offering, but to Cain and his offering [God] paid no heed. Cain was much distressed and his face fell. And God said to Cain,
>
> > "Why are you distressed,
> > And why is your face fallen?
> > Surely, if you do right,
> > There is uplift.
> > But if you do not do right
> > Sin couches at the door;
> > Its urge is toward you,
> > Yet you can be its master. . . ."
>
> And when they were in the field, Cain set upon his brother Abel and killed him. God said to Cain, "Where is your brother Abel?" And he said, "I do not know. Am I my brother's keeper?"

"What have you done? Hark, your brother's blood cries out to Me from the ground! Therefore, you shall be more cursed than the ground, which opened its mouth to receive your brother's blood from your hand. If you till the soil, it shall no longer yield its strength to you. You shall become a ceaseless wanderer on earth."

Cain said to God, "My punishment is too great to bear! Since You have banished me this day from the soil, and I must avoid Your presence and become a restless wanderer on earth—anyone who meets me may kill me!" God said to him, "I promise, if anyone kills Cain, sevenfold vengeance shall be exacted." And God put a mark on Cain, lest anyone who met him should kill him. Cain left the presence of God and settled in the land of Nod, east of Eden.

Cain knew his wife, and she conceived and bore Enoch. And he then founded a city, and named the city after his son Enoch. To Enoch was born Irad, and Irad begot Mehujael, and Mehujael begot Methusael, and Methusael begot Lamech. Lamech took to himself two wives: the name of the one was Adah, and the name of the other was Zillah. Adah bore Jabal; he was the ancestor of those who dwell in tents and amidst herds. And the name of his brother was Jubal; he was the ancestor of all who play the lyre and the pipe. As for Zillah, she bore Tubal-cain, who forged all implements of copper and iron. And the sister of Tubal-cain was Naamah.

And Lamech said to his wives,

"Adah and Zillah, hear my voice;
O wives of Lamech, give ear to my speech.
I have slain a rival for wounding me,
And a lad for bruising me.
If Cain is avenged sevenfold,
Then Lamech seventy-sevenfold."

Adam knew his wife again, and she bore a son and named him Seth, meaning, "God has provided me with another offspring in place of Abel," for Cain had killed him. And to Seth, in turn, a son was born, and he named him Enosh. It was then that God began to be invoked by name.[10]

The Preservation of Jews

In the third century, the Parthian prophet Mani (216–274 or 277) founded Manichaeism, which became a major rival to both Christianity and classical paganism. Its believers repudiated the "Old Testament" completely and had absolutely nothing positive to say about biblical or contemporary Jews. Early on, Augustine of Hippo (354–430 CE) was influenced by Manichaeism, but later turned against it and attacked it strongly. In this passage he counters Faustus, a powerful spokesman of Manichaeism who justified the physical annihilation of Jews, by professing that the preservation of Jews scattered throughout the world is important as a continual reminder of the truth of Christianity. Augustine's position certainly does not pass muster by modern standards, but his insistence on toleration in exile as an alternative to Faustus was certainly appreciated.

> AUGUSTINE, "REPLY TO FAUSTUS THE MANICHEAN" (CA. 400)
>
> "Groaning and trembling shall you be on the earth" (see Gen. 4:12 [Septuagint translation]). Here no one can fail to see that in every land where the Jews are scattered they mourn for the loss of the kingdom, and are in terrified subjection to the immensely superior number of Christians. So Cain answered and said, "My case is worse, if you drive me out this day from the face of the earth, and from Your face shall I be hid, and I shall be a mourner and an outcast on the earth, then it shall be that 'everyone that finds me shall slay me'" (Gen. 4:14). . . .
>
> What does God reply? "Not so," He says; "whoever shall kill Cain, vengeance shall be taken on him sevenfold" (Gen. 4:15). That is, it is not as you say; not by bodily death shall the ungodly race of carnal Jews perish. For whoever destroys them in this way shall suffer sevenfold vengeance, that is, shall bring upon himself the sevenfold penalty under which the Jews lie for the crucifixion of Christ. So to the end of the seven days of time, the continued preservation of the Jews will be a proof to believing Christians of the subjection merited by those who, in the pride of their kingdom, put the Lord to death.[11]

EXILE AS PENANCE AND ATONEMENT

The Inescapability of God's Presence

Aspects of the following passage seem extraordinarily distant from reality. The animals, wild and tame, recognize that Cain (unlike Adam and Eve) was a strange being; realize that he killed his brother and that God was punishing him; and all agree that Cain should be destroyed. This is followed by Cain's citation of a verse from Psalms, written a thousand years later. In the original psalm, the omnipresence of God is read only as a positive, whereas *Tanḥuma* Bereshit opens up questions and nuances regarding the psalm's broader meaning: is it a lament against the inescapability of God, a contradiction of verse 16 (*"Cain left the presence of God"*), or an explanation of the previous verse (*"The Lord said whosoever slays Cain will be seventy times avenged, and set a sign for Cain, that no one harms him"* — Gen. 4:15)?

> TANḤUMA, BERESHIT 9 (CA. 400–600 CE)
>
> [Cain] *My sin is greater than I can bear* (Gen. 4:13). [God] said: Since you confessed and repented, go forth in exile from this place, as it is said, *Cain left the presence of the Lord and lived in the land as a wanderer* (Gen. 4:16).
>
> Wherever he went forth walking, the land shook under him, and the animals and beasts shook and asked, "What is this?" They told each other, "Cain killed his brother Abel; so the Holy One decreed for Cain, '*You will be an eternal wanderer*'" (Gen. 4:12). They said, "Let's go and devour him," and they surrounded him.
>
>> The tears flowed from Cain's eyes as he said:
>> To where should I go from Your spirit?
>> To where should I flee from Your Presence?
>> If I seek the heavens, You are there;
>> If I descend to the depths You are there.
>> If I take the wings of dawn, and dwell at the ends of the sea,
>> Even there Your hand will lay me,
>> And Your right hand grasp me. (Ps. 139:7–10).

Exile as Volitional Penance

Israel ben Ḥaim of Brunn, born around 1400, trained under Jacob Weil (his father-in-law), established a school in Regensburg, and served there for some thirty years.

The case at hand is one of murder perpetrated by two individuals, apparently in response to provocative behavior by the man who was killed. The acts of the case do not permit punishment, but the judge can impose a penitential regimen, including one year of exile from the perpetrators' home community, with many detailed acts of contrition and humiliation. Strikingly, these apply only to Simḥah, who struck the final blow, but who claimed to have been drunk and has shown apparently sincere remorse. The other perpetrator, who struck the first deadly blow, has shown no remorse, and therefore cannot be punished according to Jewish law.

Thus, exile is a voluntary mode of atonement, applied only to the individual who wants to find a means of penance, and not imposed as a punishment. Exile is apparently not a judicial decision according to Torah law.

> ISRAEL BRUNN, *SHE'ELOT U-TESHUVOT* (RESPONSA) NOS. 265, 166 (15TH CENTURY, PUBLISHED 1798)
>
> *Question*: Greetings to the community of Lemberg (Posen).... On the matter of the murder that occurred in your city: a certain wicked fellow, Nahman, struck the first murderous blow, and a certain Simhah finished the murderous deed. It has been deposed that Nahman stabbed Nissan in the head with a knife, wounding him in the head. According to testimony given in the community of Frieslow[?], whose members had received a report from the eyewitnesses to the murder, he (Nahman) also wounded him so that he could not rise to his feet any more. Nahman moved the wounded man about by his head; then he called to Simhah, "Get him." Simhah ran and struck Nissan with a cudgel until he fell to the floor.[12] While Nissan was on the floor Simhah struck him three more times.[13]

Moses b. Asher testified that Simhah was drunk at the time. He testified concerning Nissan that he was ignorant and illiterate, had never even put on *tefillin*, and there was not even a veneer of piety about the man. He (Nissan) had begun the fracas by hurling two chunks of wood at Simhah. It is also inscribed how Simhah is filled with remorse and seeks to repent; Nahman has shown no remorse or inclination to repent. Nissan died that night. . . .

Answer: You have called Nahman by his name Nahman; you have called Simhah "a murderer." I *name them both murderers*, utterly guilty before the divine tribunal, but (alas) beyond the jurisdiction of the human court! In *b. Sanh.* 78a, we have the provision that if the assailants strike a man mortally, whether they do so simultaneously or consecutively, they cannot be tried for murder under Jewish Law because the Bible clearly states, *If one kills a man* (Lev. 24:18), which is interpreted as meaning that one murderer must perform the entire act of killing. . . .

As for Simhah, the testimony of the witness that Simhah was drunk is irrelevant, as long as he had not become as drunk as Lot. . . . Simhah confessed his part in the whole matter the next morning; he was completely rational. . . .[14]

Concerning that scoundrel Nahman, I shall prescribe no procedure for atonement because he spurns repentance; he is not shaken and remorseful over his iniquity. . . .

Now I shall prescribe the procedure for repentance required of Simhah, according to what appears to be correct on the basis of the documents (which describe such matters). However, I do not know the man (Simhah), his manner, or his nature. Thus, if it seems (correct) to the scholars of Posen to add or detract (from the program I shall propose) they are free to do so. This is the program of his repentance:

He shall journey about *as an exile* for a full year. Every day he shall appear at a synagogue—or at least on every Monday and Thursday. He shall make for himself three iron bands, one to be worn on each of his two hands, which were the instruments of his transgressions, and one to be worn about his body. When he enters the synagogue, he shall put them on and pray with them on. In the evening he shall go barefoot to the synagogue. The *hazzan* shall seat him (publicly) prior to the *Vehu Rahum* prayer.[15] He shall then receive a (symbolic [?] public) flogging and make the following declaration: "Know ye, my masters, that I am a murderer. I wantonly killed Nissan. This is my atonement. Pray for me." When he leaves the synagogue he is to prostrate himself across the doorsill; the worshipers are to step over him, not on him.[16] Afterwards he is to remove the iron bands.

He is to fast every day for a full year, except for those days on which penitential prayers are not said (e.g., Sabbaths, holidays). He is neither to partake of meat or wine nor to become drunk on strong liquors, and it is particularly appropriate for him to refrain from the type of drink he had on the night of the murder, because drunkenness from it caused the tragedy. He is not to sleep on a soft bed except on Sabbaths and holidays, including Hanukkah and Purim. During his exile he is not to trim his hair or his beard, for this is a mode of repentance noted in *b. Sanh.* 25a. He is not to wash with hot water except on the eves of Sabbaths and holidays. He is to cleanse his hair once a month. He is to wash his clothes once a season. He is not to frequent taverns, for in such a place did the mischief first occur. He is not to engage in any game of chance: the killing occurred because of an argument over a game of chance.[17] If people insult him with the epithet "Murderer!" he is to hold his peace and accept in love whatever insults are hurled at him; he is to say: "This is my atonement." He is to be very careful in reciting the *Shema* and *Tefillah* portions of the public liturgy. He is to make the well-known formal confession of sins three times each day and to declare after each recitation: "Please, O Lord, accept my repentance, for I have transgressed and shed innocent blood; may my humiliation and shame be my atonement."

After one year he shall continue his fasts on Mondays and Thursdays. He shall, for the rest of his days, carefully observe the anniversary month and the anniversary date of the killing. He shall fast at that time (the date) three consecutive days if he is healthy or only two days, the day of the wounding and the next day, the day of Nissan's death, if he is infirm. He shall, for the rest of his days, be active in all enterprises to free imprisoned Jews,[18] charity, and the saving of lives. He shall work out an arrangement with his (Nissan's) heirs (i.e., his orphans) to support them properly. He shall ask their pardon and the widow's pardon. He shall return to God, and He shall have mercy on him.

And since Simhah has expressed remorse and seeks repentance and atonement, immediately upon his submission to the program of public degradations, he becomes our brother once again for every religious purpose.[19]

Exile and Heresy

The prolific Don Isaac Abravanel's commentary on Pirkei Avot (Ethics or Chapters of the Fathers), a compilation of wisdom advice and ethical teachings of the Rabbis, brings together his exegetical and philosophical efforts. The following passage explains the verse that posits exile as the sentence for incautious speech. Abravanel's description of exile—a place rife with heretical ideas that lead to sin—reverses the causal relationship; exile becomes a fate to be avoided not only for its own sake, but for the dangers it contains.

> DON ISAAC ABRAVANEL, *SEFER NAḤALAT AVOT*, PIRKEI AVOT 1:11 (1505)
>
> [Late first-century Rabbinic sage] *Avtalyon says, "Scholars, be cautious with your words, for you may incur the penalty of exile and be banished to a place of putrid waters, and the students who come after you will drink and die, and consequently the Name of Heaven will be desecrated."*
>
> There is no doubt that this teaching applies to every person who is explaining what he intends to say, but for the sages this is even more important, for their words are more interesting, for there is a greater danger in understanding an incorrect meaning in the words, and considering their teaching to be applicable to everyone. That is why Avtalyon said, "for you may incur the penalty of exile," he was

observing and seeing, in his wisdom, that the Second Temple would be destroyed, and the people would go into exile among the nations who believe in harmful ideas. This is what is meant by the statement that they would be "banished to a place of putrid waters," which is a pseudonym for heresy. Thus he says, "and the students who come after you will drink," meaning that in the future they will imbibe these evil ideas from the inhabitants of that land, thinking that these were their own beliefs. "They will die" within their souls because of these beliefs. All of this is a desecration of the divine name, because the loss of the [true] beliefs continues from generation to generation, and they will attribute these [false beliefs] to the wise of Israel, who straighten out whatever seems wrong (*meyasherim kol ikuv*). . . .

Thus in their exile among the gentiles, the Jews will encounter evil and dangerous beliefs, which was not the case when the Jews were in their own land.[20]

Exile for the Sake of Heaven

Moses Cordovero was a highly respected scholar of Jewish mysticism based on the Zohar and other kabbalistic works. Born in 1522, he became a leader of the flourishing Jewish community in Safed. His ethical treatise *The Palm Tree of Deborah* focuses on the ideal of the imitation of God. First published in Venice in 1588, it would later be translated by Rabbi Louis Jacobs, one of the great Jewish scholars of the twentieth century.

> MOSES CORDOVERO, *THE PALM TREE OF DEBORAH* (1588)
>
> How should a man train himself to acquire the quality of Sovereignty (*malkhut*)? . . .
>
> A second method is explained in the Zohar and it is very important. He should exile himself from place to place for the sake of Heaven and in this way he will become a chariot to the Exiled *Shekhinah*. He should imagine: "Behold I have gone into exile but, behold, my utensils go with me. What shall be with the honor of the Most High seeing that the *Shekhinah* is in exile without Her utensils, which are lacking as a result of the exile?" Because of this he should be

satisfied with as little as possible, as Scripture says, *'Prepare thee stuff for exile'* (Jer. 46:19; Ezek. 12:3). He should humble his heart in exile and bind himself to the Torah, and then the *Shekhinah* will be with him. And he should carry out divorces, by divorcing himself (*gerushim*), constantly banishing himself from his house of rest, after the fashion of R. Simeon and his company, who divorced themselves to study the Torah. And how much better if he bruises his feet wandering from place to place without horse and chariot. Concerning him, the Bible says, *His hope* (sibhro) *is with the Lord his God* (Ps. 146:5); they explained this as derived from the word *shebher*, "break," for he breaks his body in the service of the Most High (see *Zohar* II,198a).[21]

Endless Exile and Everlasting Redemption

Yisroel Hopstein (1737–1814), the Maggid of Koznitz (also Kozhnitz), a student of Dov Baer, the Maggid of Mezritch, founded the Koznitz Hasidic dynasty and wrote on Hasidism and Kabbalah. The following passage is taken from his best-known work, a commentary on the Torah and Pirkei Avot.

ISRAEL OF KOZNITZ, "AVODAT YISRAEL
TO VAYETZEI" (CA. 1750–1810)

It is the way of the zaddik that when he is distressed or in exile, he is not preoccupied with his own soul's anguish but is concerned because the souls of Israel are the limbs of the *Shekhinah*, and in all likelihood His mighty *Shekinah* is impaired. It is about this that the zaddik protests. . . .

This is alluded to in the verse, "And Jacob awoke from his sleep . . . and he was afraid" (Gen. 28:16–17). When he foresaw the length of the last exile [following upon the destruction of the Second Temple], he was seized with fear, [wondering] when will the final redemption occur? *This is none other than . . . the gate of heaven* (Gen. 28:17), meaning that he consoled himself [with the thought] that in all probability this destruction was a prelude to the [Third] Temple, which is called the fixed abode [of the Lord] for all eternity; and proportional to the magnitude of the light of redemption is the magnitude of the destruction [and exile which precedes it].

That is why this [last] exile is so long and endless: to teach us that the future redemption will be of boundless and unlimited radiance....

It is for this reason that our Sages state, "Israel in exile worship idols in purity."[22] This means that when Israel has to obtain *shefa* [divine grace] by means of the guardian angels [of the other nations], it is regarded as comparable to idolatry, for the Children of Israel should deliver sustenance directly from their Father's table [i.e., from God Himself]. The nations of the world, upon receiving [divine grace directly as a result of Israel's lowly plight], imagine that they are in the ascent, but actually [it is a descent], for the order [of the flow of grace] should be evoked only by those who perform God's will.[23]

6 Life in Exile

Most of the Jewish sources on exile approach the subject from philosophical, theological, and religious positions (see, for example, chapters 4, 5, 7, 10). Others depict or react to historical events (chapters 2, 8). This chapter, in contrast, considers the actual experience of living in exile, and allows a positive reading of the experience.

It begins with the prophet Jeremiah's unexpected advice to the Babylonian exiles to settle and flourish in their new home, which counters the dominant theme of exile both as an affliction and as temporary. The idea of a prophet exhorting his people to establish themselves outside the Land of Israel and to work for the good of the community where they have been exiled appears nothing short of startling.

From Jeremiah's prophecy we proceed to more literary responses to his advice.

The Andalusian poet Dunash ibn Labrat seemingly reverts to the conventional response of the faithful to exile. He almost echoes the words of Psalm 137—how can life be enjoyed while in exile?—and yet, nearly every verse leading up to the angst-afflicted rebuke depicts abundance, luxury, and celebration. His description of life in exile as lush and appealing dominates the work, despite the reproach at the end. We sense the poet's mixed feelings—his pleasure in libations fighting with his sense of duty.

Benjamin of Tudela reported on multiple communities of Jews in the Diaspora. According to the excerpt from his "Exilarch" included here, the Jews of Baghdad, descendants of Jeremiah's original addressees, did indeed flourish, and well beyond Jeremiah's imagination. The historic document introduces the office of the exilarch, demonstrating political organization considerably beyond homesteading and a degree of rootedness hitherto unimagined.

Next are excerpts from the sermons of three rabbis, one from sixteenth-century Salonika and two from the seventeenth century, Amsterdam and Modena, Italy, respectively. The first warns his congregation that the exilic condition is precarious. Success leads to envy, and envy to subsequent exile. The second admonishes his listeners against arrogance and flaunting their wealth lest they anger their neighbors and God. The third cautions his audience about the dangers of assimilation. From these sermons the extent of the communities' prosperity is apparent; there would have been no need for rabbinic reprimands were it not for the exiles' opulence, growing comfort, and increasing distance from Jewish culture. The concept of exile continues to be salient and relevant so many generations after the destruction of the Temple.

At the end of the chapter we return to Jeremiah, whose letter has inspired many modern poets. Charles Reznikoff takes up Jeremiah's words, imagining the exiles' experience and foreseeing their reluctance to return to the Land of Israel after three generations of settling and flourishing. Myron Ernst uses three verses from the prophet's passage as his epigraph, reversing the direction of the previous poem. Instead of bringing the reader to the time of Jeremiah, Ernst refers to the verses to offer commentary on contemporary Jewish life.

Advice and Rebuke

Jeremiah (ca. 655–ca. 597 BCE), one of the major prophets, is considered the author of the books of Jeremiah, Kings, and Lamentations. His letter to the exiles, written in the wake of the Babylonian exile from Jerusalem and found in the middle of his prophetic book, includes expected exhortations to put faith in God, admonishments against idol worship, and assurances that God has not forsaken them. What is surprising is his additional advice to the exiles: to settle in their new home—to build houses, plant gardens, marry off their children—and to work for the good of the place to which they have been banished. Although exile is not presented as a permanent situation, it is unlikely to be over in the lifetime of the exiled. The prophet sets a pragmatic tone, advocating for an approach that allows the exiles to adjust and even flourish.

> JEREMIAH 29
>
> This is the text of the letter that the prophet Jeremiah sent from Jerusalem to the priests, the prophets, the rest of the elders of the exile community, and to all the people whom Nebuchadnezzar had exiled from Jerusalem to Babylon—after King Jeconiah, the queen mother, the eunuchs, the officials of Judah and Jerusalem, and the artisans and smiths had left Jerusalem. [The letter was sent] through Elasah son of Shaphan and Gemariah son of Hilkiah, whom King Zedekiah of Judah had dispatched to Babylon, to King Nebuchadnezzar of Babylon.
>
> Thus said God of Hosts, the God of Israel, to the whole community that I exiled from Jerusalem to Babylon: Build houses and live in them, plant gardens and eat their fruit. You should take wives and beget sons and daughters; and you should take wives for your sons, and give your daughters to husbands, that they may bear sons and daughters. Multiply there, do not decrease. And seek the welfare of the city to which I have exiled you and pray to God in its behalf; for in its prosperity you shall prosper.
>
> For thus said God of Hosts, the God of Israel: Let not the prophets and diviners in your midst deceive you, and pay no heed to the dreams they dream. For they prophesy to you in My name falsely; I did not send them—declares God.
>
> For thus said God: When Babylon's seventy years are over, I will take note of you, and I will fulfill to you My promise of favor—to bring you back to this place. For I am mindful of the plans I have made concerning you—declares God—plans for your welfare, not for disaster, to give you a hopeful future. When you call Me, and come and pray to Me, I will give heed to you. You will search for Me and find Me, if only you seek Me wholeheartedly. I will be at hand for you—declares God—and I will restore your fortunes. And I will gather you from all the nations and from all the places to which I

have banished you—declares God—and I will bring you back to the place from which I have exiled you.

But you say, "God has raised up prophets for us in Babylon."

Thus said God concerning the king who sits on the throne of David, and concerning all the people who dwell in this city, your kinsfolk who did not go out with you into exile—thus said God of Hosts: I am going to let loose sword, famine, and pestilence against them and I will treat them as loathsome figs, so bad that they cannot be eaten. I will pursue them with the sword, with famine, and with pestilence; and I will make them a horror to all the kingdoms of the earth, an execration and an object of horror and hissing and scorn among all the nations to which I shall banish them, because they did not heed My words—declares God—when I persistently sent to them My servants, the prophets, and they did not heed—declares God.

But you, the whole exile community that I banished from Jerusalem to Babylon, hear the word of God! Thus said God of Hosts, the God of Israel, concerning Ahab son of Kolaiah and Zedekiah son of Maaseiah, who prophesy falsely to you in My name: I am going to deliver them into the hands of King Nebuchadrezzar of Babylon, and he shall put them to death before your eyes. And the whole community of Judah in Babylonia shall use a curse derived from their fate: "May God make you like Zedekiah and Ahab, whom the king of Babylon consigned to the flames!"—because they did vile things in Israel, committing adultery with the wives of their fellows and speaking in My name false words that I had not commanded them. I am the One who knows and bears witness—declares God.

Concerning Shemaiah the Nehelamite you shall say: Thus said God of Hosts, the God of Israel: Because you sent letters in your own name to all the people in Jerusalem, to Zephaniah son of Maaseiah and to the rest of the priests, as follows, "God appointed you priest in place of the priest Jehoiada, to exercise authority in the House of God over every maniac who wants to play the prophet, to put them into the stocks and into the pillory. Now why have you not rebuked Jeremiah the Anathothite, who plays the prophet among you? For he has actually sent a message to us in Babylon to this effect: It will be a long time. Build houses and live in them, plant gardens and enjoy their fruit."

When the priest Zephaniah read this letter in the hearing of the prophet Jeremiah, the word of God came to Jeremiah: Send a message to the entire exile community: "Thus said God concerning Shemaiah the Nehelamite: Because Shemaiah prophesied to you, though I did not send him, and made you false promises, assuredly, thus said God: I am going to punish Shemaiah the Nehelamite and his offspring. There shall be no one of his line dwelling among this people or seeing the good things I am going to do for My people—declares God—for he has urged disloyalty toward God."[1]

"You Rejoice—and in Zion Foxes Roam"

Born in Fez and educated in Baghdad, Dunash ibn Labrat played a major role in the history of medieval Jewish poetry. Immigrating to Andalusia in the middle of the tenth century, he became associated with the celebrated Jewish courtier Hasdai ibn Shaprut in Cordoba. There he introduced a new technique of writing Hebrew poems in metrical patterns taken from Arabic poetics; this became standard in the poetry of the greatest Hebrew poets of the "Golden Age," lasting until the Almohad invasion of the 1140s. He also introduced new themes to the Jews of the Iberian Peninsula.

The following poem is filled with motifs derived from Arabic literature, especially the genre of the wine poem: a description of the garden, with its flowers and fruits, the sound of the music, the aromas and tastes, the appeal of good wine shared among friends throughout the night. The message is to seize the moment, to enjoy the present fully and without restraint.

All this is placed in the mouth of an associate inviting the poet (or his persona) to share in these seductive pleasures. But it is all rejected, not merely as self-indulgent, but as sinful for a Jew living during the period of *galut*. The issue at hand is not external in nature—that such behavior might seem inappropriate to the Muslims in power (as we will see in later texts), but based purely on internal considerations.

LIFE IN EXILE

Gentile powers control the Temple Mount, foxes now roam the site where sacrifices were offered and the Levites sang their hymns: How is it possible for Jews to forget Jerusalem while they indulge in sensual pleasures? The poem thus concludes as an antiwine poem, a repudiation of hedonism on historical and religious grounds. So long as Jews are in exile, they must restrain their enjoyment.

And yet ... The poet could certainly have conveyed this message without the lyrical evocation of what he feels compelled to forgo. Why spend three-quarters of the poem describing in such alluring language that which is forbidden? Poised at the threshold of a new, secular culture, Dunash seems to express not simplistic condemnation but ambivalence, which would soon disappear from the Jewish poets of Andalusia. The successors of Dunash would feel free to write the most lyrical descriptions of the wine party without any accompanying note of chastisement.

> DUNASH IBN LABRAT, "REPLY TO AN INVITATION
> TO A FEAST" (10TH CENTURY)
>
> He said, "Don't sleep! / Drink aged wine—
> Henna with lily / and myrrh with aromatics
> In an orchard of pomegranates / date palms and grapevines
> Sweet seedlings / tamarisks,
> And streams / [like] the humming of violins
> On the lips of singers / with harps and lyres
> There, every tree is laden / with fruit on every branch
> Birds of every wing / sing among the leaves,
> The doves coo / as if thinking melodies,
> The turtledoves reply / their cooing like flutes.
> We will drink with pleasure / among the lilies,
> Put sorrows to flight / with revelry,
> We will eat sweets / and drink fountains
> We will act like giants / and drink from goblets,
> I will arise in the mornings / to slaughter the choicest

And healthiest bulls / deer and calves,
We will slather fine oil / and harvest fresh wood
Before the end of days / we will live to the fullest."
I rebuked him, "Silence! Quiet! / How can you go on
When the Temple and God's footstool / are to the heathens!
Foolishly you have spoken / indolence you have chosen
Folly you have said / like jesters and buffoons,
You have forsaken / the reason of God's Torah
You rejoice—and in Zion foxes roam.
How can we drink wine / and how can we raise our eyes—
When we are nothing / reviled and despised!"[2]

The Exilarch

For most medieval Jewish travelers who left their homes to reach important destinations, the purpose was to visit the Holy Land, and especially Jerusalem. This was not the case for the most celebrated medieval Jewish traveler, Benjamin of Tudela, who ventured to the East and back between 1169 and 1171, and produced a detailed written account of his experience. He describes his visits to cities of southern France, Rome, Sorrento, Constantinople, Sidon, Tyre, Haifa, and then Jerusalem. But unlike other Jewish visitors for whom Jerusalem was the goal and conclusion of their ventures, Benjamin continued traveling to the east.

The highlight of his travels was Baghdad, where Caliph Emir al-Muminini al-Abbasi, the most powerful and respected ruler in the Islamic world—greater than any Christian king—provided free medical care for the sick, something apparently unheard of in Christian Europe. And Benjamin reveals rather astonishing respect—almost reverence—for the exilarch, the Jewish leader whose ancestry went back deep in antiquity. Some of Benjamin's statements about the Babylonian exilarch's authority over distant Jewish communities seem exaggerated, but the underlying message is clear: here is a world in which exile from the Holy Land did not prevent Jews and Muslims from living in mutual respect.

BENJAMIN OF TUDELA, "EXILARCH" (LATE 12TH CENTURY)

In Baghdad there are about 40,000 Jews, and they dwell in security, prosperity and honour under the great Caliph; amongst them are great sages, the heads of the Academies engaged in the study of the Law.... At the head of them all is Daniel, the son of Hisdai who is styled, "Our Lord, the Exilarch [*Adonenu Rosh ha-Galut*] of all Israel." He possesses a book of pedigrees going back as far as David, King of Israel. The Jews call him "Our Lord, the Exilarch," and the Mohammedans call him "Saidna ben Daoud"; he has been invested with authority over all the congregations of Israel at the hands of the Emir al-Muminin, the Lord of Islam. For thus Mohammed commanded concerning him and his descendants; and he granted him a seal of office over all the congregations that dwell under his rule, and ordered that everyone, whether Mohammedan or Jew, or belonging to any other nation in his dominion, should rise up before him (the Exilarch) and salute him....

Every fifth day when he goes to pay a visit to the great Caliph, horsemen, Gentiles as well as Jews, escort him, and heralds proclaim in advance, "Make way before our Lord, the son of David."... He is mounted on a horse, and is attired in robes of silk and embroidery, with a large turban on his head, and from the turban is suspended a long white cloth adorned with a chain upon which the cipher of Mohammed is engraved. Then he appears before the Caliph and kisses his hand and the Caliph rises and places him on a throne which Mohammed had ordered to be made for him, and all the Mohammedan princes who attend the court of the Caliph rise up before him. The Exilarch is seated on his throne opposite the Caliph, in compliance with the command of Mohammed.... The authority of the Exilarch extends over all the communities of Shinar, Persia, Khurasan, and Sheba which is El-Yemen, and Diyar Kalach, and the land of Aram Naharaim (Mesopotamia).... His authority extends also over the land of Siberia, ... to the gates of Samarkand, the land of Tibet, and the land of India. In respect of all these countries the Exilarch gives the communities power to appoint Rabbis and Ministers who come unto him to be consecrated and to receive his authority....

The Exilarch appoints the Chiefs of the Academies by placing his hand upon their heads, thus installing them in their office. . . .

The great synagogue of the Exilarch has columns of marble of various colours overlaid with silver and gold, and on these columns are sentences of the Psalms in golden letters. In front of the ark are about ten steps of marble; on the topmost step are the seats of the Exilarch and of the Princes of the House of David.[3]

Pattern of Persecution

Solomon Levi was born in Salonika in 1521 to a distinguished family of Jews who fled from Portugal following the universal forced conversion in 1497 of all Jews living in Portugal. He excelled in studies of the Talmud, mastered the classics of Jewish philosophical and kabbalistic literature, and even studied some of the "gentile languages" in order to gain access to non-Jewish literature.

In 1568 he became rabbi of a community in Yugoslavia, where he delivered sermons on virtually all Sabbaths and holidays. In 1571 he returned to Salonika, where he held positions in two important congregations until his death in 1600. The book *Divrei Shlomo*, published in 1596, is an extensive record of his preaching from 1571 to 1574, with 314 folio pages, each with four columns of fifty-three lines. And this is a record of only four years of a thirty-year career as a preacher.

Characteristically of traditional Jewish exegesis, Jacob is presented as having been persecuted by his older brother Esau, rather than having deceived his father and stolen Esau's birthright. What is important for our purpose is the presentation of the biblical narrative as an adumbration of Jewish experience in exile. Jews will settle in a new country, work hard and prosper, and thereby arouse hostility and contempt in the native population, so that eventually they will need to flee to another country. This would be their experience of exile until the Messianic Age.

SOLOMON LEVI, *DIVREI SHLOMO* ON VA-YETSE' (1573)

All this [the narratives of Jacob persecuted by Esau and by Laban because of their jealousy] is an instructive sign that our people would be expelled and persecuted, moving from kingdom to kingdom, from one ruler who hates them to another. Within a relatively few years they would become more powerful and wealthier than the native inhabitants of the land, who would eventually come to despise them, so that they would have to flee from that land to yet another. Such would be the pattern until the messianic age. For God would arrange it that when they were persecuted by one who hated them, as was the case with Esau, they would find another who would welcome them warmly, as was the case with Laban.

We learn also that the industriousness of our people, [enabling them] to earn money and acquire wealth, is similar to that found in our father Jacob. But his industriousness was rooted in justice and truth.... That is not the case among the people in this evil generation, for they are *filled with lies and violence* (Ps. 10:7). The meaning [of this passage] is that our people should not be blamed because they are so energetic and devote such effort to acquire wealth and capital in a land not their own, so long as they amass it justly and equitably, for this is what our father Jacob did, and this is what has preserved us among the gentiles. At first, they see that God brings them blessing because of us. But later on they begin to despise us and think of taking it all from us. They therefore trump up charges against us in order to enslave us. Such events have occurred to our people throughout the thousands of years we are in exile, many, many times as history reveals.[4]

Against Acculturation

Aaron Berechiah of Modena, a cousin of the polymath Venetian rabbi Leon Modena, was himself a man of many talents: a kabbalist disciple of Menahem Azariah of Fano, a poet, and a preacher. He is best known for *Derashot Ma'avar Yabbok* (Mantua, 1626), one of the most important books collecting material on Jewish attitudes toward dying and death and the rituals and customs of burial and mourning.

His sermon on the Torah portion Shemot, delivered in early 1619, concludes by addressing the matter of exile. He begins this discussion with a well-known Rabbinic statement about the Israelites in Egypt, asserting that they were worthy of redemption because they did not change their names or their language, or (in one version) their style of clothing. This leads Berechiah to rebuke his listeners for behavior that violates this imagined model of steadfast loyalty to tradition. Exile for the Italian Jews means precisely changing names, neglecting the Hebrew language, and imitating gentile styles of dress—behaviors that must delay the ultimate redemption.

AARON BERECHIAH OF MODENA, "SHEMOT," *DERASHOT MA'AVAR YABBOK* (1619)

Thus the exiles in Babylonia behaved antithetically to the manner of the exiles in Egypt, who did not change [their names, or their manner of clothing, or their language].[5] Those in Egypt were worthy of increasing and spreading out (Exod. 1:11), since they maintained their distinctiveness in these three areas from all the other nations.[6] But the exiles in Babylonia, who did change, were unworthy of increasing.

What then shall we say of the Jews in the present exile who change their names? Mordecai becomes Marco, Shimshon becomes Diofebo,[7] Shimon becomes Simone, and similarly with most of the women's names.[8] Also our clothes: they are of a style that arouses the impulse to evil—more those of the women than of the men. In addition to the waste of money, they inspire jealousy against us in the hearts of those who say that we are making ourselves equal to them, who are the masters here. This is the cause of the edicts requiring special hats and other distinctive marks on our clothing—the antithesis of the honor we seek to attain.[9] We do not remember that it is incumbent upon us to mourn constantly for the destruction of the Temple.

As for the holy tongue, there are few who accustom themselves to write in the Hebrew language. As a punishment measure for measure, in many places we are required to write our communal records in their language and their style, so that (*ye'emnu ba'ad ha-otiyot*).[10] This is quite serious, for the result of this is that our internal affairs are open to them. See that because of our sins, we have not been worthy of increasing and spreading out, as were those who went out of Egypt, for theirs is the true way. Let us then behave like those in Egypt, who did not change [their names, clothing style, and language]. Then we will be worthy of increasing and spreading out among the idolaters. And God will remember us as He remembered our ancestors because of the merit of the fathers, as the Bible says, *God remembered His covenant [with Abraham and Isaac and Jacob]* (Exod. 23:24).[11]

In Praise of Modest Living

Saul Levi Morteira (see chapter 4) begins a beautifully structured and elegantly developed sermon (excerpted here) with the very upbeat biblical verse Exodus 1:7 ("The Israelites were fertile . . . very greatly, so that the land was full with them"), but immediately follows with a Rabbinic statement that introduces "exile" as an important means of punishment for Jews because of their lavishly improper behavior. Morteira's message is clear: arrogant behavior, ostentatious apparel, and high living by the immigrant Jews in their new environment angers their Calvinist gentile neighbors, and God as well. Therefore the Jews must recognize that even in this new environment of freedom, they are still living in exile.

SAUL LEVI MORTEIRA, "THE PEOPLE'S ENVY" (1622)

It is clear that the Egyptian exile was called an *iron blast furnace* (Deut. 4:20) because it affected us the way a blast furnace works upon silver or gold placed within it. These are refined by the removal of all dross, prepared to withstand fire, strengthened for the testing stone and the blows of the hammer. So the calamities of Egypt taught Israel to endure as slaves, thereby preparing her to endure the calamities of later exiles. . . .

But God used that exile to teach us even more. If we would only open our eyes, we could learn lessons of great import, extremely beneficial to us in this current exile. These lessons might even alleviate the misfortunes that weigh upon us. For everything God did to our ancestors was intended to help us learn, so that we might behave properly. . . .

God showed us all this in Egypt, so that we might learn from the past and not repeat the same foolish mistake, but it has been to no avail. . . .

There is a serious problem in our theme-verse: *The Israelites were fertile and prolific, they multiplied and increased* [vayishretsu vayirbu vaya'atsmu] *very greatly, so that the land was full of them* (Exod. 1:7). All of these phrases seem repetitious; the strongest expression would have sufficed.[12] Nor is it proper to say simply, "The same content is repeated in different words." No, each phrase refers to an essential matter. We therefore maintain that God has taught us from the first exile how to act in all future exiles. It would be well for us if only we paid attention. . . .

Now when the Israelites in Egypt recognized their alien status and behaved like foreigners in exile, they lived in peace and tranquility. But when they forgot their original situation and aspired to be princes and nobles, God made them feel the full weight of the yoke, and many disasters befell them, for they had forgotten the meaning of exile. This has been the cause of all the misfortunes of Israel in all exiles through the ages.

The present passage from the Torah testifies to this fact. It says, *Joseph died, and all his brothers, and all that generation* (Exod. 1:6). This means that the first generation of our ancestors who left the land of Canaan, who knew that they were aliens and behaved moderately, at an appropriate social level, died in peace. Then a new generation arose after them who did not know their place of origin. They began to behave in a domineering and arrogant manner, bringing the evil that eventually occurred upon themselves. The Egyptians grew envious of them and devised nefarious plots, ultimately oppressing them with a heavy yoke. All this was in accordance with God's will, so that they would remember that they were in exile.

Then the Torah says, *The Israelites were fertile*, after the death of their parents. Then, having reproduced abundantly, they were no longer content to live in their original space. They refused to endure crowded conditions and to remain content with little, so as to avoid the hostile glares of their enemies. Rather, *va-yishretsu*, meaning that they spread out.... After they were fecund, they expanded; becoming numerous, they wanted wider spaces.

This is inappropriate for those who live in exile. They should be prepared to endure hardship; happy are those who have what they need and no more. But such a contented disposition is not what we see today. This is not befitting a people living outside its land, in the land of its enemies....[13]

Indeed, all Jews living in exile should refrain from purchasing houses or vineyards. These make Jews forget God, and they are a troublesome burden in time of expulsion. They isolate Jews from their fellow Jews and cause them to mix in among the Gentiles. Moreover, these possessions are readily seen by all, arousing great envy.[14]

Jews should rather live "in tents," meaning "in the manner of a tent dweller," as one who tarries for the night, not in large houses with expensive ornaments. For in this manner they will "long live on the land where they sojourn," and their enemies will not envy them....

Then the verse says, *vayirbu*. It was not only that they expanded in their houses quantitatively, but also qualitatively *they became great* and magnificent. This refers to their manner of dress and to other externals. They began to have expensive clothes and horses and chariots with men running before them, all of which is inappropriate for aliens and exiles in a land not theirs. In addition to increasing envy, it prolongs the exile....[15]

All this happened to us in the Egyptian exile so that we might learn a lesson for the other exiles. But we have gone astray like a flock of sheep, repeating the same mistake wherever we have been exiled, by dressing more ostentatiously than the nobles of the land. We have caused our own destruction during the period of the exile. And our enemies have responded with general expulsions both out of envy and as a punishment....

So it is with the Jewish people. If they would willingly accept their exile, behaving moderately—rather than arrogantly overshadowing the inhabitants of the lands where they dwell—they would pass through their exile in fair condition, without suffering, until God favors the remnant of Joseph.... That is why sorrows afflict them: so they will remember that they are slaves and exiles....

All this is implied by the verse about the Israelites in Egypt, *The Israelites were fertile, va-yishresu vayirbu*: they *became great* in magnificence and grandeur. Then Pharaoh afflicted them with servitude.¹⁶

After this, the verse says, *vaya'atsmu, very greatly*. This refers to the fact that their arrogance was manifest in yet another way over and above the spaciousness of their homes and the costliness of their clothing, namely, in sumptuous foods and magnificent furniture. . . . It is improper for anyone to act immoderately in this respect, especially those in exile, for they should consider it a great kindness if they have enough to sustain themselves, without anything extra. . . .

In addition to this personal disaster that befalls them, the exile is made more onerous. For God despises this, and He makes the Gentiles among whom they are exiled despise them, as was the case with the Egyptians. The verse says, *va-ya'atsmu, very greatly*, and then, *the land was full of them*. This means that the land and its inhabitants were fed up with them and their deeds. . . . Then *a new king arose* (Exod. 1:8), and sorrows increased. What was even worse, *the more they afflicted them, the grander they became* (Exod. 1:12). This means that, in the midst of their affliction, they remained arrogant. Such is our way today. All of us complain and weep about hard times, but when we get something, we spend a fortune on banquets with wine. The same is true of all the other unnecessary things. . . .

We must remember our exile before God. May it be His will to send us our righteous Messiah, soon and in our days. Amen.¹⁷

Perseverance

The poet, playwright, and novelist Charles Reznikoff (1894–1976), born to Russian Jewish immigrants, grew up in New York and graduated from law school when only twenty-one, although he practiced law only briefly. Poet Louis Zukofsky coined the term Objectivist to describe Reznikoff and fellow poets. Objectivists regarded the poem as object, and considered historical particulars to be at least as significant as sensory impressions.

Issues of social injustice, the plight of the poor and marginalized, and themes of exile recur in Reznikoff's work. In the poem "Babylon:

539 B.C.E.," he recreates the historic moment when the exiled Judeans are offered the opportunity to return to Judah. Recognizing that the majority of the exiled—descendants of the original Babylonian captives—chose not to return, he explains the reasons why—and, by extension, why Jews choose to live in exile even now. The "now" of the poem, of course, teems with irony, at least in hindsight, since it was published on the cusp of the greatest threat to Jewish existence in modern times. The poem also celebrates Jewish perseverance: "we Jews are as the dew, / on every blade of grass, / trodden under foot today / and here tomorrow morning."

> CHARLES REZNIKOFF, "BABYLON 539 B.C.E." (1934)
>
> AN ELDER. Our fathers were saved from the deaths
> others died by hunger, plague, or sword,
> when the cities of Judah and Jerusalem itself were taken,
> and from the deaths so many died
> along the journey that left our fathers
> —the hills of Judah and the sea
> out of sight many months and years
> —exiles by the quiet waters and willows of Babylon;[18]
> but for us the noise of battle, not the battle itself,
> is over; there is no shouting of soldiers
> to warn us; no arrows no shrieks
> of the wounded;
> only the suction
> of this city
> to pull us off our feet
> until the remnant of Judah—Jerusalem and our God forgotten—
> are particles in the dust of Babylon,
> like other thousands and tens of thousands
> Babylon has taken.
>
> ANOTHER ELDER. Did the Lord, whom our fathers served,
> come from the sky to stand beside them,

or even from the safety of the clouds with His lightnings
save His citadel?—
an aloof God, saving a few alive
of all Judah's thousands and tens of thousands.
Is there another people who, their cities taken,
the temple of their God become the stones it had been,
and they themselves scattered from the land,
are still worshippers of its God?
Nor, as it might have happened, are we captives among a savage people,
a brutish people, living in tents or caves:
these Babylonians are a great people,
living in palaces and gardens—
but we were only shepherds and herdsmen,
tenders of vineyards and of trees, ploughmen;
this is a nation of merchants and warriors,
priests of triumphant gods.
It was meant for ill to us,
but it has been for good, as to Joseph[19]
who was brought to Egypt among slaves
to be second in his master's and in the king's house.

MESSENGER. To all you Jews,
captives of Babylon,
Cyrus the Persian, worshipper of one god and hater of idols,
proclaims,
Joy and rejoicing!
Your enemy is about to fall
and Babylon become a proverb among the nations!
Return to Judah,
rebuild Jerusalem and the temple of your God;
your captivity is ended!

THE FIRST ELDER. Surely the sun rises in the east!
Let it not be said that God has forgotten Judah,

or that the Lord was aloof
when puddles of blood stood in the streets of Jerusalem;
we looked for one of us—
and our deliverer is a stranger;
now let us hear no more of the God of Judah,
but tell us of the Lord of the Universe and of Eternity,
before whom the multitudes of Babylonia
are as powerless
as when their cities,
the great angels of granite before their palaces,
the great gods and the lesser gods,
will be looked for with spoons in the desert
and remembered
only because Judah has remembered them for evil.

AN ELDER. It was hard for our fathers when they were slaves in Egypt,
building a mountain range
of granite along the flat banks of the Nile
under the quick fists and staffs of taskmasters,
to leave the pots of fish that were theirs for the taking[20]
and the plentiful sweet water
for the wilderness and the knives of its tribes;
how much harder will it be for you, Judah,
to leave the gardens of Babylon,
the suits of linen and the cloaks of wool,
the meats and the cool fruits and wine
to become again dusty shepherds and herdsmen
on your barren hills, Judah;
to toil in your fields
eating only of what they shall plant,
if locusts and grasshoppers
leave what is saved from drought and the storm,[21]
and thieves and armed bands

what is spared by the locusts and worms.[22]
Now shall the longings of your heart
and the words of your mouth, Jacob,
the sighs and groans, the cries and outcries of fifty years,
be put to the proof;
for the time is come of choosing and refusing:
your deliverer
calls upon Judah with the crash of thunder,
speaking your name with the voice of the earthquake.

THE PRINCE OF THE CAPTIVITY. Servant of Cyrus,
who hates even as we do
the vanity of idols,
in a world where their worshippers are like the sands for number,
those who love the truth are drawn to each other
like particles of iron that have known the loadstone;
build on each other like coral in the sea
against the waves, the tides and spring tides, tempests and typhoons,
that would sweep us all way!
The Jews are few; Judah is small among the nations,
without cities and land,
and you Persians have become a mighty people;
but in the battle we have known pebble in a sling
to do as much
as a spear weighing many shekels of brass,[23]
and Judah will not forget the friendliness of Cyrus.
Now let the young men who are ill at ease
where all the ground is field and garden, street and square,
and all the water is canals,
or the smooth river flowing between steps,
men who like the taste of salt better than that of honey,
try their strength against the hills
and from the rubbish heaps that are Jerusalem
rebuild the city;

LIFE IN EXILE

    replant the land
with olive trees and fig trees, with vineyards and fields of
    barley, fields of wheat;
so shall Judah like a tree that has seen many tribes—
many cities become mounds and heaps—
flourish and renew itself;
for here we are only so much timber,
although smoothed and polished.
And there is other work to do in Babylon—
in courtyards, where flowers and leaves are brilliant
against a white-washed wall, the only noise
that of the fountain and the long leaves of the palms;
in cool rooms
where one need only put out his hand
to take food from the dish
or lift the cup to his lips
while the noise of the street
touches the listener no more than rain;
here others have their work,
like the stars in their orbits, seemingly motionless,
but shining, not without influence,
upon the action of the world.
Let hands build the walls
hands more numerous
may pull down again,
but we must build in Babylon
another Zion
of precepts, laws, ordinances and commandments
to outlast stone or metal,
between every Jew and the fury or blandishment of any land—
that shall keep up a man as much as bread
and swallows of water in his belly, strengthen him
like links of armor on his body.

> Let other people come as streams
> that overflow a valley
> and leave dead bodies, uprooted trees and fields of sand;
> we Jews are as the dew,
> on every blade of grass,
> trodden under foot today
> and here tomorrow morning.[24]

Abundance in Exile

In the following poem, published in the Zionist journal *Midstream*, Myron Ernst (b. 1937), author of the collection *God, Time, Creosote* and the chapbook *Geographies*, draws from both the contemporary (a fruit bowl, speckled trout, birches and hemlocks) and the biblical (begotten children, Moab, wadis, and the prophet Jeremiah's passage normalizing exile) to portray life in exile as delightful. Faintly echoing the medieval poet Judah Halevi (see chapter 10) in describing "all the good things," the speaker eschews the idyllic present with its abundance, concluding with the paradoxical "need for the lack of it."

MYRON ERNST, "EXILE" (1988)

> *Thus saith the Lord of Hosts, the God of Israel, unto all that are carried away captive, whom I have caused to be carried away captive, whom I have caused to be carried away from Jerusalem unto Babylon; Build ye houses and dwell in them; and plant gardens, and eat the fruit of them; take ye wives and beget sons and daughters. . . .*
> —Jeremiah 29:4,5,6

> This I have done,
> and she arranges the fruit
> nicely on an English dish, just so
> at the center of the oaken
> table where the begotten children sit.

LIFE IN EXILE

I went and bought a little
wooden motorboat too;
I take it on the sweet,
teeming lake where You've sent me;
I know where the speckled
trout sleep; troll
for the wicked-toothed pickerel.

I still remember
staring into Moab,
the wadis' deep rootworks,
until I learned them by heart,
as if naming all of a cadaver's
dry veins laid bare
around the bones.

In that other time
their flesh must have crept,
their nape's hair risen,
like mine, watching darkness lower
over the reddened bones of hills,
into the dry gullies first—

It's too rich here, birches,
thick hemlocks flesh out the hills
around this cool exilic lake,
and too green—
so much water,
I am in need of a lack of it.[25]

7 Internalized Exile

The Hebrew terms *galut* and *galutiyut* are not well represented by an English equivalent. They imperfectly translate to "exile" and "exilicness" respectively, capturing the generally negative connotations. *Galut* (n.) is used to refer to the place of exile (outside of the homeland); the forced uprooting of someone condemned to live in exile; the involuntary departure from the homeland that leads the person to that place; the state in which that person now lives, away from the homeland. It has come to mean the captivity, banishment, and scattering—diaspora—of a people exiled. Alexander Altmann's Rosh Hashanah sermon presented in chapter 5 uses the Yiddish equivalent, *golus*, and emphasizes the difficulties inherent in the experience, the necessity of it being endured.

Galutiyut, also a noun, is in the form of a noun derived from an adjective—a place, an experience, or most commonly a person, that/who embodies the state of *galut*. In modern times *galutiyut* became the antithesis of the characteristics envisioned and desired by the Zionist dream of the new Jew. It was the condition of being passive, weak, and vulnerable, or the culture and conditions that led to these traits.

In this chapter we present a range of perspectives on the experience of *galut*, internalized exile, from the sense of its inevitability—and invariably leading to antisemitism—to an experience or state that is both productive and corruptive in turn, full of suffering and majesty.

Communal Identity in Exile

Yitzhak Baer is best known to English-language historians for his massive two-volume *A History of the Jews in Christian Europe* (1961 and 1966), covering the period from the beginning of the Christian Reconquest of Spain from Muslim control in the late eleventh century to the 1492 expulsion: one thousand pages in all. His book *Galut* is quite different. Originally written in German and published in Berlin in 1936, an English-language edition published by Schocken Books in 1947 totals 123 small pages. Obviously intended for a general readership, it is a fine presentation of a broad topic that became especially important in the wake of Nazi persecution and its totalitarian movement.

The following passages, taken from the very beginning and the very end of the book, speak to the paradoxically enduring experience of exile for Jews.

> YITZHAK BAER, *GALUT* (1947)
>
> The word "*Galut*" embraces a whole world of facts and ideas that have appeared with varying strength and clarity in every age of Jewish history. Political servitude and dispersion, the longing for liberation and reunion, sin and repentance and atonement: these are the larger elements that must go to make up the concept of *Galut* if the word is to retain any real meaning.
>
> The picture begins to take shape at the time of the Second Temple. A national state still exists in Palestine, and the holy place embodying a power sufficient to redeem all humanity still stands. The goal is to bring the whole world under the leadership of the Jews and to the salvation of their religion; the Diaspora is not simply a consequence of political enslavement—it serves also to spread the knowledge of the true Teaching throughout the world. True, the political situation of the Jews does not permit the attainment of this ideal. Enslaved, contemned, and rejected, all over the world the Jews pray that they may be politically reunited on their own soil—only then will it be possible to fulfil the whole Law. For *politeia* (the order of law and doctrine), nation and soil belong together.
>
> Thus in the Hellenistic-Roman Diaspora we can already distinguish all the essential elements of the medieval *Galut*. And antisemitism, too, makes its appearance. Antisemitism is the inevitable consequence of the Jews' exalted consciousness of religious superiority and of their mission among the nations, a consciousness all the more infuriating

because it exists in a nation totally without power. The problem of being a Jew is inseparably bound up with the *Galut*. Already it is a distinguishing mark of *Galut* that there is persecution, outrage, and injustice from which specious [privileges give no relief]. . . .[1]

It is during this age [the second age of our history] and on this very soil of Palestine that the first martyrs for the sake of faith arose. We taught the world the idea of martyrdom, and in the third great age of our history—the real age of the *Galut*—this idea was realized in the very body of the people. For two thousand years we suffered for the sake of the redemption of mankind; we were driven forth and scattered over every part of the earth because of the fateful interaction of the religious and political factors determining our history.

We went among the nations neither to exploit them nor to help them build their civilizations. All that we did on foreign soil was a betrayal of our own spirit. Nor, finally, did we go among the nations of Europe in order to convert them in the sense of that missionary ardor which animated our people in antiquity and which later animated the followers of Christianity. Once political limitations had destroyed the possibilities of conversion, our people had to content itself with testifying to its missionary vocation in the world by its mere existence.[2]

Exile as Discord and Dialogue

Born in Romania, Eliezer Berkovits studied at the Pressburg Yeshiva, received rabbinical ordination in 1934 at the Rabbinical Seminary of Berlin, and earned a doctorate in philosophy at the University of Berlin. He served as a congregational rabbi in Berlin before escaping Germany in 1939. He proceeded to hold positions as rabbi in Leeds, England (1940–46), Sydney, Australia (1946–50), and Boston (1950–56); then served as chair of the Department of Philosophy at the Hebrew Theological Seminary in Skokie, Illinois (1958–75); and finally moved to Jerusalem, where he lived until his death in 1992.

As an Orthodox rabbi, he took an unusually courageous position in repudiating the common belief that the Jewish people's exile and suffering served as punishment for the sins of the Jews. In many writings he insisted that this traditional belief, incorporated into the traditional liturgy ("Because of our sins we were exiled from our land"), should no longer be accepted. His exhortation that exile—*galut*—is *not* simply a punishment for sinful Jews is readily apparent in the three powerful passages below.

ELIEZER BERKOVITS, "GALUT, OR THE BREACH BETWEEN THE TORAH AND LIFE—THE REAL PROBLEM" (1943)

[B]y the time the Talmud was closed, Judaism had in fact reached a point where development was no more possible, for the great partner of Torah—Jewish reality—was lost. From then on the Jewish nation has more and more been subjected to living conditions in the shaping of which as Jews they had no say whatsoever. The examples of Jewish communal autonomy in the centuries that followed were of great cultural and religious importance in their days, but they could not normalise the basic anomaly of Jewish existence. For Jews from now on had to bear in sufferance an existence imposed upon them by others. The great spiritual tragedy of the Galut consists in the breach between Torah and Life, for Galut means the loss of Jewish-controlled environment, which as far as Jews are concerned is the crux of the whole problem.[3]

ELIEZER BERKOVITS, "GALUT AND ERETZ ISRAEL" (1943)

The present task must be shared between Eretz Israel and the Galut. The place for the creation of the full Jewish existence is, of course, the Jewish National Home, but the rediscovery of Judaism will, to a very large extent, probably be better done in the Galut, firstly because of the great material resources of the Galut, with the incomparably larger Jewish masses in need of it there, and secondly, because a rapidly expanding community in Eretz Israel will not be able to exercise the patience and care necessary for the success of such an endeavor. But although the preparatory task will have to be divided between Galut and Eretz Israel, organically regenerated Judaism can arise nowhere except in Eretz Israel. Even if the great majority of Jews still remain in the Galut, from Zion alone can the teaching come, from Jerusalem the word of God, for which modern Jewry is waiting. Though the conflict between Judaism and the "Christian existence" of Jews in the Galut will always remain, for this is the inevitable discord between the two different rhythms of living, it will no more penetrate the mind and heart of the Galut Jew.[4]

ELIEZER BERKOVITS, "GALUT" (1973)

Galut, exile, seems to be the dominant feature of Jewish history. The Jewish people have lived longer in exile than in their homeland in Eretz Yisrael, yet *Galut* is considered an abnormal condition both politically and spiritually. The Jew in the *Galut* is fenced in on all sides: politically, socially, economically; his very life is continually in jeopardy. The area too in which Judaism may grow and live is narrowly circumscribed—it is largely limited to the synagogue and the home.

How did Jews understand their exile? How did they explain it to themselves? They looked upon it as part of the great dialogue between God and Israel. . . . Indeed, there exists a deep-rooted tradition that *Galut* is a punishment for sins. It is the old *Mipnei Hataeinu* ("Because of our sins [we were exiled from our land]" idea). . . .

It was not easy to maintain such an idea. Exile has gone on much too long; the suffering was often too heavy to bear. The questions were unavoidable: Are we so much worse than the others? Are our transgressions so much more grievous? A great deal of ingenuity was spent in order to justify the idea of punishment. . . . The righteous are judged much more strictly, because they ought to know better. One could also take refuge from the searching questions of threatening disbelief by recalling the words of Amos 3:2:

> You only have I known of all the families of the earth,
> Therefore I will visit upon you all your iniquities.

Although . . . even in the Bible and the Talmud it was not accepted as the only satisfactory explanation, Jews through the ages clung to it stubbornly. It is understandable; there was solace in it.... Israel's very closeness to God explained Israel's destiny in exile.

Such ideas were supported by another trend in Jewish thought—the positive value of suffering. Rightly endured, suffering purifies and deepens the human personality. It induces man to turn inward; to foreswear the superficial pleasures of the passing moment and to concentrate on the enduring values of human existence, perhaps to seek ultimate meaning where alone it may be found—in a realm beyond time and space.... [These] enabled the Jew to carry on, to move from catastrophe to catastrophe without surrendering either faith or hope.... Jews could believe ... through suffering they had atoned for their sins, they were purified, they ... stood the test. Because of suffering they were ready for the Messiah, worthy of him.... If the Messiah did not come, there was always an explanation. Somehow, Jews failed again. The explanation was not always convincing. The *Galut* had gone on too long, it was too cruel.... "All exiles come to an end, only mine increases; all questions are answered, but my question returns ever to the place from which it came."[5]

Is there nothing but punishment, purification, and waiting only to be disappointed? Needless to say, there is also another approach to the problem, more valid and equally well rooted in the teaching. Exile as a single event may well be punishment. But exile as an enduring condition, and entailing survival in spite of it, belongs to a fundamentally different category.... *Galut*, the specifically Jewish form of exile, is rather different: it does not follow; it is at the beginning.

Jewish history begins with God's words to Abraham: "Get thee out of thy country, and from thy kindred, and from thy father's house, unto the land which I will show thee" (Gen. 12:1). The history of Judaism commences with *Galut*. If exile is at the very start, then there must be something in the nature of Judaism, in God's plan for the Jewish people, which is inseparable from it. Abraham, in order to become the patriarch of Israel, had to leave his father's house and the land of his birth.... He went into exile, because in the world as it existed then, Abraham could not find a home. He had the choice: either to be true to himself and become a stranger, or wanderer, or to become one with his surroundings and remain at home. He chose himself, his own personal destiny; but in order to do that he had to go into exile. . . .

The children of Israel, whom the natural course of events had taken to Egypt, could have merged with the Egyptian people and have been completely absorbed by Egypt's civilization. But if they were to remain Jews and loyal to the obligation of their descent, they had to remain apart. Again, like their father Abraham, they had a choice: to surrender their identity and submerge in the majority, or to remain true to themselves and become strangers and live in exile.

What is the significance of *Galut* as a starting point? One might generalize and say: There are certain ideals that are not easily absorbed by the order of the world; . . . ideas and values that are strangers among men and are of tragic necessity forced into exile. Such a stranger in history is the idea represented by the Jewish people in the history of mankind. The history of a people of God, a people that enters on the scene of history on the strength of a covenant with God, that sees its responsibility as a people to obey God's word and to do his will, must be in a condition of *Galut*. As Abraham did not fit into the local world of his birthplace, so do his children not fit into the universal world of the nations to the extent that it is dominated by materialistic self-interest and ambitions of power. We say in our prayers, "Because of our sins we have been exiled from our land,"[6] but the truth is that during the period of the Second Temple the Jewish people had already completely given up every form of idolatry. It was the period of the great teachers of the Mishnah. During that time Israel was probably closer to God than in any previous phase in its history. Yet, this generation was overtaken by the catastrophe of the *ḥurban*, the destruction of the Temple and the state and the scattering of the people into the four corners of the world. . . . [I]n the world as it existed then, a world ruled by the Roman Empire, there was indeed no room for the people of the prophets. . . .

There are many passages in Talmud and Midrash that describe God as weeping over the exile of his children. . . .[7] Why should exile involve the kind of suffering Israel had to endure? It is taken for granted that a minority scattered all over the world that attempts to retain its identity will be oppressed and persecuted. . . . Whenever a minority is persecuted, justice, humanity, decency are all in a state of exile from the affairs of men. The case of the Jew is, of course, aggravated by the fact that, not by what he does, but by what he is, indeed by the fact that he is, represents a challenge to the principle by which nations "normally" live. And God himself is "powerless.". . . This, of course, means that exile is a cosmic condition. God Himself is a refugee in the world. This is the final meaning of the Jewish concept of *sh'khinta b'Galuta*, the Divine Presence in exile in the world. The *Galut* of the Jewish people is a specific case of this cosmic condition and a necessary outcome of it.

In spite of the suffering involved there is also majesty in exile, the majestic loyalty of a people that in an unprecedented and unparalleled manner has kept faith with an ideal. Even Jews are often inclined to look upon their *Galut* as a phase of passivity in which the Jewish people are a mere object for the butt end of history. The truth is that their condition was a matter of choice. But for the Nazi period, Jews could always escape persecution through apostasy, by conversion, through assimilation and complete surrender of identity. . . .

[E]very day that the Jew endured and remained loyal to his God or to his identity was a day of choice and decision. To accept the day-by-day challenge and not to surrender, no matter what the consequences, has been a deed of the spirit that for intensity, duration, and willingness for self-sacrifice remains unique in the history of mankind.[8]

Self-Identity in the Diaspora

Isaac ben Yedaiah, author of the next text, lived in southern France in the middle of the thirteenth century. Passionately committed to a philosophical exposition of Judaism, he wrote his commentary to demonstrate that all of the Rabbis' statements, as irrational or implausible as they might seem on the surface, were in fact compatible with philosophy if understood correctly.[9]

In the passage he explicates the following talmudic statement that marital relations were no longer pleasurable following the destruction of the Temple: "R. Isaac said, From the day when the Temple was destroyed, the pleasure of [marital] intercourse was taken [from Jews] and given to the sinners, as the Bible says, *Bread eaten in secret is pleasurable* (Prov. 9:17)."[10]

Ben Yedaiah's comment on this passage strongly evokes the difficulties of exilic Jewish life in terms not generally associated with Jews in medieval Europe. By day's end, the exertion involved in hard physical labor, necessary to sustain a family and pay heavy taxes, purportedly left the Jewish male exhausted, interested only in eating and falling asleep, his desire to make love to his wife all but extinguished. Ben Yedaiah vividly contrasts this with the days when Jews lived on their own lands and Jewish men of leisure were expected to satisfy their wives' sexual needs daily.

This explication is complicated, however, by the commentator's commitment to a philosophical tradition (derived from Aristotle, and classically stated by Maimonides) that considered sexual relations, like everything pertaining to the sense of touch, as shameful. In his commentary ben Yedaiah insists that frequent indulgence in sexual relations is a perversion of energies that should be devoted to cultivation of the intellect. Why then is the suppression of sexual desire in the exile bad?

Here he presents a psychological reading of the Rabbinic statement: the pressures of exile suppress the Jewish male's normal drive for sexual fulfillment with his wife, but leave intact the much stronger drive for the illicit relationship: with a gentile woman or the wife of another man. *Galut* essentially robs Jewish men of their manhood in relation to their wives, thereby extinguishing the most important safeguard against acting out on the desire to sin. Even an exhausting day of physical labor does not suppress the desire for this forbidden pleasure.

ISAAC BEN YEDAIAH, *COMMENTARY ON THE AGGADOT OF THE TALMUD* (LATE 13TH CENTURY)

Before the Temple was destroyed, God's Chosen People was spread through its own land; the entire nation settled tranquilly on its lees [Jer. 48:11].[11] Among them were men of leisure, who enjoyed every sort of debasing pleasure. Among the many pleasures and superfluous things they sought, they enjoyed indulging in sexual intercourse every day, because of the abundant fluids that welled up in them due to their pursuit of superfluous things. Thus the Sages said, "Those at leisure [should engage in sexual relations with their wives] every day."[12] They taught that the man who is pampered and strong can perform the commandment to "be fruitful and multiply" (Gen. 1:28) every day. . . .

But when the people went into exile, and became subservient to their enemies, slaves at forced labor [Gen. 49:15, Josh. 16:10], year after year, exhausting themselves throughout the day in order to provide for their household needs, and pay their onerous taxes [or, perform their onerous compulsory tasks], their manliness was lost, and they became effeminate. When evening comes, and the [Jewish] male returns from his work and eats to his satisfaction, he soon dozes off—sleep being so appealing because of the burdensome drain on him during the day—the sweet sleep of the laborer. As he rests, it does not even occur to him to perform that shameful act, even when it is permissible for him, with his wife, ordained only for him, because he is so weary and exhausted. He has no desire for this act—unless there is an opportunity to sin.

If *another* woman should make herself available to him, he will embrace the bosom of this alien [Prov. 5:20]. His great toil [necessary to earn a livelihood] will not prevent him from doing so, because of the impulse that causes him to sin and feeds him that which is forbidden and shameful, while he has no desire for what is permissible for him. This is human nature: a man wants to fulfill his desire to sin. Solomon, the wise, taught us this in the verse, *Bread eaten in secret is sweet* (Prov. 9:17), and he also said, *She eats and wipes her mouth* (Prov. 30:20). In these verses, "eating" is a metaphor for the pleasant transgression of sinning.

The Sages intended to teach about the sinner that his impure bread, his secret bread, which he digs in the darkness [Job 24:16], in the dead of night [Prov. 7:9], is more pleasurable than what is pure; it is as sweet to his taste as honey, even though he is weary and exhausted because of his onerous labor. He does not fear God, nor does he toil to become rich [cf. Prov. 23:4], but only to taste of that which brings pleasure to his flesh. Solomon also said, *Stolen water is sweet* (Prov. 9:17), teaching the adulterer that whatever he may steal from his neighbor, such as deceiving him and having relations with his neighbor's wife, the woman prohibited to him will be sweeter than the woman permitted him.[13] Knowing this, his God will bring him and justly castigate him [cf. Jer. 10:24].[14]

Zionist Ideas and Ideology

In the context of debates over their civil emancipation and other social reforms, European Jews found themselves no longer confined geographically or metaphorically to the shtetls. Influenced by the goals of the Enlightenment, consciously or not, many Jews tried to become full citizens, integrated into the European societies in which they lived. The limitations they faced—especially the intractability of antisemitism— led some to rethink their position, and to confront what came to be called "the Jewish question" or "the Jewish problem" in a new way. Below are three responses from the late nineteenth and early twentieth centuries addressing this issue.

Judah Leib (Leon) Pinsker (1821–91) was the founder of the Ḥibbat Tziyon (Love of Zion) movement. Born in Russian Poland, he initially believed that citizenship rights would solve the Jews' problem. He studied both law (in Odessa) and medicine (in Moscow), and became an important figure in the Society for the Promotion of Enlightenment among Jews, advocating assimilation into Russian culture. Yet in the wake of the 1881 pogroms he changed his mind, and called for Jews to emancipate themselves in an unsigned pamphlet, *Auto-Emancipation: An Appeal to His People by a Russian Jew*.

In the excerpt below, he asserts that assimilation is no longer possible. Until Jews address their need for a common language, shared customs, and land, they will neither be a nation nor avoid the consequences of antisemitism. Hence, Jews must emancipate themselves and become a nation in their own right. In this pamphlet Pinsker did not specify location, and in fact focused on the Land of Israel only belatedly.

JUDAH LEIB PINSKER, *AUTO-EMANCIPATION* (1882)

Among the living nations of the earth the Jews occupy the position of a nation long since dead. With the loss of their fatherland, the Jews lost their independence and fell into a state of decay which is incompatible with the existence of a whole and vital organism.... This ghostlike apparition of a people without unity or organization, without land or other bond of union, no longer alive, and yet moving about among the living ... unlike anything that preceded or followed it, could not fail to make a strange and peculiar impression upon the imagination of the nations....

Fear of the Jewish ghost has been handed down and strengthened for generations and centuries. It led to a prejudice which ... paved the way for Judeophobia.

Along with a number of other subconscious and superstitious ideas, instincts, and idiosyncrasies, Judeophobia, too, has become rooted and naturalized among all the peoples of the earth with whom the Jews have had intercourse....

Judeophobia is a psychic aberration. As a psychic aberration, it is hereditary; as a disease transmitted for two thousand years, it is incurable....

Friend and foe alike have tried to explain or to justify this hatred of the Jews by bringing all sorts of charges against them. They are said to have crucified Jesus, to have drunk blood of Christians, to have poisoned wells, to have taken usury, to have exploited the peasant, and so on. These charges—and a thousand and one others of like nature—against an entire people have been proved groundless.... Though the Jews may justly be charged with many shortcomings, those shortcomings are, at all events, not such great vices, not such capital crimes, as to justify the condemnation of the entire people. In individual cases, indeed, we find these accusations contradicted by the fact that the Jews get along fairly well in close intercourse with their gentile neighbors. This is the reason that the charges preferred are usually of the most general character, made up out of whole cloth ... and true, at most, in individual cases, but untrue as regards the whole people.

Thus have Judaism and anti-Semitism passed for centuries through history as inseparable companions. . . . No matter how much the nations are at variance with one another, no matter how diverse in their instincts and aims, they join hands in their hatred of the Jews; on this one matter all are agreed. . . .

Having analyzed Judeophobia as an hereditary form of demonopathy, peculiar to the human race, and having represented anti-Semitism as based upon an inherited aberration of the human mind, we must draw the important conclusion: the fight against this hatred, like any fight against inherited predispositions, can only be in vain. . . . Prejudice or instinctive ill will can be satisfied by no reasoning, however forceful and clear. These sinister powers must either be kept within bounds by material coercion, like every other blind natural force, or simply ignored. . . .

In the psychology of the peoples, then, we find the basis of the prejudice against the Jewish nation; but we must also consider other, no less important factors, which render impossible the fusion or equalization of the Jews with the other peoples.

No people, generally speaking, has any predilection for foreigners. . . . The aversion which meets the foreigner in a strange land can be repaid in equal coin in his home country. . . . The foreigner has no need to *be*, or to *seem to be*, a patriot. But as for the Jew, he is not a native in his own home country, but he is also not a foreigner; he is, in very truth, the stranger par excellence. He is regarded as neither friend nor foe, but as an alien, of whom the only thing known is that he has no home. . . .[15]

The Fetters That Bind

British poet and writer Amy Levy (1861–89) grew up in a middle-class family in London's West End. Her feelings of alienation—as a woman, as a Sephardic Jew, as single and without child—are expressed in her identification with the figure of the poet in exile, such as Judah Halevi, whom she read through Heinrich Heine's poetic interpretation. Both the title and the symbol of the lion (Ezek. 19) recall the story of the Children of Israel held captive by the Babylonians.

In the poem neither lion nor bird can return to its homeland. The poem ends with a personal sense of exile that could be read to include spiritual captivity. Levy died by suicide before her twenty-eighth birthday.

> AMY LEVY, "CAPTIVITY" (1889)
>
> The lion remembers the forest,
> The lion in chains;
> To the bird that is captive a vision
> Of woodland remains.
>
> One strains with his strength at the fetter,
> In impotent rage;
> One flutters in flights of a moment,
> And beats at the cage.
>
> If the lion were loosed from the fetter,
> To wander again;
> He would seek the wide silence and shadow
> Of his jungle in vain.
>
> He would rage in his fury, destroying;
> Let him rage, let him roam!
> Shall he traverse the pitiless mountain,
> Or swim through the foam?
>
> If they opened the cage and the casement,
> And the bird flew away;
> He would come back at evening, heartbroken,
> A captive for aye.
>
> Would come if his kindred had spared him,
> Free birds from afar—
> There was wrought what is stronger than iron
> In fetter and bar.

I cannot remember my country,
The land whence I came;
Whence they brought me and chained me and made me
Nor wild thing nor tame.

This only I know of my country,
This only repeat: —
It was free as the forest, and sweeter
Than woodland retreat.

When the chain shall at last be broken,
The window set wide;
And I step in the largeness and freedom
Of sunlight outside;

Shall I wander in vain for my country?
Shall I seek and not find?
Shall I cry for the bars that encage me
The fetters that bind?[16]

"Indeed This People Is Grass"

This opening phrase of the next poem, taken from Isaiah 40:7, evokes an earlier historical moment of return from exile: the end of the Babylonian captivity, when the Jewish people was permitted to return to their land and an anonymous prophet called upon them to respond accordingly. One exegetical tradition is that Isaiah 40:6-8, contrasting human glory with God's word, pertained to the Babylonians' illusions of power and permanence, and the line "indeed this people is grass" (40:7) referred to the Babylonian Empire, whose time had now ended. Here, in a shocking inversion, Hayyim Nahman Bialik (see chapter 4) applies the verse to the Jewish people.

The first stanza evokes a people who is passive and indifferent to important events, and particularly "God's voice." The word "voice," appearing four times in the stanza, echoes the beginning of Isaiah 40:6, the celebrated voice crying in the wilderness. Great events are occurring, God is summoning the people to action, but they remain engrossed in their worship of "golden idols," oblivious to the opportunity for radical change.

This apparently reflects the poet's deep disappointment resulting from the absence of a popular Jewish response to Leon Pinsker and other pre-Herzl Zionist writers, and to the Ḥibbat Tziyon movement of emigration and settlement in the Land of Israel. With this movement apparently sputtering, and the new Zionist movement having not yet emerged, Bialik gives vent to fears that the burdens of exile have rendered the people incapable of responding to the opportunities at hand.

In the second stanza Bialik limns a picture of the ideal national leader needed by the Jewish people. Some have seen this passage as a prophetic evocation of Herzl, who was just about to emerge in his historic role, but when the poem was written, and when it appeared, Herzl was still off the stage of Jewish consciousness. Moreover, the poet's complaint is that the people has not produced such a leader; the leader's absence, rather than his imminent appearance, suffuses these lines.

The third stanza returns to an utterly bleak description of the Jewish people, explaining it as a result of the centuries of suffering in exile. The final lines raise a haunting question: Has the negative impact of the exile so dessicated or deadened the people that Jews will be impervious even to the sounds and symbols of the long-awaited messianic redemption? A studied ambiguity in the final line makes it applicable both to the traditional resurrection of the dead and the metaphorical demise of the people—so sapped of life force that Jews are impervious even to the signal that the end of the exile has come. The rhetorical questions seem to expect the answer "No."

Fundamentally, "Indeed This People Is Grass" is one of the most pessimistic visions in Jewish literature. Historian and Hebrew literary scholar Joseph Klausner wrote that "such terrifying words as these exist only in the very harshest rebukes of the prophets." Still, Klausner manages to find some basis for hope that the poet may or may not have intended: "Yet this kind of embitterment is the first step toward the great hope that all can change for the better. For to dead men and corpses, one does not bother addressing vigorous rebukes."[17] Perhaps, indeed, the bitter negativism is a rhetorical ploy intended to shock.

> HAYYIM NAHMAN BIALIK, "INDEED THIS
> PEOPLE IS GRASS" (1897)
>
> *For the wind blew in it . . . indeed this people is grass* (Isa. 40:7).
>
> Indeed this people is grass, dry it is like wood;
> indeed this people is hollow, hollow and heavy without end;
> that the Lord's voice thunders from here and there—
> and none stirs and none trembles and the people is not seared.[18]
> It does not rise like a lion or shake like a king of beasts
> and not one man in all the city fears the voice.
> And the heart of the people did not stir with joy at once
> from left to right or sea to sea,
> when they revealed themselves to it, its sons, the seed of the living God,
> that came from afar to the call of the Lord.
> Nor did it reach a hand, nor ask after the health
> of all that call its name in innocence and faith.
> And in the hubbub of an idle race around idols of gold[19]
> the voice of God is hidden, is swallowed his mighty roar.
> And in a heart low and base, and with insults and spittle
> the word of God is mocked, and turned away with guffaws.
>
> Indeed this people are withered, full of holes and hemlock;
> all rot and decay from its head to its feet!
> That did not raise from its midst in a day of sickness and suffering
> a living man, of action, in whom a heart beats,
> and in that heart a spark burns, a spark to boil the blood up
> and in whose head will rise a light to light the way for the multitude;
> to whom is dear the name of the race and its God
> more than wealth and gold—those falsest idols;
> and a little vision, a lot of truth and courage,

fierce hate for the lot of life of slavery and outrage,
pity great as the sea, mercy as multitudinous
as the trouble of his people and the weight of its burdens—
all these moan in his heart, moan and pitch like the sea;
all these burn like fire, burn and set alight his veins;
all these thunder like an echo constantly both night and day:
"Rise up and work, rise up and do, for with us is the hand of God!"

Indeed this people is lost, yearning for shame and spittle;
its deeds have no foundations and its actions no regulation.
Thousands of years of wandering, an exile too great to bear,
have turned the heart falsely back; the race has lost its way.
The study of rod and whip[20]—will it be sensible to pain
of soul's disgrace and subjugation other than by whips on its back?
Or is it capable of worrying other than for the day[21]
this people rolling in the valley of exile dark as the abyss?
To bear its soul for the day and foretell the light
to steer its course to the end, to prophesy for these days?
It will not rise if not stung awake by the whip.
It will not rise if not raised by violence.
A leaf drying from the tree, weed rising in the heap,
a vine layed to waste, a bud mildewed—will we be revived by dew?
Even in the blow of the horn and waving on high of the banner[22]—
will the dead be aroused? Can the dead be stirred?[23]

"Always Quite Content to Remain Where They Were"

Joseph Hayyim Brenner (1881-1921) is best known today as a literary figure whose work vies with that of S. Y. Agnon in quality and reputation.[24]

Born in Ukraine, he received the traditional yeshiva education. He supported himself by teaching Hebrew, began writing stories, and became active in the Jewish labor movement. When in England—having fled the tsarist army—he joined the Po'alei Zion (Workers of Zion) movement.

Arriving in Palestine in 1909 during the midpoint of the second wave of immigration (1904–14), he soon began contributing to several local newspapers. He paved roads as part of the Labor Battalion (Gedud Ha'avodah) and helped found the Histadrut (labor union) that was to establish or prompt much of the infrastructure of the Jewish settlement in the Land of Israel.

Committed to socialist Zionism, Brenner was convinced of the need for a colonial-territorial movement fueled by the proletariat (the working class). In his essays and fiction promoting a secular Hebrew culture he depicted Jewish life in exile in almost unrelentingly critical terms, his pessimism relieved only by his commitment to Zionism. His 1914 article "Self-Criticism" (excerpted below) pushed Jews past minimal achievement—"Survival alone is not a virtue"—and especially disparaged those Jews who, he said, are content to stay in exile and embody "our sick character."

> JOSEPH HAYYIM BRENNER, "SELF-CRITICISM" (1914)
>
> In their prayers, their liturgy, and sacred books the Jews complained to God for not redeeming them, for not restoring them forever to their homeland, while they were doing so much for His Great Name's sake, despite the bitter exile which prevented them from observing all the laws and commandments properly. At the same time, however, they were always quite content to remain where they were, among the wicked gentiles, so long as the latter allowed them to remain. Naturally, they paid for their lives with money, withdrew into their shells, their tortoise shells, whenever they were subjected to oppression, peered through the chinks in their cave walls, looking forward all the while to better days when they would be able to emerge, spread out over the land, and do business with it. Not a history of Sanctification of the Name, but a history of awaiting the chance to assimilate—such is our history.
>
> The expulsions and the ghettos—these assured our survival. Even the Golden Jewry of Spain—who knows what would have remained of them, of those Spaniards of Mosaic Persuasion, beyond what remained

of their Marranos [sic] of Christian Persuasion! It is only because they were suddenly expelled by the tens of thousands to a strange land of a lower cultural level, in which, as a result, they did not fare as well as in the land which expelled them, that we have today our Arabic-Sephardim, Turco-Sephardim, Serbo-Sephardim, and the Bulgarians of Mosaic Persuasion in the Ottoman Empire and the Balkan lands.

History! History! But what has history to tell? It can tell that wherever the majority population, by some fluke, did not hate the Jews among them, the Jews immediately started aping them in everything, gave in on everything, and mustered the last of their meager strength to be like everyone else. Even when the yoke of ghetto weighed most heavily upon them—how many broke through the walls? How many lost all self-respect in the face of the culture and beautiful way of life of the others! How many envied the others! How many yearned to approach them!

It had been the consensus of our literature until recently that our forefathers, the Jews of the old ghetto, felt within their hearts a pride and a superiority to the gentile, even while kissing his hand and abasing themselves before him. This thesis is: There was outward humiliation and servility, but inward pride and beauty.

It is possible, of course, that some Jews who were sensitive to their mortification consoled themselves with the promise to Jews of a better life in the world to come. Perhaps they assured themselves that despite all the gentile's earthly possessions of large estates, horses, carriages, minstrels, and all the pleasures of this world, he would never inherit Paradise with us. This was a consolation, but nothing more.

But whence this disdain of, and sense of superiority over, the gentile? Was the Jew really so insensitive, so dead to the world, as not even to realize how much more beautiful and rich was the gentile's life than his own? No, this is impossible! This we cannot believe! If there was disdain of the gentile, it was but the natural envy that the poor man has for the rich, the monk for the knight, and the weak man for the strong. Such disdain was really but a shrug of resignation of our share in this world, some sort of consolation—depending upon the mood—in hopes of the world to come, followed by a quiet gritting of the teeth and conscious or subconscious inner turmoil.[25]

Liberation from Exile

Jacob Klatzkin (1882–1948), son of the well-known Russian rabbi Elijah Klatzkin, was not especially interested in rabbinic Judaism. He studied in yeshiva in Lithuania, moved to Germany to study philosophy under Hermann Cohen, eventually completing his doctorate in Switzerland. Known as an opponent of Ahad Ha'am, he became an important editor of the German *Encyclopedia Judaica* together with Nahum Goldmann. Most of his writings were published in Berlin.

When war broke out, he moved to the United States, where he taught at the College of Jewish Studies in Chicago and wrote *In Praise of Wisdom: Everyday Life and the Art of Living*. He returned to Switzerland in 1947, shortly before his death.

Klatzkin's 1914 essay, "Boundaries," demonstrates his commitment to Zionism and his repudiation of Jewish life in exile, even though that was where he spent his entire life.

> JACOB KLATZKIN, "BOUNDARIES" (1914)
>
> *The Galut is unworthy of survival.* Let us assume that the Galut can survive and that *total* assimilation will not inevitably follow the abandonment of religion. Nonetheless we must assert: The Judaism of the Galut is not worthy of survival.
>
> *The Galut falsifies our national character.* Perhaps our people can maintain itself in the Galut, but it will not exist in its true dimensions—not in the prime of its national character. . . . At the very most it can maintain us in a state of national impurity and breed some sort of outlandish creature in an environment of disintegration of cultures and of darkening spiritual horizons. The result will be something neither Jew nor gentile—in any case, not a pure national type.
>
> Perhaps it is conceivable that, even after the disintegration of our national existence in foreign lands, there will yet remain for many generations some sort of oddity among the peoples going by the name—Jew. Indeed, both we and the nations of the world are already quite accustomed to showing our lack of respect for this

designation by applying it even to ultra-assimilationists who were conceived, born, educated, and grew to maturity in denial of their Jewishness. . . .

Does it make any sense for us to struggle to maintain this empty label? Why prolong its existence and cling to a slight difference that, possessing only a negative and not a positive national significance, has outlived its meaning?

The Galut is corrupting our human character and dignity. Such a life, even if it continues to exist, will represent no more than a rootless and restless wandering between two worlds. It will cause rent and broken human beings to persist—individuals diseased by ambivalence, consumed by contradictions, and spent by relentless inner conflict. . . .

And our thousands of years of Galut—were they a total waste? Did we create no national values in the Galut? Though we were suffering the Exile, were we not among the leaders of human civilization? If it was so in the midst of distress and poverty, how much greater will be our achievement after we shall have acquired equality among the nations of the world? . . .

No, the argument is not valid. So long as our religion was strong, it was a solid wall protecting us and enabling us to live a national life, almost a political life, on alien soil. In effect, even in the Galut we lived a sovereign life. The Crown of the Torah accompanied us; our Book of Laws was our companion in our wanderings.

The Galut must be preserved long enough to be transcended. And what about the Galut? Will it simply wither away? Its function will be to serve as a source of supply for the renaissance of our people in its homeland. Eretz Israel will need the Galut for many generations to come. It will draw upon the Galut for energy and vitality; it will gradually strip that Jewry, which is doomed to oblivion, and *to the extent that it will strip it, it will save it.* . . .

Galut Jewry cannot survive and all our efforts to keep it alive are simply an act of coercion, the maintenance of an unnatural existence. These efforts, however, are not entirely useless. . . . We are simply hoping to delay its end for a short while so that we may have the time to salvage some bricks for a new structure. . . .

The Galut has a right to life for the sake of liberation from the Galut. In essence, it is the vision of the homeland which validates the Galut. Without this *raison d'être*, without the goal of a homeland, the Galut is nothing more than a life of deterioration and degeneration, a disgrace to the nation and a disgrace to the individual, a life of pointless struggle and futile suffering, of ambivalence, confusion, and eternal impotence. . . .

From this point of view we affirm the importance of the national effort in the Galut, an affirmation based both on negation of the Galut and definition of its purpose. Without negation of the Galut there is no basis for such an affirmation.

We must conserve Galut Jewry to the very best of our abilities. We must cultivate a national culture despite existing conditions and inevitable trends. We must increase self-restrictions and prohibitions, for the sake of protecting our identity and apartness, and we must define boundary after boundary between ourselves and the nations among whom we are assimilating. . . . We know that the struggle against assimilation has no chance of victory. . . . It is our task to delay the end and to slow the process of disintegration so that, meanwhile, our people may be rebuilt. . . . This transitional existence is of significance, precisely because it is transitional.[26]

Jewish Homelessness

Max Nussbaum (1908–74) served as a congregational rabbi in Berlin from 1935 until the summer of 1940, when he fled Germany for the United States. He became rabbi of an Oklahoma congregation for three years, and then moved to Los Angeles, where he remained for the rest of his career. Ruth Nussbaum's biography, *Max Nussbaum: From Berlin to Hollywood*, includes an important chapter, "Ministry under Stress: A Rabbi's Recollection of Nazi Berlin, 1935–1940."

Rabbis preaching under the Nazi regime in Germany, and especially in Berlin, were permitted to deliver sermons, but—with a member of the Gestapo sitting in the front row of every synagogue during their Shabbat services—there were severe limits to what could be said from the pulpit. Often, pulpit rabbis would reference biblical figures and events to communicate a message that could not be fully articulated when applied to the present.

The following sermon, which Nussbaum delivered fewer than two months after the outbreak of war, focuses on the patriarch Abraham—but not, as was common, on Abraham's role as the founder of Jewish life in what would become the Land of Israel. Rather, Nussbaum elaborates upon a different aspect of Abraham's life: his traveling, his wandering, first from his homeland for a location unknown to him, and then away from his new home into Egypt.

An important point in this sermon is the emphasis on the uniqueness of Jewish homelessness, a condition Nussbaum titles *galut*, or exile. Despite the uprooting traumas experienced by other nations, he insists that none of them have experienced the Jewish tragedy of *galut*.

> MAX NUSSBAUM, "TO TRAVEL AND TO FLEE" (1939)
>
> The story of Abraham's life may be expressed in a single word, which dominated his life: "Wandering." No wonder, therefore, that his life has become the symbolic model of ours throughout the centuries, and it need no longer be disputed why Abraham's years of wonderings are the very center of our current attention....
>
> If mankind should once succeed in reconstructing in such a way that on each spot of the soil only one people would live, and indeed it would be a nation that truly belongs to that spot, so that Land and People would coincide with each other, then we would have solved one of the most difficult problems of human history....
>
> Many people will be struck by the idea that the time has now come when nations other than our own also feel what is called *Galut*. Of course, it cannot be denied that all these above-mentioned cases were not lacking in personal grief. Country, homeland, and father's house are also important conceptions for them. But nevertheless, this parallel is not quite right; this problem reminds us of ours and it attracts our attention, but it does not at all mean *Galut*. Only we Jews can truly feel what it means when ships of their own nation enter a harbor. It is true that their passengers may have been torn away from

their homes, but on the other hand they are welcomed, cared for, and led to that place that had previously been established and that would become their future home. They know where they come from and where they are going. In spite of all the personal grief, this is an exchange of population, a re-organization or whatever else it may be called, but by no means *Galut*. We alone—who no longer think it to be peculiar when ships are leaving for an uncertain destination, but not arriving there, being forbidden to go on shore—we alone can judge and feel this fine yet deep difference between those events occurring among the other nations and our own historical fate.[27]

"Tomorrow Will Be Better"

Natan Zach (1930–2020), born as Harry Seitelbach in Germany, moved with his family to Mandatory Palestine as a child. The manifesto he wrote as a member of the literary movement Likrat would revolutionize the direction of contemporary Israeli poetry. One of its most important innovators, Zach formulated new rules that broke from tradition, favoring brevity over sentimentality, directness over ideology, and colloquial language over the more formalized locutions of his predecessors.

> NATAN ZACH, "AN EXILE POEM" (1966)
>
> Dreamers of dreams
> Tomorrow will be better
> The wonders have been set for tomorrow
> Menachem Mendels of the coming disaster[28]
> The tribulation drawing near
> And they do not tremble nor do they feel
> Spinning their webs in secret
> An international accord of future Rothschilds
> In their beds and in their dreams at night.
>
> A barefoot beggar Jew steps out in the world
> He does not yet have a wife, or a child
> But the child will be an Einstein, or a lawyer

And will compensate him for his market stall and for his thrombosis
Meanwhile, the dream ends in a suit and a pose
That is all poetry without a bit of prose

For real, with which it is possible to live in this valley of tears
Where we were born to stepmothers
And to oppressed, downtrodden fathers, who lash
Their own bodies, like devout Muslims on their holy day,
While their God watches and jeers:
"Go away, old fool, go away, old fool!"[29]

The Second Babylonian Exile

Eli Amir's novel *Tarnegol Kapparot* (translated as *Scapegoat*; lit. "Fowl of atonement") is written in the tradition of *sifrut hama'abarah* (transit camp literature), stories of immigrants—mostly from Arab and Islamic lands—resettling in Israel. In this genre, the crises of identity provoked by the uprooting are understood to result from the disparities between expectations and reality, the discrepancies between previous status and standards of life in one's original land and in Israel, the fragmentation of family, and the clash of Western and Eastern cultures.

The experiences of Amir's protagonist, seen here reacting to both his Israeli counselor's exhortations to adapt and his peers' resistance, echo his own. Amir (b. 1938) was one of more than 120,000 Jews brought to Israel in the mass immigration from Iraq in the first years following the State of Israel's establishment. At the time of its demise the Baghdadi Jewish community comprised the plurality of the city's population. Baghdadi Jews were influential participants in the professions, in politics, and especially in business. But ultimately the majority of the Jewish community moved to Israel out of necessity, not ideology, as Iraq became increasingly inhospitable to its Jewish population. They left behind a history dating back to the Babylonian Exile, a proud legacy of accomplishment and coexistence.

The departure from Iraq was a community exile: an uprooting of almost an entire community. The exile *from* Babylonia thus created "the

Second Babylonian Exile"[30]—reversing the earlier exile *to* Babylonia. In the following excerpt the first paragraph is the voice of the Polish-born Israeli counselor; the Iraqi teen's response follows.

> ELI AMIR, *TARNEGOL KAPPAROT* (1982)
>
> You're different from the "regionals," and there's nothing wrong with that! It's natural. Our children are different from us too. Masul is mistaken if he thinks that people here hate Baghdad. Everyone knows that our movement stands for equality between Jews and Arabs and calls for cooperation between them. There's simply no room in our lives here for Baghdad or for the way of life in the Jewish *shtetl* of Eastern Europe either. We came to this country because we rebelled against that way of life. Zionism is a revolt, a revolution, and every revolution has a price. . . . We don't have to deny our cultural origins, neither those of Eastern Europe nor those of the Middle East, to which we have returned. Do you think we didn't suffer the infantile diseases of cultural adjustment ourselves? Didn't we try to imitate the East when we first came here? I told you about the mounted guards of HaShomer who wore *abbayehs* and Circassian hats. Didn't they put up Bedouin tents and try to imitate the Bedouin way of life? And it was precisely the HaShomer people who fascinated us in Poland. We didn't bring Poland here with us and you're not going to bring Iraq with you either. We cast the yoke of the past off our necks for the sake of the future, and that is your mission too. We rebelled against our parents. You already know the poem, 'Do not listen, son, to the teachings of your father.' If only our fathers had listened to us. Perhaps they wouldn't have ended up the way they did. . . .[31]
>
> After all, they [the local teens who had been born in Israel] were the princes of the valley. . . . They were the new and I was the old, they were the redemption and I the diaspora. I wanted to be like them, a new man, and I was neither one nor the other. I thought it would be enough if I ate the food they did, did the work they did, even in the manure if necessary, but none of it helped. I was flooded by a tide of self-pity, and when I raised my eyes to the fronds of the

palm tree I remembered the palm tree that stood in our garden in Baghdad, a real palm tree, not like the one I was lying under now, flimsy, slightly hollow, not well-rooted in the soil, like me. . . .

When we arrived here I had sworn I would root myself in Kiryat Oranim, that I would become part of it. And now I was neither here nor there, a drifting plant in a no man's land.[32]

Sex, Character, and Soul of a Jew

In his drama *Soul of a Jew: The Last Night of Otto Weininger*, Joshua Sobol (b. 1939), one of Israel's most prolific and successful playwrights, gives voice to the ideas of the exilic Jew proposed by the Austrian philosopher Otto Weininger (1880–1903).

A brilliant and tortured intellectual from fin-de-siècle Vienna, Weininger was also a born Jew who influenced Wittgenstein, Strindberg, and James Joyce (among others), and famously converted to Protestantism shortly after receiving his doctorate from the University of Vienna. In his thesis *Sex and Character*, published shortly before his suicide in 1903, Weininger stated:

> It is notable that the Jews, even now when at least a relative security of tenure is possible, prefer moveable property, and, in spite of their acquisitiveness, have little real sense of personal property, especially in its most characteristic form, landed property. . . . For these reasons Zionism must remain an impracticable ideal, notwithstanding the fashion in which it has brought together some of the noblest qualities of the Jews. Zionism is the negation of Judaism, for the conception of Judaism involves a worldwide distribution of the Jews. Citizenship is an un-Jewish thing, and there has never been and never will be a true Jewish State. . . . The true conception of the State is foreign to the Jew. . . . Nor will Zionism solve that question. . . . Before Zionism is possible, the Jew must first conquer Judaism. . . . Therefore the Jewish question can only be solved individually; every single Jew must try to solve it in his proper person. There is no other solution to the question and can be no other; Zionism will never succeed in answering it.[33]

Eighty years later, in 1983, Sobol, known for his dramas based on historical documents (including his trilogy of Holocaust plays), offered a fictional recreation of the last night in Otto Weininger's life, from which two short excerpts appear below. The play combines the personal, political, and psychological domains against the backdrop of rising antisemitism in the Vienna of Karl Lueger and Sigmund Freud. Weininger's theories about sexuality—rejected by Freud and admired by Hitler—overlie his attitude toward his Jewish identity. His own response—rejecting his Judaism by converting to Christianity—ultimately fails.

The play's title, *Nefesh Yehudi* (*Soul of a Jew*), taken from the Israeli national anthem "Hatikvah," is laden with irony. The reference to the anthem contradicts Weininger's dire predictions for the Zionist movement, yet simultaneously puts the very success of Zionism into question.

Different characters represent various contemporary attitudes of and toward the Jews in Europe. Otto's father, an ardent and impassioned devotee of Wagner, and indeed of all Germanic culture, expresses considerable ambivalence toward the nascent Zionist movement: he believes that Zionism was all that remained noble in Jewish life, but holds that it can only succeed when freed from Judaism. His friends range from a militant Zionist to an ambivalent Jew and a non-Jewish philosemite.

The main character speaks of exile as illness. According to Weininger as portrayed in Sobol's play, Judaism, like the female, is weak. Exile is the most befitting form of existence for the Jew; because of the weakness of the Jew, antisemitism is inevitable and thus endemic to Jewish life in exile.

Sobol presents Weininger's more extreme ideas as, nonetheless, having certain commonalities with the ideologies of the Zionist writers Herzl, Pinsker, and Brenner, who—especially Herzl—lived in a similar milieu and shared like-minded experiences. Each thinker asserts the inevitability of antisemitism and the necessity of nationhood. Weininger's character is portrayed as self-hating and self-destructive, whereas the others are lauded as important figures in the history of Zionism.

JOSHUA SOBOL, *SOUL OF A JEW: THE LAST
NIGHT OF OTTO WEININGER* (1983)

OTTO: Judaism is on an even lower level than femininity. Woman believes in man; the Jew believes in nothing. The Jew is the enemy of form. The Jew is a born anarchist. The Jew elects to live in exile: it is his natural way of life. He felt this way even before the destruction of the Temple. The Jew will prefer this way of life even when he has his own country.

DOUBLE: The Jew, like woman, knows that
he is matter without form,
creature without ego,
a human being without soul,
nil and naught, moral chaos.
Therefore, the Jew
doesn't believe
in himself, or
in law and order....[34]

OTTO (to his Double): Leave them alone! I told them Zionism is not the solution. I warned you this adventure will end up in disaster. I told you you'd return to exile, I told you that you can't defeat the Jewishness in you.[35]

8 Exile in Medieval and Modern History

This chapter returns to the topic of historical exile but from a later period. The exiles under exploration—within Spain, from Spain, from elsewhere, and of the other—are well documented and have played a major role in the perception and narrative of the Jewish people. Several perspectives on the experience of exile are offered here, suggesting that even as exiles share the experiences of uprooting and dislocation, the particulars—from where they are uprooted, to where they are dislocated, the timing and duration of the exile—make each exile uniquely individual.

The expulsion of the Jews from Spain was, to some extent, the culmination of a series of expulsions from Europe (England in 1290, France from 1182 to 1384, several German states at different times) but ultimately diverged in size, duration, and motivation. The Jews who had come to England under the Norman Conquest were declared to be direct servants of the kings, faced intermittent outbreaks of anti-Jewish violence especially with regard to the Crusades, and averted a major attempt at expulsion from 1275 only to be finally expelled under Edward I in 1290. Jews living in France faced an edict of expulsion under Philip Augustus in 1182 but were recalled in 1198; faced another edict under Philip the Fair in 1306 but were recalled in 1315; and then experienced a final expulsion by Charles VI in 1394. As for Jews in the Western German Holy Roman Empire, especially in the Rhineland, they faced major persecution in the context of the First Crusade, and many thousands were burned to death during the Black Death of 1348–49.

Jews had lived in Spain the longest of anywhere. Where financial gain—whether through taxes levied or assets seized—motivated these earlier expulsions, the 1492 Alhambra Decree that demanded conversion or banishment was religiously motivated. The Church desired to spread Catholicism and feared Jewish influence on the recently converted.

Muslim Spain (Andalusia) was initially hospitable to Jews, yet the invasion of Berbers forced them to convert (to Islam) or flee to Christian Spain. It was not long, historically speaking, before the Reconquista—the efforts to reclaim Iberia for Christendom—forced a similar choice. Faced with the Alhambra Decree, an estimated two-thirds of the Jews converted and the other third, approximately one hundred thousand Jews, left their homes behind. Those seeking refuge in Portugal found the briefest respite; others fled to North Africa, Italy, and the Ottoman Empire.

The Spanish Expulsion is remarkable both for its singularity and its commonality. That not every Jewish exile is from Israel-Jerusalem-Zion, and that not everyone exiled from Israel-Jerusalem-Zion is a Jew, adds more layers to the intersection of the collective and the personal.

Muslim Spain

Born and raised in Granada, Spain, Moses ibn Ezra survived the destruction of the Jewish community there in 1066 and became part of an impressive group of scholars and poets (including Judah Halevi) in rebuilt Granada—but a powerful attack by the Berbers in 1090 had a major impact on his life. Unable to flee from the enemy while his family was spread far and wide, he remained in the devastated city until finally he escaped, finding refuge in Christian Spain.

Yet his new refuge made him feel as if he was indeed in exile. Apparently he had little interaction with other Jews living in the Christian environment; he had felt much more at home in the Arabic environment. Thus the final part of his life was an ongoing encounter with exile—not from the Land of Israel, but from Arab Spain.

The first poem below, "Ad An ba-Galut" (How far in exile), is a poignant example of the sense of exile Jews experienced after being forced to leave countries far away from the Land of Israel but in which they had felt at home. The hope ibn Ezra expresses so powerfully is for a return not to Jerusalem, but to Granada. So, too, in the second poem,

"Aḥar Yemei ha-Shaḥarut" (When the morning of life), regarding the painful question near the conclusion—"Oh, when will God call unto me, 'Go free!'"—the question is actually: "When will I be able to return to Granada?" The answer, unfortunately for him, was "never."

> MOSES IBN EZRA, "AD AN BA-GALUT" (11TH CENTURY)
>
> How far yet must my feet, at Fate's behest,
> Bear me o'er exile's path, and find no rest?
>
> The sword of Separation hath he drawn
> To harrow me over the earth;
> And with the battle-ax of Wandering,
> From each new refuge doth he drive me forth.
> Upon me he hath loosed his brood of ills;
> I totter, yea I fall, before their might—
> Whilst like a fading shadow, day by day,
> My life takes flight.
>
> Misfortune's marshalled hosts trampled my heart in youth;
> Still in mine age, they march unwearied on,
> Trampling, untouched by truth,
> The breaches of its walls they daub with woe,
> Then throng again to smite it, blow by blow.
>
> Marvel it seems, that the fierce fires of hell
> Should rage within my breast, albeit mine eyes
> Pour torrents passing all the rains that fell
> From beyond Noah's skies!
> Alas, they draw my tears from sulphurous streams,
> And drench my heart only to feed its flames!
>
> Oh, foolish eyes! They wake at morn to weep,
> And urge to lamentation in the night, whilst others sleep.
> They trust in tears for stay, where stay is none,
> They seek in tears for hope when hope is gone.

Misfortunes, hold! My body is too frail to bear new pains;
And with my soul deal gently; for in her no strength remains.

Speak now: Am I a sea no storm can quell?
A monster of the deep, whose scale-clad sides the sharpened dart repel?
Am I of Anak's giant progeny,[1]
Or Samson-like, strongest in misery?
Behold, my skin is black, my flesh is gone,
Dried is the marrow in my crumbling bone;
How shall my heart endure the shock of ills
Would rive in train the everlasting hills!

If in mine exile, I might meet but one
With whom to hold sweet converse of the mind,
Then would I willingly forgive Fate's spite
That sent me forth, so dear a friend to find.
From town to town I haste, but everywhere
It is to Folly's tents that men repair;
To Learning's gate they cannot find the way—
Yet never do I bar it night or day,
And none need weary to gain entrance there.

Dullards! They cannot see the stars of fame,
That in the firmament of letters rise to blazon forth my name.
My words of wisdom could not please their ear,
Though these had power to make the deaf to hear.
Say to the pilferers of song, that steal my words,
And fain would make my thoughts their prey,
That they indeed their thievish hands may fill
With fragments of my precious gems, to lay among their pebbles;
Plant amid their briers slips of my myrtle—but 'tis labor lost;
They cannot vie with me, until their feet
The mighty rivers of my tears have crossed.
How shall men liken to the lion's roar

The futile yelpings of an angry cur?
To catch a race-horse, shall a blind man try?
Or sparrows chase an eagle through the sky?

My songs shall live while earth and sun
Their ordered daily course shall run;
But songs in falsehood wrought shall be,
Within a day, forgotten utterly.

Oh how can I, whose wont was to consort
With the great-minded nobles of the west, take joy in life?
How shall my lonely heart, even in sleep, find rest?

Yet may not Fate, that hath been harsh so long, relent at last;
And grant my heart's desire—and lead me back
To that fair city where my youth was passed?
There wait the roofs of friends, and there might I
Sit by a loved one's threshold, and exchange
Greetings of friendship with the passers-by.

Or peradventure, after I am dead
Some spark of life may in my dust remain,
To sprout in bud and blossom, when the tears
Of faithful friends upon my grave shall rain.

But who can say if those dear, distant ones
Cherish or scorn the love I treasure yet?
If I forget them, may my hand forget its cunning[2]
If, from them apart, one thought of joy can enter in my heart.

Oh, if indeed, the Lord would me restore
To beautiful Granada-land, my paths
Would be the paths of pleasantness once more;
For in that land my life was very sweet—
A kindly Fate laid homage at my feet,
And deep I quaffed at Friendship's fount,
As now I fain would quaff the waters of Senir,[3]

Whose snowfall current bears the swimmer high
When Eden's streams run scant and sluggishly.

Though hope be long deferred, though heart be faint,
On God I wait, unto whose mercy there is no restraint,
And whose decree can break the shackles and unbar the gate,
And send the prisoner of exile free.

MOSES IBN EZRA, "AḤAR YEMEI HA-SHAḤARUT"
(11TH CENTURY)

When the morning of life had passed as a shadow,
And the path of my years was shortened,
Exile [*nedod*] called to me: "O thou, that dwellest at ease, arise!"
At the sound of his voice, mine ears tingled;
I arose, with shaken heart,
To go forth, a wanderer—
And my children cried unto God!

But they are the fount of my life—
How shall I exist without them,
And the light of mine eyes be not with me?

Fate has led me to a land
Wherein my mind is bewildered and my thoughts confused—
To a people rude of speech and obscure in word;
Before the insolence of their gaze, my face is cast down.
Oh, when will God call unto me, "Go free!"
That I may escape from them—if only by the skin of my teeth![4]

Christian Spain

The massive expulsion of the Jews in 1492 from the Spanish territory governed by Ferdinand and Isabella created a powerful new exile. Previous expulsions—such as those aforementioned from England and France—were of course shattering for Jews who had made their homes in these countries, but nothing comparable to this; Jewish life on the Iberian Peninsula had lasted more than a thousand years.

Notably, the Jews were given a choice: they could remain in Spain if they would accept conversion. The overwhelming majority of those who had not previously converted did not take this option.

Jews authored many texts on the 1492 expulsion. Their uprooting from their homes and their need to find new settlement in countries where they did not know the language made them feel as if they were indeed going into exile.

The final paragraph of the following selection, "An Anonymous Chronicle of the 1492 Expulsion," is rather astounding in the author's assertion that God's hatred of Jews (possibly meaning divine anger at their transgressive behavior) drove God to make Ferdinand more powerful than any previous king.[5] (Although Isabella was a monarch of equal status to Ferdinand, and her contempt for the Jews was even greater than his, she is not mentioned in the passage.)

"AN ANONYMOUS CHRONICLE OF THE
1492 EXPULSION" (CA. 1492)

Draw near, O nations, to hear, and peoples hearken and listen. Gather together, O you people, and be amazed. Stand by the wayside and see, and ask about the earlier days and the days which were before you. Was there anything such as this in your days and the days of your fathers? Did a nation hear the voice of God, the voice of the Lord smashing cedars, a voice emanating from the Master of Mercy, to destroy and to kill and annihilate all the House of Israel, His close nation? He even came in judgment against the elders of His nation and ministers, as we have seen with our eyes, for in our days the earth was divided and destroyed. God has mixed the language of all the sons of Ever [the "Hebrews"], and has sent forth His arm with anger and fury against them to exile them. The Lord roars from on High, and from His holy abode His voice issues forth to bring scorn upon all in captivity and to extinguish the western light, namely the exile of Jerusalem in Spain, making them as dust to be trampled and as water to be poured down from a steep place, a nation scattered and divided. . . .

As for those in the Spanish exile—one that was a marvel for the nations, where the beloved and precious Jews said, "We will live in the shadows of the nations"—they became an astonishment, an example and a byword. Their glory was brought down to the grave, along with their brilliance and their multitudes, their wares and their riches. And the people of the Lord, who had been exalted above all the nations of The Earth, the Lord burst out against them in the breach, and gave them into the hands of worthless beings who afflicted and plundered them, as fish caught [in a net]. . . . For every [former] happy and illustrious community, I will raise my voice as a woman in travail at the birth of her first child. . . .

But now, where has all our good turned aside? Where has our grandeur and our radiance and our glory gone? How did the remnant of Judah remain orphaned and alone in exile, forced to wander to and fro, with none to guide it and none to take its hand? *Where are they*—our heads, our leaders, our kings, our ministers and all the great men of our nation, who would stand in the breach to fight our battles and avert this decree? They [i.e., the leaders] were righteous and honorable and had many good qualities and in their days the Jews knew light and joy, and there was no breach and no complaint. Now, though, our souls are dry, there is nothing, there is no staff to support us, and there is none to return our glory to its earlier times. For those who go out and those who come in there is no peace, for there is no redeemer. He that is helped still falls down and all fail together, for the glory of Israel has departed.

How was our glory dissipated, leaving the Daughter of Zion plundered and a restless wanderer? The nights of my pleasure have turned to fear. *Where are they*, the 277 holy communities, overflowing with good, which once lived in Castile at ease and in contentment, who produced among them great scholars and heads of *yeshivot*? In the other communities too, there were glorious communities by the thousands and tens of thousands, and we could not count them. All were settled on their land, in their towns and by their castles, and all of Israel had light in their settlements. . . .

Y. L. GORDON, "IN THE DEPTHS OF THE SEA" (1884)

For many years the exiled Hebrews dwelt
On Spanish soil, and most secure they felt.
Contented with the gentle Moslem rule,
Their lives of joy and happiness were full.
Like brethren dwelt they, civic rights they shared;
Quite peaceful was their stay, and well they fared;
Until a power, wicked and corrupt,
With heart of stone like Cain, the fratricide,
Uprooted them, and did their homes disrupt,
And thousands slew, who for God's glory died.

Thus Jacob's children exiled were from Spain;
To enter Portugal they tried in vain.
Dame Europe to the wand'rers turned her back;
A grave alone for them she oped, alack!
On Africa's sharp rocks were crushed their bones,
And flowed their blood on Asia's craggy stones.
The many corpses turned the oceans dry;
On dry land did their blood like water flow.
Their God did hide, enshrouded in the sky!
Nor were their tears avenged on earth below.

Avenged thou wilt not be, crushed Judah's seed!
Each deed of thine oppressors doth succeed.
Was strength bestowed on Spain her foe to quell
That merciless thy sons she might expel?
And did her seamen's fleet a land lay bare
Because thy banishment Spain did declare?
Yea, e'en in Portugal thy gifts she sought
Wherewith to find to India a lane—
The dynasty which housed thy tribe—stands not;
Still firm are standing Portugal and Spain.

In books of chronicles I read and hear
The groans of victims seized with deadly fear,

The captive's voice from prisons and from stocks,
And cries of men while dashed 'gainst craggy rocks,
A voice from iron threshing boards aghast,
And flaming pyres in which alive they're cast.
It is the voice of Jacob, e'er pursued;
To dunghills forced by bigotry's mad raids;
His woes increased and constantly renewed
By holy wars and ritual crusades.

From sea-shores which 'neath Cartagena lie,
Sail num'rous merchant ships, their trades to ply
In ships but three, nigh thousand crowd in rows.
The sails are spread and pointed are the bows.
With ropes the riggers hurry and press on,
The seamen rush and sailors haste and run.
O floating city, whither art thou bound?
Why dost thou leave a haven for dim skies?
Dost thou seek markets new and foreign ground?
These souls thy merchants are, or merchandise?

And who are these that crowd in yonder ships—
Like mourners sit, and silent are their lips?
Their faces wan betray great grief and fear;
Both blind and sick, and men and women drear.
O cringing herd! who are ye, trav'lers? Say!—
Their faces tell, why do ye ask them, pray?
Yea, scattered straws which fly the threshing blast;
Yea, pigeons that from vultures' talons flee;
From fire to water and from tree to mast;
From earth, which quakes beneath them, to the sea!

Canst thou not tell the burned, sunken cheek,
Unchanged with changing eras, humble, meek?
O wretched tribe, pray, whither dost thou flee?
"Where lists the wind, yea thither wander we.

Nor care we whether north or south we stray;
If we our God, our Father, worship may.
Nor care we if we're carried east or west,
There where our faith will e'er sustain our breath;
And where a clod of earth we'll find to rest
Therein our weary bodies after death."

The flagstaffs' standards flutter in the gale;
The anchors lifted are, the ships set sail.
The air resounds with sudden thund'rous yell:
"Beloved native land, ah fare thee well!"
Great hosts forsake thy shores, on journeys go;
Will they return or not?—what man doth know!—
The land that to your heart was ever dear
No longer will, O Hebrews, ye retain;
Your treasures fond behind ye now leave here;
If to return ye dare, ye will be slain!

Yea, all your treasures fond ye leave behind!
Here parted they whose souls did friendship bind;
And one a brother left incarcerate;
And one his sire, to an uncertain fate;
One left his houses, vineyards, fields in haste,
And books, effects that ne'er can be replaced;
And one did banish pleasures from his heart,
And farewell bade to mirthfulness of old;
Most grieves he from his father's grave to part;
His soul doth mourn, and will not be consoled.

Ah, flee from here, ye wretches, steeped in woe.
Yea, flee—yet where? Ah, whither can ye go?
Who will commiserate a nation lost
And gather thee, forever driven, tossed?
The curse of all the world doth o'er thee spread;
At thy grim cruel fate all shake their head.

Oh, tell your sons unto the end of days,
Conjure your children and your kin, I pray,
Never to show in bloody Spain their face,
Nor tread upon its soil fore'er and aye.[8]

Exile from Elsewhere
Exile from Isfahan

Bābā'ī ibn Lutf (1617–62) wrote what is thought to be the first history from the Iranian Jewish community. He lived in Isfahan, home to one of the oldest Jewish communities in Persia, first referenced before 400 CE. The city grew in significance once the fifth Savafid shah, Abbas I (1571–1629), established it as his capital in 1598. Under his rule and that of his great-grandson, Shah Abbas II (1632–66), Jews were subject to severe restrictions, persecution, and forced conversion under the threat of expulsion.

Ibn Lutf writes about the expulsion of 1656 in his chronicle *Kitāb-i Anusī* (Book of the forced convert) from which the following excerpt has been taken. According to historian Vera Moreen, ibn Lutf offers a first-person account, having risked his own safety to bear witness.

> BĀBĀ'Ī IBN LUTF, "HOW THE GRAND VIZIER FOUND
> A PRETEXT AGAINST THE JEWS OF ISFAHAN AND
> DROVE THEM OUT OF THEIR HOMES" (CA. 1660)
>
> No previous generation has ever seen a day such as we have seen, full of hundreds of lamentations and griefs. The Āṣaf[9] of those times summoned the Jewish community of Isfahan and said, "You are all poor, you are unclean and impure as far as our faith is concerned, yet your bodies come in constant contact with our own. You touch everything: is there no difference between wine and vinegar? The order of the shah, the Master of Favors, is that you leave the city this very day. I will show you an empty place where you can build new houses." ...
>
> Afflicted and crying, the Jews answered: "We have all paid the *jizya* [the poll tax demanded from non-Muslims in Muslim states]; moreover, for several reigns now our homes have been in Isfahan.

The Jewish quarter has remained as before; it has seen no additional building or repairs these past few years.[10] Moreover we pray for the shah and we always ask the Almighty to preserve his life." Āṣaf said, "We know nothing of this; we will drive you out of Isfahan. Whether you accept this or not I shall expel you from your [present] realm." ...

The shah's Āṣaf said quickly, "Go, all of you to hell! Go wherever you want; no people will allow even one of you among them!" Having said this he chased them away from his presence saying, "Don't come again in flight!" They left, crying, wailing, and with burning hearts, they headed toward the desert.

By chance this happened on a Friday night. They were all crying near the Torah when, in the city and in the bazaar, a proclamation was suddenly heard: "All Jews must leave quickly tonight, male and female! Whoever shall be seen tomorrow will lose his head." When the people heard that proclamation late at night all became greatly agitated. They were saying, "What shall we do? Woe to us! If tomorrow arrives we risk our lives staying here. The night is dark and there are guards everywhere! We won't be able to see our way and we will fall into the trap, suddenly, like helpless children!" The men jumped up in confusion carrying their wives and children on their shoulders. Thus, in the dark night fearing the sword, they took the road toward the tomb of Seraḥ bath Asher. On the same Friday they [others?] arrived there despairing. ... They were crying, full of suffering there, young and old, even children, all standing up. Wailing in God's abode they kept saying, "O God, turn this misfortune away from us!"

When Saturday morning came all went to the synagogue. Āṣaf was informed of the situation and chose the most cruel soldiers saying to them, "Bring the Jews to me at dawn. Moreover, you must bring to me their leaders again." By chance, the leader of the Jews of Isfahan ... was a good man, like balm to the soul. The name of that great man was Sa'īd. He was a friend to all and a jeweler by profession. The night on which Āṣaf said to the Jews, "You must get out of town," one group set out to the tomb of Seraḥ bath Asher, another became great wanderers, while still another group dispersed, crying in great confusion. ... All at once, on Saturday, they saw royal servants armed with bows that were drawn taut. They were leading some Jews in deplorable conditions, hands tied behind them ignominiously. They were after the leaders of the community, Sa'īd, Obadiah and Sason. After they found their dwellings they seized them and tied their hands at once. They were dragged before Āṣaf in this condition and lined up in a row before him.

Āṣaf said, "O dirty Jews, all of you cause me anguish, go, all of you, men and women, and leave your property behind. Leave our region and choose for yourselves another place, or become sincere Muslims at the hand of Shah Abbās." When the helpless Jews heard this they gave up hope of life. With hands tied behind their backs they went out, following the previous group of Jews. Thus on the Sabbath they too set out stupefied toward the tomb of Seraḥ bath Asher. The people who were already there suddenly heard a great clamor. When they saw Sa'īd and Sason they became alarmed. Instead of the sound of Sabbath songs, wailing was heard on account of this day of sorrow. They mourned everywhere. The cruel soldiers killed many of them mercilessly. Like captive pigeons they were forced to relinquish their women and children. Such a Sabbath they spent in that desert; all of them grieving, they had to set out once again....

[O God . . . grant us Deliverance from the hands of the oppressor! Come to our rescue in this exile; let no one remember this affliction.] . . .

When this news arrived, in every region hundreds of cries rose from everywhere. The Jews proclaimed many fasts, made many sacrifices and treated orphans and widows generously, like beloved sons. They blew the *shofar* and sounded the *teru'ah*. But because of God's decree they were unable to contrive a plan before the shah.

[O Bābāī, be mindful of preordained fate! Find some expedient to help you!][11]

Exile from Warsaw

Isaac Bashevis Singer (1902-91) grew up in Radzymin, a distant suburb of Warsaw. The Rebbe of Radzymin, Aaron Menaḥem Mendel Guterman (1860-1934), was considered one of the leading rabbis in Poland. Singer's father, also a rabbi, served as head of the yeshiva in the suburb. After the yeshiva burned down, the family moved to the city where Singer was educated in the Warsaw Rabbinical Seminary. His older brother by nine years, Israel Joshua Singer, had published several collections of short stories and one novel before immigrating to the United States in 1933. Two years later Isaac Bashevis joined his brother in Brooklyn. In the United States his own reputation as a novelist flourished.

Despite the title of the book below, the selected text does not make reference to "exile." The Singer family was not expelled from Poland; like hundreds of thousands of Jews, Israel and Isaac chose to leave their home country. Yet the passage is a powerful expression of coming to a new country that—at least at first—seemed so totally different from being at home.

ISAAC BASHEVIS SINGER, *LOVE AND EXILE* (1986)

After a long hesitation I decided to take a walk. Outside I made a mental note—there were two white columns at the front of the porch. No other house on the street had them. I walked slowly and each time glanced back at the house with the two columns. I had read accounts of spies, revolutionaries, of such explorers as Sven Hedin, Amundsen, and Captain Scott who wandered over deserts, ice fields, and jungles.[12] They were able to determine their locations under the most bewildering conditions, and here I trembled about getting lost in such a tiny community as Seagate.[13] I had walked, not knowing where, and had come to the beach. . . . It smelled here of dead fish and something else marinelike and unfamiliar. I trod on seashells. I picked one up and studied it—the armor of a creature that had been born in the sea and apparently had died there as well, or had been eaten despite its protection.

I looked for a star in the sky but the glow of New York City, or maybe Coney Island, made the sky opaque and reddish. . . . Maybe simply walk into the sea and put an end to the whole mess? After long brooding, I headed back. It was my impression that I had been following a straight path, but I had already walked quite a distance back and the house with the white columns was nowhere in sight. . . .

I turned around to go back. Someone had once advised me to always carry a compass. I'm the worst fumbler and clod under the sun, I scolded myself. A compass wouldn't have helped me. It would only have confused me further.... I suffered from a kind of disorientation complex.... The fact is that it was inherited. My mother and father lived for years in Warsaw and they never knew the way to Nalewki Street.[14] In our house there hovered the fear of the outside, of Gentile languages, of trains, cars, of the hustle and bustle of business, even of Jews who had dealings with lawyers, the police, could speak Russian or even Polish. I had gone away from God, but not from my heritage.

What now? I asked myself. I felt like laughing at my own helplessness. I turned back and saw the house with the two white columns. It had materialized as if from the ground.... I went back to my room and lay down on the sofa. I did not put on the light. I lay there in the darkness. I was still young, not yet thirty, but I was overcome by a fatigue that most probably comes with old age. I had cut off whatever roots I had in Poland yet I knew that I would remain a stranger here until my last day. I tried to imagine myself in Hitler's Dachau, or in a labor camp in Siberia.[15] Nothing was left for me in the future.

Exile from Egypt

Andre Aciman was born in 1951 in Alexandria, Egypt, to Sephardic Jewish parents of Turkish and Italian origin. Despite having lived in Egypt since 1905, the family was not eligible for Egyptian citizenship. When conditions became increasingly difficult for Jews they left the country, settling in New York by way of Rome. Andre grew up speaking French at home, studied in Arab and British schools in Alexandria, left bearing an Italian passport, and completed his academic training in the United States.

After teaching at Princeton University and Bard College, Aciman became a distinguished professor and director of the Writers' Institute at the City University of New York Graduate Center. The author of novels, essays, and memoirs, he is perhaps best known for his novel *Call Me by My Name* (2007).

In his well-received memoir, *Out of Egypt* (1995), he writes movingly and memorably about living on the eve of exile and the Passover seder his family held the night before their departure. "It never occurred to us that a seder in Egypt was a contradiction in terms," he wrote in the *New York Times*, continuing with the question of just what was being celebrated, and which departure of the Jews, exactly, did the seder commemorate. "Caught in these loops and coils [of exile and diaspora], my family forgot to remember the obvious—that Egypt was never our home, that we should never have come back after Moses, that we didn't even know where our home was."[16]

The final chapter of Aciman's memoir details the process of exile, beginning with invasive phone calls and government surveillance, continuing with the seizure of the family business, and ending with the final decree.

ANDRE ACIMAN, *OUT OF EGYPT* (1995)

[My father] said he could still remember witnessing his parents' emptied home thirty years before on the day they had left Constantinople. As had his father seen his own father's home. And our ancestors as well....

[The evening he died], I slipped into Uncle Nessim's bedroom. I sat on his bed, looking out the window, catching the flicker of city lights, remembering how he spoke of London and Paris, how he said that all gentlemen, of whom he fancied himself one, would have a glass of scotch whiskey every evening. "It will kill me one day," he prophesied, "but I do love to sit here and watch the city and think about things for a while before dinnertime." And now, I too would do the same, think about things, as he put it, think about leaving, and about all the people I would never see again, and about this city, so inseparable from who I was at that very instant, and how it would slip into time and become stranger than dreamland. That too would be like dying. To be dead meant that others could come into your room and never know it had once been yours. Little by little they would remove all traces of you. Even your smell would go. Then they'd even forget you had died....

My father telephoned in the morning. "They don't want us anymore," he said in English. I didn't understand him. "They don't want us in Egypt." But we had always known that, I thought. Then he blurted it out: we had been officially expelled and had a week to get our things together. "Abbatoir?"[17] I asked. "Abbatoir," he replied. . . .

Facing the night, I looked out at the stars and thought to myself, over there is Spain, then France, to the right Italy, and, straight ahead, the land of Solon and Pericles. The world is timeless and boundless, and I thought of all the shipwrecked, homeless mariners who had strayed to this very land and for years had tinkered away at their damaged boats, praying for a wind, only to grow soft and reluctant when their time came. . . .

And suddenly I knew, as I touched the damp, grainy surface of the seawall, that I would remember this night, that in years to come I would remember sitting here, swept with confused longing as I listened to the water lapping the giant boulders beneath the promenade and watched the children head toward the shore in a winding, lambent procession. I wanted to come back tomorrow night, and the night after, and the one after that as well, sensing that what made leaving so fiercely painful was the knowledge that there would never be another night like this, that I would never eat soggy cakes along the coast road in the evening, not this year or any other year, nor feel the baffling, sudden beauty of that moment when, if only for an instant, I had caught myself longing for a city I never knew I loved.[18]

From Home

Dina Elenbogen is a poet and memoirist. Her 2015 memoir, *Drawn from Water: An American Poet, an Ethiopian Family, an Israeli Story*,[19] tells of her relationship with Israel, and with the Ethiopian immigrants who were brought to Ma'alot, a small city in the northern periphery, in 1991. Operation Solomon was the third and largest rescue of Beta Israel, airlifting over fourteen thousand Ethiopian Jews in under thirty-six hours. Elenbogen's long friendship with several of the immigrants led her to ponder the experiences of immigration and exile and the meaning of home.

The short essay, first published in *Tikkun* magazine, offers multiple notions of home, exile, and return. These range from the Jewish idea of Israel as homeland, to the reality of its realization for both Ethiopian

Jews ("what it meant . . . to return to a homeland that didn't always feel like home") and Palestinians, to the very personal conception of one's own mother as "the most essential place . . . home."

DINA ELENBOGEN, "EXILE: LOSING THE MOTHERLAND" (1999)

In 1983, in his living room on Van Buren Street, where wandering Jew plants dropped their leaves against his western window, the poet Gerald Stern puts this question to the students gathered around him: is there any place where, if you could never return to it, you would want to die? As one of Stern's young, romantic graduate students, I blurted out "Jerusalem." Others said Paris, the Greek islands; I think someone muttered something about home. When I said Jerusalem then, I think I also meant love, that I would want to die if I could never return to the man I loved, who, at the time, lived in Jerusalem.

Over the decade and more that followed that conversation, my travels would take me into the lives of Ethiopian Jews, who after decades of longing for Jerusalem had finally reached their dream. Watching Ethiopian children become Israelis, teaching the teenagers English, sharing *enjara* [a fermented bread, spongy and sour, traditionally made from teff] as part of their family, and studying their lives brought me to Jerusalem numerous times between the years of 1984 and 1998. I thought a lot, during these visits, about exile and about what it meant for my Ethiopian friends to return to a homeland that didn't always feel like home. Before each departure, as I watched the golden light fade against Jerusalem stone, I knew these journeys were a luxury. Yet, even in these moments, I changed Gerald Stern's words from "die" to "suffer greatly." I would have suffered but would not have wanted to die if I could not return to Jerusalem.

In the middle of the Intifada, in 1989, I reunited with a Palestinian friend from Jerusalem who was living in Chicago, and who for political reasons could not return to Jerusalem, his home. I felt his pain as I prepared for my return and packed his unsealed letters and gifts for our mutual American poet friend in Jerusalem. I understood in a more profound way than ever before what a privilege it was to return, year after year, to my spiritual home. And I understood too, a different kind of suffering.

This past summer, my husband Steve and I pushed our daughter Sarina in her stroller over the harsh stone of the Jerusalem streets, carried her through the narrow passages of the Old City, and gave her name at the Wall. As I watched Sarina dance in her father's arms in the men's section of the *kotel*, from which I stood with so many generations of Jewish women, I knew I would be sad if I could not return to this place. But I would no longer equate suffering with not being able to return to a physical place. And thoughts of dying I could now only imagine having if, for some reason, I could never return to my daughter.

My fourteen-year journey in and out of the lives of Ethiopian Jews, back and forth from Chicago to Jerusalem, from one homeland to another, had turned into a book. And on this trip, I felt that I had everything I needed; the journey had come full circle. As I said goodbye to Osnat, an Ethiopian former student who I had watched grow from a shy thirteen-year-old into a bold young woman, and who, throughout this visit, had carried my daughter along the sea and sang to her in Hebrew, there were no tears: I knew I had the security of return.

The tears came instead, this time, upon my return to America. My mother's illness, diagnosed as a non-threatening form of scleroderma, had entered her pulmonary system in the short time we'd been away; she was in critical care. As she lay in her hospital bed in Evanston, her mind as sharp as ever, I read her Sholom Aleichem stories, remembering the lilt in her voice when she read to me as a child. This time I listened to the sound of her lungs struggling to take in more air.

Three weeks later, as I was trying to find a babysitter one morning so I could return to the hospital, my father called with the words, "She died." I fell on the floor in sobs larger and deeper than any pain I'd known. When I couldn't get up to comfort my daughter, who was crying from her crib, I understood for the first time what exile really means: how it feels to never be able to return again to the most essential place, to the giver of life, the source, mother, home.[20]

Exile of the Other

Sophia Parnok (1885–1933) was a poet, translator, journalist, and librettist born to a wealthy Jewish family in Russia, outside the Pale of Settlement. She converted to Russian Orthodoxy mostly for nationalist reasons, and still identified as Jewish. Her poem "Hagar" expresses her identification as an outsider, due in large part to her religious identity, her lesbianism, and her hyperthyroidism.

Hagar, Sarah's handmaiden in the Bible, is arguably the symbol of exile par excellence. Hagar's story humanizes the experience of exile, bringing it out of the specific Jewish context and connecting it with both the national and the universal.

> SOPHIA PARNOK, "HAGAR" (CA. 1920)
>
> So Hagar sits in obloquy
> And gushing forth in streams
> The spring pours out a threnody
> *Beerlachai-royi*.[21]
>
> Those lands belong to Abraham
> But this expanse—to none.
> Around her, only wilderness
> To Shur itself does run.
>
> Despair, despair instinctual!
> In her Egyptian eyes,
> Disconsolate, elongated,
> A nascent teardrop cries.
> The frigid torment's shimmering,
> A dagger's cutting edge—
> O, terrifying, childless,
> O, dread proprietress!
>
> "Hagar!"—And then her countenance
> Dark-skinned is drained of blood.

> She looks—her eyebrows lifted at
> An angel of the Lord. . . .[22]

Exile's Embrace

This text from the poet Lea Goldberg (see chapter 2) is unfinished, yet reads as a complete poem. The speaker identifies both with Hagar—exiled because she was a threat to Sarah the matriarch, and with Antigone—exiled because she defied the patriarchy. Why the speaker herself is exiled we don't know.

The desert is the site of wanderings and Jewish exile, but the poem reclaims and embraces the desert as the end of such wanderings. Goldberg is revising the idea of exile as the binary opposite of home.[23]

"Sand" and "star" recall the blessing of Abraham (Gen. 22:17) and the beginning of both Jewish and Arab nationhoods.

> LEA GOLDBERG, "FRAGMENT" (CA. 1970)
>
> The clasp of sand and stone.
> Hagar's,
> Antigone's, mine.
>
> The clasp of sand and stone.
> The tight-lipped love.
> The downcast pride,
> The proud insult.
>
> On the exiles' path
> The clasp of sand and stone—
> The sky nearby—
> And in the sky
> Star cacti.[24]
>
> ©All rights to Lea Goldberg's poems reserved to
> Hakibbutz Hameuchad Publishers Ltd.

Exile from Palestine

Originally published in *Harper's Magazine* as a travelogue, Edward Said's "Palestine, Then and Now" essay recounts his trip back to his childhood home after many years of absence during which he had become an eminent professor of comparative literature. A diagnosis of leukemia (which eventually did kill him, but not until more than a decade later) had impelled him to return, and to bring his family with him.

As a Palestinian visiting a place now known (by most) as Israel, Said incorporates the dominant motifs of modern exilic writing: the sense of being an outsider and the desire to belong; the connection to the land, the physical place; how history interrupts and even violates one's personal life. He tempers his nostalgia for his homeland with political realities and even with doubts regarding the reliability of memory.

He points out the penchant for barbed wire, the utilitarian architecture blighting the landscape, the omnipresence of the military. He introduces us to a friend's cousin, Haifa, her very name expressing the family's intimate connection with the city. He relates stories of Jewish settlers encroaching on Palestinian territory and displacing Israeli Arabs, of the extreme crowding within the refugee camp. He studs his narrative with the words "purged," "violated," "fragmented," "gloomy," "stagnant," and "appalling." But he also exposes his unfounded paranoia as he proceeds unimpeded through the usual port-of-entry formalities, his unsentimental reminiscences regarding the Church of the Holy Sepulchre, his unease in meeting with refugees, and the forced nature of his anti-Israel analogy regarding the barbed wire.

While he well conveys the sadness of the exile's experience, he also admits that at the end of his trip he views exile as "a more liberated state," and mentions "the pleasures . . . of exile." The success of Zionism and the establishment of the State of Israel has made exiles out of the Palestinians,[25] but whether those forced from the land, or those who have stayed in the land but are forced from their homes, suffer more from the burdens of exile, Said leaves the reader to ponder.

EDWARD W. SAID, "PALESTINE, THEN AND NOW:
AN EXILE'S JOURNEY THROUGH ISRAEL AND
THE OCCUPIED TERRITORIES" (1992)

Mine was the generation raised in an Arab world that accorded the Jewish state no recognition at all; even the idea of Israel was anathema. This odd proposition, that Israel did not exist, made possible a policy of non-knowledge, a void that erected a wall around itself, allowing both Israeli and Arab leaders to get away with literally everything in the name of security. Until 1967 the Arab world, including the millions of Palestinians floundering in exile, nearly forgot about their compatriots who remained in Israel after 1948. Until 1967 it was nearly impossible to use the world "Israel" in Arabic writing. All this was supposed to cost Israel in legitimacy and resolve, so that if we didn't acknowledge its presence it would go away. Of course it didn't, although even those many of us whose passports and safe jobs made it feasible to return needed a long time to make the trip, cross the barrier, and confront the difficult reality.

It took only a few moments and we were out of the airport.... Tentatively at first, boldly later, I found myself repeating to myself that I did have a right to be here, that I was a native, and that nearly everything in my early life could be graced to the city of my birth [Jerusalem]. I was baptized in the Anglican St. George's Cathedral (built in 1898), a couple of hundred yards from the hotel; along with most of the male members of my family, I had attended the cathedral school, St. George's; my family had owned property in Jerusalem barely a mile away from where I now stood, was connected to a whole network of other families—was, in fact, as Palestinian as one could be. What remained now? I asked myself. What could be reconstituted through memory and then experience in a ten-day visit, despite the politics of extreme antagonism that I had lived for forty-five years?...

It took almost two hours to find the old family house, and it is a tribute to my cousin's memory that only by sticking very carefully to his map did we finally locate it. Today the street is called Nahum Sokolow, the sandy little square now an elegant, even manicured park. My daughter later told me that, using her camera with manic excitement, I reeled off twenty-six photos of the house.

It bore the nameplate "International Christian Embassy" at the gate. To have found my family's house now occupied not by an Israeli Jewish family but by a right-wing fundamentalist Christian and militantly pro-Zionist group run by a South-African Boer no less! Anger overtook me, so that when an American woman came out of the house holding an armful of laundry and asked if she could help, I could not bring myself to ask to go inside.

More than anything else, perhaps, it was the house I did not, could not, enter that symbolized the eerie finality of a history. It seemed to stare down at me from behind its shaded windows. Palestine as I had known it was over. . . .

I would find it very hard to live there, I think: exile seems to me a more liberated state, but, I have to admit, I am privileged and can afford to experience the pleasures rather than the burdens, of exile. Yet I also feel that, as a family the four of us need the connection, need the assurances that Palestine and Palestinians have really survived, and this we now have. I think I needed the change metaphorically to bury the dead, and, what with the large number of funerary associations for me what had been Palestine was indeed a mournful place. But I can feel and sometimes actually see a different future as I couldn't before.[26]

9 Language as the Locus of Exile

Among the many aspects of exile are the uprooting of the individual and the scattering of the collective. The estrangement from language is both specific to the individual and significant to the community; language is what allows people to communicate and to form community.

The story of the Tower of Babel, ostensibly about hubris leading to the punishment of dispersal, is also about the formation of different languages and the ways in which different languages lead to divisions among people. As a consequence of trying to compete with the Divine, the people trying to build the tower are doomed to be separated by languages. As such, in the biblical tale, the multiplicity of languages is not celebrated but rather presented as retribution.

For many exiles, the inability to communicate easily with neighbors in their new homes is another form of linguistic estrangement. A means of both communication and self-expression, language has a significant affective aspect. Most people—even those who learn the language of their new country—are more comfortable communicating in their first language, which we call their mother tongue for a reason. Parents in exile are challenged to bring up their children in their mother tongue; as one poet writes, "My mother's tongue is not my mother tongue." The second generation experiences exile a degree removed, often in language fluency as well.

Babel and Afterward

The Tower of Babel is the third in a series of brief narratives at the beginning of the first book of the Bible that presents the initial paradigm of exile. Adam and Eve are banished, Cain is sentenced to wander,

LANGUAGE AS THE LOCUS OF EXILE

and Babel ends with scattering. In each case, exile is punishment, and a harsh one at that. These three tales also form a progression—from interspecies communication (in Eden before the Fall, the snake and the humans converse without difficulty) to the complete confounding of the human language.

When the Tower of Babel story begins, there is unification of language, but soon thereafter, God jumbles the tower builders' speech and sends the people into exile—that is, taking away communication and community. The exile is alone, and unable to communicate.

By one understanding, the punishment of exile was necessary because the builders were rebellious and refused to "fill the earth." An alternative reading views the culprits as being too settled, too centralized, and too urban: the picture of bourgeois contentment. Where Adam is meant to work the land with great effort, and Cain is to work the land with little reward, the tower builders are even more disconnected from the land. In effect, their sin is one of self-aggrandizement, of not knowing one's place.

The story is full of irony, because these people who did not know their place are sent away from the only place they have ever known. The very fear that has motivated them to build the tower, "lest we be scattered," is indeed realized as a consequence: "Thus the Lord scattered them from there over the face of the whole earth."

> GENESIS 11:1–9
>
> Everyone on earth had the same language and the same words. And as they migrated from the east, they came upon a valley in the land of Shinar and settled there. They said to one another, "Come, let us make bricks and burn them hard."—Brick served them as stone, and bitumen served them as mortar.—And they said, "Come, let us build us a city, and a tower with its top in the sky, to make a name for ourselves; else we shall be scattered all over the world." God came down to look at the city and tower that the mortals had built, and God said, "If, as one people with one language for all, this is how they have begun to act, then nothing that they may propose to do will be out of their reach. Let us, then, go down and confound their

speech there, so that they shall not understand one another's speech." Thus God scattered them from there over the face of the whole earth; and they stopped building the city. That is why it was called Babel, because there God confounded the speech of the whole earth; and from there God scattered them over the face of the whole earth.[1]

Language as Homeland

Anton Shammas (b. 1950, Fassuta, Israel), an Arab Christian, is best known for his 1986 Hebrew novel *Arabeskot* (*Arabesques*). He has also published poetry in both Arabic and Hebrew, and articles in English.

Shammas's essay below, originally presented at a conference on writing held in Jerusalem's Yemin Moshe neighborhood, looks at the experience of exile through the prism of language. He draws from a number of literary examples, among them the thirteenth-century poet and *The Divine Comedy* author Dante Alighieri, who was forced to leave his home in 1302 for political reasons but kept Florence with him by continuing to write in his native dialect.

Shammas also refers to the poet Uri Zvi Greenberg, who adopted the Hebrew language for ideological reasons after moving to Palestine in 1924, and eventually represented the right-wing Herut Party in the first Israeli parliament. Presumably Shammas chose to include Greenberg because of his ultranationalistic belief in the State of Israel's establishment as Jewish historical destiny.

ANTON SHAMMAS, "ON EXILE AND LITERATURE" (1985)

As someone who can, on a good day, lay claim to a measure or two of that Borgesian "polite arrogance" of exiles, I'm almost tempted to open the following remarks with the immortal lines of the Florentine poet who "was the first to give political exile the dignity of an institution":

> Midway upon the journey of our life
> I found myself within a dark forest,
> For the straightforward pathway had been lost.
> [tr. Longfellow]

For I, too, am thirty-five, "midway upon the journey" of my life. But that's all there is, I'm afraid, as I can't, unfortunately, claim to have any other thing in common with the poet who "opened the long line of Europe's banished intellectuals"—Dante Alighieri. In my case, it was nothing but sheer luck that saved my family the wandering inside that dense thicket of the dark forest of 1948, in which thousands upon thousands of Palestinian families found themselves, having been driven out of their homes by the invading newcomers who, in turn, and according to the twisted logic of history, bestowed upon them their own state of exile. Thus, I was spared the fate of the refugee and given, instead, the dubious status of an exile in my own homeland. The Jewish state of Israel, as it defines itself, treats me as a Palestinian *yored*, an expatriate who's expected one day "to make *Aliyah*" to the Palestinian state, when it will be allegedly established in the very distant, uncertain future, if ever. It follows that I am the constant Palestinian-on-probation, whose mother tongue is Arabic, but prefers, for some outlandish reason, to write in his stepmother tongue—Hebrew.

Be that as it may, could language, as such, be homeland enough? Could language be a homeland of any kind?

A dear friend of mine from Jerusalem, who currently teaches modern Arabic literature at an American university, was preparing himself at the time, in the early 'eighties, for the big move, and decided to tie the knot with his Palestinian sweetheart, so they both can equally share the burden of the self-imposed exile. I asked him half-jokingly if it wouldn't be a better move to wait until he arrives at his final destination and then find himself an American, green-carding bride, courtesy of Uncle Sam. "No," he said, "I want a wife who, when I lay my head on her arm, I'll be able to listen to her blood flowing in Arabic." They have been listening to each other's blood happily ever after.

Uri Zvi Greenberg regarded Hebrew as "the language of [his] blood" because the fate of wanderers assigned him a different mother tongue. He had been exiled from his ancestral mother tongue for hundreds of years and then he went back home to it, or so he believed. A very problematic homecoming in his case—for those Palestinians who were driven out of their homes by Uri Zvi Greenberg were soon to realize that it would be difficult, if not totally impossible, to make do with the little that language—elusive and fleeting as it is—can offer. They may have wondered: Can language supplant the scent of orange groves for the Palestinian refugee who is running for his life in 1948? Can language be a substitute of sorts for the homeland?

Having been banished from Florence, Dante held on to his homeland through writing in the Florentine-Italian dialect, while distancing himself from what he called "the tragic style" of Latin (hence the *Commedia*). Knowing that he would never go back home, he believed that "the whole world is a homeland, like the sea to fish." Then he argues:

> a certain form of language was created by God along with the first soul. . . . In this form of language Adam spoke; in this form of language spoke all his descendants until the building of the Tower of Babel (which is interpreted as "tower of confusion"); this is the form of language inherited by the sons of Heber, who are called Hebrews because of it. To these alone it remained after the confusion, so that our Redeemer, who was to descend from them (in so far as He was human), should not speak the language of confusion, but that of grace. [*De vulgari eloquentia*, bk. 1, chap. 6, tr. Steven Botterill]

Exile, for the Palestinians, is the language of confusion; there is no grace in being a confused refugee. The Palestinians in Israel live in a state of confusion within the Jewish state of Israel. As for me, only the language of grace can articulate my confusion and add to my puzzlement a touch of grace. As for the puzzlement, I belong to the Arab minority living inside the Jewish majority living inside the Arab majority in the Middle East, Russian Babushka-doll style. Once one layer of puzzlement is removed, another is revealed, ad infinitum. It's a rather crowded Babushka, and at times it is hard to determine where the homeland ends, and exile begins. And at times it's hard to determine who is our ventriloquist—is it the homeland, or maybe exile? One thing for sure, though: we are the puppets for both.

At this point it may be instructive to put things in their German perspective, as it seems to be always lurking in the background when one thinks of Israel/Palestine. Some lines come to my Palestinian mind from "The Flood," a poem by Günter Grass:

LANGUAGE AS THE LOCUS OF EXILE

> We are waiting for the rain to stop,
> though we have grown accustomed
> to standing behind a curtain, to being invisible.
> ...
> Many things are drifting through the streets,
> things people hid away in the dry season.
> ...
> We stand now facing the water gauge,
> comparing our worries like watches.
> [tr. Paul Weinfield]

Shall we compare our puzzlements, then, our exiles?

Khalīl Sakakīnī, a Palestinian writer and educator, whose Diaries cover his life in Jerusalem over the first half of the twentieth century, built a house for his family in 1937, in the Qatamūn neighborhood, outside the walls of the Old City of Jerusalem, four years before another Jerusalemite Jewish writer, Shai Agnon, built another house not far away from Sakakīnī's, in the Talpiot neighborhood. On April 30, 1948, Sakakīnī was forced to evacuate his house, along with his family, and found refuge in Cairo, where he died in 1953. Here are some excerpts from his Diaries:

> Cairo, Saturday, Oct. 11, 1948 . . . and January 1, 1949
> We left Jerusalem on Friday, April 30, 1948, at 6:00 am, heading to Egypt. . . . We had packed clothes we needed and left everything else in the house, hoping soon to return. I intended to take with me my papers and my notebooks but forgot everything. I meant to take my hookah, which is my second brain, but took the tube and forgot the glass bowl. . . . Farewell, my library! Farewell, my precious books! I don't know whatever happened to you after our departure—were you looted, were you burned, were you ceremoniously relocated to another private or public library? Will an old man like myself, who's not left with many more years to live, be able to start a new library?

Sakakīnī died in exile in Cairo in September of 1953; his huge library which he was very proud of had been looted by a special biblio-squad working for the Hebrew University during the 1948 war, and whose mission was to evacuate private Palestinian libraries. His books were "ceremoniously relocated" and stored together in a special room until 1968, when they were exiled to the stacks, according to the logic of the Dewey Decimal System. Sakakīnī's house, which he endearingly called "The Island," was turned later into a daycare facility, and the street on which it was built was renamed *Yordei Hasirah*—The Seafarers. An island on the street of sailors—yet another irony of exile.

Sakakīnī was a master of my mother tongue. His incisively crystalline Arabic style is the embodiment of the Palestinian National Home. Later, when it waned away in his Cairene exile, it took away from him what Aldous Huxley would call the "local validity" of his identity. Grace turned into confusion, into puzzlement, and I'm adopting the language of grace to verbalize the vicissitudes of his confusion. Some might consider this act cultural trespassing, for which I might still, some day, be punished. Sakakīnī had no choice but be an exile, and even if he was surrounded by many Arabic-speaking countries, he felt desolate, if not a pariah. The Palestinian Arabic of his Island-house in Qatamūn was lost forever, and he couldn't find a substitute for it in the Cairene Arabic, as he couldn't find a substitute for his lost homeland. Exiles would often preserve the dying ember of their homeland's language.

I left my native village in the Galilee when I was twelve and haven't seen stars since. My late uncle used to say: "The only difference between the village and the city is that in the city you can't see the night stars." In essence, whoever is left outside their homes would never see stars in the night sky.

At the end of his *Inferno*, Dante climbs out of earth, following his Guide, to find himself under the Jerusalem sky:

> Up we climbed, he first and I second, until I saw
> the beautiful things the heavens carry, through a round opening.
> And thence we came forth to look again at the stars.
> [tr. Robert M. Durling]

Will those stars ever tarry and wait for us so we can look at them again?[2]

Linguistic Exile

Eva Hoffman (b. 1945) emigrated with her family from Poland to Canada when she was thirteen. Moving to the United States for college, she subsequently became a professor of literature and creative writing at several universities and served as senior editor of the *New York Times Book Review* for thirteen years. She also authored the nonfiction works *Exit into History, Shtetl, After Such Knowledge, Time: Big Ideas, Small Books* and *How to Be Bored*; the novels *The Secret* and *Illuminations* (also published as *Appassionata*); and the memoir *Lost in Translation: A Life in a New Language*.

The following two short excerpts from Hoffman's memoir stress the significance of language to the uprooted individual. In this first excerpt she writes of trying to choose the language for her diary, being torn between intimacy and proximity:

> EVA HOFFMAN, *LOST IN TRANSLATION* (1989)
>
> For my birthday, Penny gives me a diary, complete with a little lock and key to keep what I write from the eyes of all intruders. It is that little lock . . . that creates my dilemma. If I am indeed to write something entirely for myself, in what language do I write? Several times, I open the diary and close it again. I can't decide. Writing in Polish at this point would be a little like resorting to Latin or ancient Greek—an eccentric thing to do in a diary, in which you're supposed to set down your most immediate experiences and unpremeditated thoughts in the most unmediated language. Polish is becoming a dead language, the language of the untranslatable past. But writing for nobody's eyes in English? That's like . . . performing in front of yourself, a slightly perverse act of self-voyeurism.
>
> Because I have to choose something, I finally choose English. If I'm to write in the present, I have to write in the language of the present, even if it's not the language of the self. . . .
>
> The diary is an earnest attempt to create a part of my persona that I imagine I would have grown into in Polish. In the solitude of this most private act, I write, in my public language, in order to update

what might have been my other self. The diary is about me and not about me at all.... When I write (or for that matter, think) in English, I am unable to use the word "I." ... driven, as by a compulsion, to the double, the Siamese-twin "you."[3]

This second excerpt speaks to Hoffman's anxious embrace of her adopted tongue. She is working her way through her exile, finding her community and her voice.

I've become obsessed with words. I gather them, put them away like a squirrel saving nuts for winter, swallow them and hunger for more. If I take in enough, maybe I can incorporate the language, make it part of my psyche and my body. I will not leave an image unworded, will not let anything cross my mind until I find the right phrase to pin the shadow down.... "Beveled, chiseled, sculpted, ribbed," I think as a wooden lampstand I like flashes through my mind. I see myself... a comical figure, mouthing a litany of adjectives....

The thought that there are parts of the language I am missing can induce a small panic in me, as if such gaps were missing parts of the world or my mind—as if the totality of the world and mind were coeval with the totality of language. Or rather, as if language were an enormous, fine net in which reality is contained—and if there are holes in it, then a bit of reality can escape, cease to exist. When I write, I want to use every word in the lexicon, to accumulate a thickness and weight of words so that they yield the specific gravity of things. I want to re-create, from the discrete particles of words, that wholeness of a childhood language that had no words.[4]

Dispossessed of Language

Haviva Pedaya is an Israeli poet, writer, and professor of Jewish history at Ben-Gurion University. Born in Jerusalem in 1957 to Iraqi Jewish immigrants and descended from renowned kabbalists, she identifies as a Mizrahi feminist and directs the Elyachar Center for Sephardi Heritage Studies. Her research into Jewish mysticism, trauma, and the Spanish Expulsion informs her creative works.

LANGUAGE AS THE LOCUS OF EXILE

Her poem "A Man Walks" addresses many aspects of exile—its biblical roots; its relationship to freedom and redemption; its universality; the individual experience; the significance of homeland; the desert as no place; different exiles and kinds of exiles—but ends with one's estrangement from the Hebrew language.

HAVIVA PEDAYA, "A MAN WALKS" (1992)

> A man walks
> from Damascus to Paris
> whether passing through a tunnel
> or slicing through the air
> that I don't know
> suddenly I saw the East wandering
> shaking without an axis
> I walked the distance of years from Jerusalem to Be'er Sheva
> without packing for exile
> like Ezekiel lying on his side
> in bed in Babylon
> 365 days
> his beloved dead and Zion exiled
> Abraham went from Be'er Sheva to Moriah
> three days
> tying and untying his son in his mind
> three days slaughtering and weeping
> we are still tied and untied
> Who are those slaughtering and weeping?
> Those slaughtering laughing?
> Here they all go
> There is already one ahead of the rest who walked to the city of
>   the dead
> Is that where we are hiking?
> If I want to be dug out of the graves
> how

long will there be nothing
except for life rushing backwards
A face mask and my own face
if I were a man imprisoned in a woman
if I were a prayer in tight sentences
if the mountains of Jerusalem were in the deserts of Be'er Sheva
I have walked many deserts
never reaching Mount Moriah
now I feel my homeland
for suddenly I understand how much this land is moving,
Its shaking discomfiting
Among my brothers I am astray
some walking from Iraq to America
some from Lebanon to Nicosia
some from Israel to Palestine
some from Israel to Israel to Israel to Israel
finding nothing because Israel is missing from Israel
You wanted to be free in your home
pack for exile
there is no one free who has not been cast out
Am I not a girl
am I not a woman
cast out from man
with neither mother nor father
Am I not a person
dispossessed of words
ousted though not in exile
Here in my land with my people
buried, but not in the desert
in the excess of my coffin
exiled but not afar
but in this dust that conquers blood and tears
in it and chokes
A man ascends and ascends

> whether by weeping or vodka
> That I don't know
> Will it always be so in the East
> whether soul or land
> Meanwhile I prefer to dwell in a word
> No other home exists yet
> if it ever did
> within my Hebrewness my blindness my Arabicness[5]
> This is music only playing itself
> My lips move
> but my voice is unheard
> Adults cursed and loved in this language
> from which I'd been banished for my redemption
> "Hebrew speak Hebrew"[6]
> while the East cries out[7]

"I Have Not Stopped Walking"

Salman Masalha (b. 1953) is an Israeli Druze poet from the village of Maghar.[8] He earned a PhD in classical Arabic literature from the Hebrew University, became coeditor of the *Concordance of Early Arabic Poetry*, and has published many volumes of his own poetry. His choice of Hebrew as both medium and subject ("I write in Hebrew") is both a personal and political statement. Masalha belongs to a burgeoning movement of Israeli Arab poets who write in Hebrew, among them Anton Shammas (profiled above), Naim Araidi, Nazih Khe'ir, and Ayat Abou Shmeiss. By writing in Hebrew they collectively make the claim — whether conscious or not — that they belong to the dominant Israeli culture as much as any other speaker of Hebrew.

The poet, like his lyrical I, is claiming the language for his art, but never as his mother tongue. Instead, he seems to favor it for its distancing qualities: "to lose myself in the world," "to cool the blood that spurts / endlessly from my heart," "to get lost in my words." He is the wandering exile: "I have not stopped walking."

He uses the foreign language that surrounds him to neutralize any foreignness. By making himself as if not at home, then at least in the world, in his adopted tongue, he makes himself comfortable anywhere he roams: "Because strangeness, mostly, / lies in man's heart."

> SALMAN MASALHA, "I WRITE HEBREW" (1997)
>
> I write in the Hebrew language
> which is not my mother tongue, to
> lose myself in the world. He who doesn't
> get lost, will never find the whole.
> Because everyone has the same
> toes. Left big toe
> by right heel.
>
> And sometimes I write Hebrew
> to cool the blood that spurts
> endlessly from my heart. It's always like that.
> There are many treasures
> in the coffer I have built in my chest.
> But the colors of the night that was spread
> over exposed walls, peel
> without ever knowing what
> all this wonder is.
>
> And I write Hebrew, to
> get lost in my words, and also to find
> a bit of interest for my footsteps.
> I have not stopped walking. Many paths
> have I traveled. Engraved by my hands.
> I shall take my feet in hand
> and meet many people. And make them all
> my friends. Who is foreign? Who far, who near?
> There is no strangeness in the ways of the world.
> Because strangeness, mostly,
> lies in man's heart.[9]

"My Mother's Tongue Is Not My Mother Tongue"

Poet, essayist, and translator Giora Leshem (1940–2011) was one of the founders of the Keshev l'Shira publishing house and the cultural magazine *Yakum Tarbut*. He also served as associate editor and frequent contributor to *Nativ*, a journal of politics and art published by the Ariel Center.

The title of his poem "My Mother's Tongue Is Not My Mother Tongue" speaks to the lingual experience of the exiled individual through the next generation. The poet-narrator, the "lyric I," is as separated from his mother's experience—and her language—as his mother is separated by her exile. While his mother's experience of exile ("complete exile," "wilderness," "abyss") is at the center, the poet extends the experience generations both before and after. His grandfather suffered from the exile because "[his] tongue was extinguished as well. . . ."

Leshem employs the European landscape ("forest streams," "chestnut trees," "woods burning," "snow") to heighten the contrast between his mother's European past and his own Israeli present, even while writing of the experience of exile on the body ("hair," "lips," "tongue," "mouth"). Exile is an experience of absence, a condition of lack and negation. For the poet himself, exile is the negation of language, of song, of memory, and of the orphan's kaddish (*Kaddish Yatom*), and leaves only "syllables of guilt."

> GIORA LESHEM, "MY MOTHER'S TONGUE IS
> NOT MY MOTHER TONGUE" (2000)
>
> My mother's tongue is not my mother tongue. And never
> will be. My youth did not hear a voice trembling with age tell,
> in Hungarian or Slovak, of her bitter youth,
> nor her songs of forest streams or the wind in the chestnut tree.
> Only the scent of the woods burning and the smoke.
> In this warm land, snow words rest on her hair.
> Woe to the land that has no sea, whose dictator
> is an admiral a complete exile brought my mother

by dry land through the sea: words and letters
adrift. Tried by water and fire, like an ember,
my grandfather's tongue was extinguished as well,
like my mother's, with gaping mouth on the trench's edge,
and who hears? The orphan kaddish
is not my mother's tongue.
My mother's tongue is not my mother's tongue
neither in the city on the Yarkon's bank,
nor in another river city nor in the
country of the sea, where the strange words
with syllables of blood and guilt are buried.
And my mother's tongue falls from my lips
another tongue, a beautiful tongue
in a gaping mouth.[10]

10 Negation, Ambivalence, and Affirmation of Exile

The collection of texts in this final chapter cover the range of attitudes toward exile, from negation to affirmation. Overall, in different periods and among diverse communities, exile has generally been seen as a state to be avoided, mitigated, or ended. Generations of Jewish leaders and thinkers pondered and debated whether exile was a natural condition for Jews and hence necessarily endured, or needed to be brought to an end.

While the negation of exile—*shelilat hagolah*—became the clarion call of modern Zionism, the concept is rooted in much earlier movements. A minority view from late ninth- to early tenth-century Karaism held that Jews must not wait for the Messiah in the Diaspora, but instead must return to Jerusalem to hasten the coming.

There were, however, other ways of viewing exile: as individual or communal opportunity for the Jews. Rather than endangering the continuity of Jewish peoplehood, exile could be seen as helping mold and perpetuate the nation. Exposure to other peoples, customs, and beliefs in exile could strengthen those of the Jews, and lead to both individual spiritual growth and community cohesion. The dispersal of Jews among non-Jews could prevent annihilation of a concentrated population of Jews on one hand, and help temper antisemitism on the other. In the modern period Jewish communities outside of Europe flourished, and Jews living among gentiles helped raise support for the modern State of Israel.

In the twentieth century, exile came to be seen to be a productive if not necessary condition—a challenge that strengthened Jews' faith. So too, various Jewish thinkers viewed the existence of multiple centers of

Jewish life in positive terms—as means to nourish one another. Jews in the Diaspora are commended for being agents of change and for the support they garner for Jews in Zion.

Negation

Daniel al-Kumisi (late ninth century to early tenth century) was part of the Karaite community, which then extended throughout many regions of the Persian Empire—including his own, North Persia. Insisting that the Hebrew Bible was the only source of true Judaism, and dismissing the claims of Rabbinite Judaism, based on the Talmud, as a perversion of the divine message, the Karaites represented a significant challenge to the rabbis' leadership. Additionally, there were frequent disagreements among the Karaites themselves.

Generally speaking, Jews throughout the world agreed that at some future time, the Messiah would come and the Jewish people would be returned to the Holy Land. The question was, did Jews need to remain in exile until the Messiah arrived, or could they themselves expedite the Messiah's arrival by returning and praying in the Holy Land, especially in Jerusalem?

Al-Kumisi, apparently one of the earliest Karaites to settle in Jerusalem, held the minority position, insisting that simply praying for the Messiah from a distance was not enough. One had to pray at the very site of the ancient Temple—then the site of the Muslim Dome of the Rock—in order for the Messianic Age to begin.

The most significant Karaite leader, Anan ben David, did not agree. Al-Kumisi makes a very strong case, but apparently his writings had very little influence even among the Karaites, and have been preserved only in fragments.

> DANIEL AL-KUMISI, "APPEAL TO THE KARAITES OF THE DISPERSION TO COME AND SETTLE IN JERUSALEM" (10TH CENTURY)
>
> Know, then, that the scoundrels who are among Israel say one to another, "It is not our duty to go to Jerusalem, until He shall gather us together, even as He had cast us abroad." These are the words

of those who draw the wrath of the Lord. . . . Even if the Lord had not made it an ordinance upon us to go to Jerusalem from the various lands of the Dispersion and to pray there with mournful and bitter tears, would we not have known . . . that it is for those who are objects of the Lord's wrath to come to the door of Him who has been moved to anger, to supplicate Him . . . ? How much more so when the Lord has commanded the men of the Exile to come to Jerusalem and to stand . . . before Him, mourning, fasting, weeping, and wailing, wearing sackcloth and bitterness, all day and all night, as it is written, *Upon thy walls, O Jerusalem, have I appointed watchmen; all day and all night, always, they shall not be silenced; ye who mention the Lord, do ye not cease and do ye not give him rest* (Isa. 62:6-7). And it is written also in Jeremiah (Jer. 31:18a-b): *I have surely heard Ephraim*—Ephraim signifying Israel—*moving to and fro*: i.e., wandering hither and thither in exile, crying and weeping, and saying before Me, Is it not Thou, O my God, *who has chastised me* and hast cast me into exile? And I in my exile . . . have become *as a calf that has not been trained* (Jer. 31:18) to bear the yoke, in as much as the shepherds of the exile have not taught me to bear the yoke of the ordinances as set forth in the Law of Moses, but rather have led me astray with *an ordinance of men learned by rote* (Isa. 29:13). *Now make me turn back, and I will so turn back, for thou art the Lord, my God* (Jer. 31:18c).

And the Lord replied to Israel in these words: My people, if thou desirest that I should turn thee back (Jer. 31:21-22): *Set up for thyself way signs*—meaning [signposts] on the road to Jerusalem to go to the House of the Lord; *make for thyself bitterness*—by weeping and wailing—*set thy heart toward the highway, the road thou hast traveled; return, O virgin of Israel, return to these thy cities!* (Jer. 31:21)—i.e., prior to the reassembly of the Exiled, go back to Jerusalem and there hold vigils before the Lord. . . . *How long wilt thou wander about, O back-sliding daughter* (Jer. 31:22), saying, I will not go to Jerusalem, to the seat of the Lord? . . . Therefore it is incumbent upon you who fear the Lord, to come to Jerusalem and to dwell in it, . . . until the day when Jerusalem shall be restored, as it is written: *And do ye not give him rest* (Isa. 62:7).[1]

NEGATION, AMBIVALENCE, AFFIRMATION

Longing for Zion

Judah (Yehuda) Halevi (1075?–1141) was a physician, poet, and philosopher writing at the height of the Golden Age of Spain (*tor hazahav*). Mentored by Moses ibn Ezra (see chapter 8), Halevi composed both secular and religious poetry in Hebrew—using Arabic metrics—as well as prose in Arabic. His foremost work, *The Book of the Kuzari*, is a defense of Jewish thought written in a compelling narrative.

The first clause of his iconic poem "My Heart Is in the East," one of the best known in all of Hebrew poetry, powerfully expresses the burden of exile in five Hebrew words.

While Halevi reportedly experienced displacement—either by being separated from his childhood home because of Muslim conquests and Christian reconquests or having been born in what was then Christian Spain and moving to Muslim-ruled territory ("Arab chains")—his yearning was for a place he had never been. His far-off Zion had been conquered by the Crusaders for the Holy Roman Empire (Edom). Not content with mere words, Halevi set off for Palestine in 1140, the year before his death; it is not known whether he died en route or shortly after his arrival.

> JUDAH HALEVI, "MY HEART IS IN THE EAST" (12TH CENTURY)
>
> My heart is in the east, and I in the uttermost west—
> How can I find savour in food? How shall it be sweet to me?
> How shall I render my vows and my bonds, while yet
> Zion lieth beneath the fetter of Edom, and I in Arab chains?[2]
> A light thing it would seem me to leave behind all the good things of Spain—
> Seeing how precious in mine eyes to behold the dust of the desolate sanctuary.[3]

Heine on Halevi

Heinrich Heine (1797–1856), one of the foremost German poets, was also one of the most famous Jewish converts to Christianity. German authorities banned his poetry because of his radical politics; as a member of the Young German movement, he advocated socialist ideas and French revolutionary thought. Subject to German censorship and attracted by the July Revolution, he moved to France. He lived his last twenty-five years as an expatriate—or exile—in Paris.

His long 1851 poem "Jehuda ben Halevy," excerpted here, draws a direct line from Psalm 137 to the "great and famous poet" Judah Halevi (same person, altered spelling), from the exile in Babylonia and the mourning of the Ninth of Av to Halevi's individual exile. Likening Halevi's exilic longing for the ancestral homeland to the yearning of a romantic lover, Heine conflates communal, national, and personal states of exile.

Despite his conversion to Lutheranism, it is quite possible that Heine identified with Halevi as a Jew, along with sharing both poetic genius and the experience of displacement. Heine penned this from the confines of his bed or "mattress grave."

> HEINRICH HEINE, "JEHUDA BEN HALEVY" (1851)
>
> 1.
> "If, Jerusalem, I ever
> "Should forget thee, let my tongue
> "To my mouth's roof cleave, let also
> "My right hand forget her cunning—"
>
> Words and melody are whirling
> In my head to-day unceasing,
> And methinks I hear sweet voices
> Singing psalms, sweet human voices.
>
> Often to the light come also
> Beards of shadowy-long proportions;
> Say, ye phantoms, which amongst you
> Is Jehuda ben Halevy?
>
> **

NEGATION, AMBIVALENCE, AFFIRMATION

And Jehuda ben Halevy
Was not merely skill'd in reading,

But in poetry a master,
And himself a first-rate poet.

Yes, he was a first-rate poet,
Star and torch of his own age,
Light and beacon of his people,
Yes, a very wondrous mighty

Fiery pillar of all song,
That preceded Israel's mournful
Caravan as it was marching
Through the desert of sad exile.

2.
"By the streams of Babylon
"Sat we down and wept, we hangèd
"Our sad harps upon the willows—"
Know'st thou not the olden song?

**

God be praised! the seething slowly
In the pot evaporates,
Then is mute. My spleen is soften'd,
My west-eastern darksome spleen.

And my Pegasus is neighing
Once more gaily, and the nightmare
Seems to shake with vigour off him,
And his wise eyes thus are asking:

Are we riding back to Spain,
To the little Talmudist there,
Who was such a first-rate poet,—
To Jehuda ben Halevy?

Yes, he was a first-rate poet,
In the realm of dreams sole ruler
With the spirit-monarch's crown,
By the grace of God a poet.

**

And the hero, whom we sing of,
Our Jehuda ben Halevy,
Also had his heart's fair lady;
But she was of special kind.

**

She the Rabbi was in love with
Was a poor and mournful loved one,
Woeful image of destruction,
And her name—Jerusalem!

**

And Jehuda ben Halevy
At his mistress' feet expired,
And his dying head, it rested
On Jerusalem's dear knees.[4]

The Failure of Assimilation

Theodor (Benjamin Zeev) Herzl (1860–1904) has long been dubbed the father of modern Zionism. Born in Budapest, at age eighteen he moved with his family to Vienna. He became a journalist and playwright instead of the lawyer his parents had wanted.

The Dreyfus Affair—in which the Jewish French army captain Alfred Dreyfus was falsely accused of treason in an atmosphere charged with overt antisemitism—raised Herzl's consciousness and inspired him to write *Der Judenstaat* (literally, "The state of Jews," 1896), which argued for the necessity of Jewish sovereignty; *The New Ghetto* (1897), a drama illustrating the difficulties Jews faced in trying to break away from the internal, psychological ghetto imposed by antisemitism; and *Altneuland* (*The Old New Land*, 1902), a novel expressing his vision of what the Jewish state would be like.

Herzl was not the first to promote the idea of a Jewish state—Moses Hess, for example, called for Jewish settlement of Palestine in *Rome and Jerusalem* (1862)—but Herzl was the first to organize a political endeavor to realize the idea. He convened the First Zionist Congress in Switzerland in 1897, writing in his diary entry of September 3, 1897, "In Basel I created the Jewish State. In . . . 50 years everyone will realize it."[5]

Understanding the importance of political action, Herzl practiced grand diplomacy, meeting with the German kaiser, the Ottoman sultan, the king of Italy, and the pope. Ever a pragmatist, he considered the offer of land in East Africa as an immediate haven for East European Jews suffering from persecution, the so-called Uganda Plan, only to abandon it in the face of great opposition.

Much of Herzl's writing and activity after the Dreyfus Affair concerned antisemitism, either directly or indirectly. As he wrote in a private letter: "I do not consider the anti-Semitic movement altogether harmful. It will inhibit the ostentatious flaunting of conspicuous wealth, curb the unscrupulous behavior of Jewish financiers, and contribute in many ways to the education of the Jews."[6]

In the excerpt below Herzl addresses "the Jewish question" through the prism of assimilation's presumed failure. Assimilation, he says, can be attained only through intermarriage, which itself is only possible when Jews advance up the social ladder by accumulation of wealth. But this, in fact, cannot happen, because resentment would increase antisemitic sentiment before assimilation could occur. He concludes that the only solution is a Jewish state, yet he treads carefully. Conscious of his mostly middle-class bourgeois audience, he reassures his readers by advocating that they not leave their comfortable homes until their new homes are ready in Palestine.

THEODOR HERZL, *DER JUDENSTAAT* (1896)

The Jewish question persists wherever Jews live in appreciable numbers. . . . We are naturally drawn into those places where we are not persecuted, and our appearance there gives rise to persecution. This is the case, and will inevitably be so, everywhere, even in highly civilized countries . . . so long as the Jewish question is not solved on the political level. . . .

Anti-Semitism is a highly complex movement, which I think I understand. I approach this movement as a Jew, yet without fear or hatred. I believe that I can see in it the elements of cruel sport, of common commercial rivalry, of inherited prejudice, of religious intolerance—but also of a supposed need for self-defense. I consider the Jewish question neither a social nor a religious one. . . . It is a national question, and to solve it we must first of all establish it as an international political problem to be discussed and settled by the civilized nations of the world in council. . . .

We have sincerely tried everywhere to merge with the national communities in which we live, seeking only to preserve the faith of our fathers. . . . In vain are we loyal patriots, sometimes super loyal; in vain do we make the same sacrifices of life and property as our fellow citizens; in vain do we strive to enhance the fame of our native lands in the arts and sciences, or her wealth by trade and commerce. In our native lands where we have lived for centuries we are still decried as aliens. . . . The majority decide who the "alien" is; this, and all else in the relations between peoples, is a matter of power. . . . It is without avail, therefore, for us to be loyal patriots. . . .

Oppression and persecution cannot exterminate us. No nation on earth has endured such struggles and sufferings as we have. Jewbaiting has merely winnowed out our weaklings; the strong among us defiantly return to their own whenever persecution breaks out. This was most clearly apparent in the period immediately following the emancipation of the Jews. . . . Wherever we remain politically secure for any length or time, we assimilate. I think this is not praiseworthy. . . .

For old prejudices against us are still deeply ingrained in the folk ethos. He who would have proof of this need only listen to the people where they speak candidly and artlessly: folk wisdom and folklore both are anti-Semitic. The people is everywhere a great child, which can be readily educated; but even in the most favorable circumstances its education would be such a long-drawn-out process that we could far sooner, as already mentioned, help ourselves by other means.[7]

We Are Aliens in Exile

Born in the Kovno region in 1843, Moses Leib Lilienblum was reared in a traditional family and received a traditional education. In his mid-twenties he came under the influence of Haskalah writers, and he began to publish articles in Haskalah journals criticizing the regimen of talmudic studies and the ignorance of broader culture prevailing in East European Jewish society. Vilified by the Orthodox as a freethinker, he moved to the more open environment of Odessa and undertook a course of studies that he hoped would prepare him for acceptance into its university. In 1876 he published *Ḥattot Ne'urim* (The sins of youth), an account of his life through 1873 that portrays the writer as a young heretic-martyr, which one scholar characterized as "the most important autobiography of the Haskalah period."[8] In 1899 he appended the section "Derekh Teshuvah" (The way back), continuing the autobiographical account through the period of the pogroms, his repudiation of the Haskalah, and his conversion to a proto-Zionist analysis of the Jewish condition.

In the passage from "Derekh Teshuvah" below, presented as the final entry in a diary written a few months after the 1881 pogrom in Odessa, Lilienblum describes his new understanding of the Jewish situation in exile. Alienation and estrangement abide. Jews will never be accepted by their neighbors; the expectations and hopes for acceptance as equals that underscore and validate the changes made as part of the Haskalah movement are a delusion. No matter the transformations in traditional Jewish society, no matter how well educated Jews may become or how much they contribute to the economic and cultural life of the society and nation, they will always be viewed as outsiders who do not belong.

Fortunately, there is a constructive alternative. Not emigration to the United States; that is still exile, and Jews will never be fully accepted there either. But the "land of our fathers . . . remains vacant." By emigrating to and settling in that land, the enduring nightmare of exile can end.

MOSES LEIB LILIENBLUM, "DEREKH TESHUVAH" (1899)

12th of Tishri [1881], at night on my couch. They write: "One should collect and assemble the data about those Jewish activities which harm the natives."[9] We, then, are not native. During the pogroms, a native woman, ragged and drunk, danced in the streets, joyously shouting: "This is our country, this is our country." Can we say the same, even without dancing . . . without being drunk? Yes, we are aliens, not only here but in all of Europe. . . .[10]

Now I understand the word "anti-semitism."[11] This is the secret of our affliction in exile. Even in Alexandria in the time of the Second Temple, and in all the lands of our dispersion, we were aliens. . . . We were aliens in Europe, when religion flourished because of our religion; now when nationalism reigns, we are aliens because of our origin. We are Semites among Aryans, the sons of Shem among the Sons of Japheth, a Palestinian tribe from Asia in the European lands.

Yet we dream we will become children of the European nations, children with equal rights. . . .

[W]e are aliens and will remain aliens. Our future is fearful, without a spark of hope or a ray of light—slaves, aliens, strangers forever. Yet why should we be aliens in alien countries if the land of our fathers has not yet been forgotten and remains vacant?[12] It can absorb our people! We must cease to be aliens, and return to our fatherland. We must buy land there, little by little, becoming rooted there, like other people who live in the land of their fathers. We are being uprooted . . . the gates are open for us to leave. We are, in fact, fleeing. Why, then, flee to America and be alien there, too, instead of to the land of our fathers?[13]

I was exalted by this lofty thought of return. It is the salvation for the Jewish people, and the assurance of their eternal existence, which hitherto only our declining religion had secured.

The oppressive weight rolled from my heart. It was a revelation. I became exalted and transfigured. The dew of renascence[14] fell upon me and melted the fearful ice which for so many years had congealed my heart.

In September, I stopped attending classes at the gymnasium.

The pogroms taught me their lesson, and I was in despair about our future. My studies seemed a sin against my unfortunate people. . . . All our hopes for equality came to naught. Our people were fleeing the sword, misfortune all around, the present bitter, the future fearful—and I was thinking of entering the university! For years I had striven toward this. But now I am convinced that our misfortune is not the lack of general education but that we are aliens.[15] We will still remain aliens when we will be stuffed with education as a pomegranate is with seeds. I terminated my studies and, with great dedication, I began to prepare myself for my new ideal, though I did not know how.[16]

Negating the Diasporic

The Hebrew essayist Asher Zvi Hirsch Ginsberg (1856–1927), best known by his Hebrew name and pen name Ahad Ha'am, is known as the founder of cultural Zionism.

His vision of Zionism was quite different from that of Herzl, the movement's most famous leader. Influenced by Leon Pinsker's *Auto-Emancipation* (1882), he visited Palestine in 1891 and developed his own ideal of creating not just a state of Jews but a "Jewish State." His goal was a secular Jewish culture based on Jewish national consciousness, the Hebrew language, and a negation of the *galut* or *golah*: the assumption that Jews were destined to live in exile.

In 1897 he attended, as an observer, the First Zionist Congress led by Herzl in Basel; the experience led him to split from Herzl's official Zionist movement. "We did not come to Basel to found a Jewish state today or tomorrow," he wrote soon after. "Rather, we came to issue a great proclamation to all the world: the Jewish people is still alive and full of the will to live."[17] He moved from Russia to London in 1908, and then in 1922 to Tel Aviv, where he died five years later.

Ahad Ha'am's vision of Zionism was considerably broader than Herzl's, allowing for both a Jewish center to be established in Palestine and a permanent Diaspora. He critiqued the Yiddishists for settling for being a minor culture ("infant toddlings") not commensurate with "the eternal people," and the autonomists for settling for less than a full national life. As he wrote in his review of the First Zionist Congress:

> After thousands of years of unfathomable calamity and misfortune, it would be impossible for the Jewish people to be happy with their lot if in the end they would reach merely the level of a small and humble people, whose state is a plaything in the hands of its mighty neighbors and exists only by means of diplomatic machinations. . . . It was not in vain that the prophets rose to the aid of Israel, envisioning the reign of justice in the world at the end of days. Their nationalism, their love for the people and for their land, led them to this.[18]

In the translation below the terms Diaspora and "dispersion" are used almost interchangeably for *galut* and *golah*. It could be argued that "exile" comes closer to Ahad Ha'am's intended meaning for both; readers are encouraged to substitute accordingly.

AHAD HA'AM, "THE NEGATION OF THE DIASPORA" (1909)

"The Negation of the Diaspora," is an expression frequently heard in discussions between the Zionists, who look beyond the Diaspora for a solution of our national problem, and the Nationalists, who do not. . . .

In the subjective sense all Jews adopt a negative attitude toward the Diaspora. With few exceptions, they all recognize that the position of a lamb among wolves is unsatisfactory, and they would gladly put an end to this state of things if it were possible. Those who profess to regard our dispersion as a heaven-sent blessing are simply weak-kneed optimists; lacking the courage to look the evil thing in the face, they find it necessary to smile on it and call it good so long as they cannot abolish it. . . .

To adopt a negative attitude toward the Diaspora means, for our present purpose, to believe that the Jews cannot survive as a scattered people now that our spiritual isolation is ended, because we have no longer any defence against the ocean of foreign culture, which threatens to obliterate our national characteristics and traditions, and thus gradually to put an end to our existence as a people.

There are, it is true, some Jews who are of that opinion; but they are not all of one way of thinking. They belong in fact to two different parties.... The one party argues that, as we are doomed to extinction, it is better to hasten the end by our action than to sit and wait for it to come of its own accord after a long and painful death agony.... But the other party argues that, since we are threatened with extinction, we ought to put an end to our exile before it puts an end to us. We must secure our future by gathering the scattered members of our race together in our historical land... where alone we shall be able to continue to live as a people. Any Jew who is both able and willing to get rid of his Judaism by assimilation may remain where he is; those who are unable or unwilling to assimilate will betake themselves to the Jewish State....

Both alike have come into conflict with something very deep-rooted and stubborn—the instinctive and unconquerable desire of the Jewish people to survive. This desire for survival, or will to live, obviously makes it impossible for the Jewish people as a whole to contemplate the disappearance of the Diaspora if that involves its own disappearance; but the case is no better if the argument is that the Diaspora must disappear in order that the people may survive.... The Jews as a people feel that they have the will and the strength to survive whatever may happen, without any ifs or ands. They cannot accept a theory which makes their survival conditional on their ceasing to be dispersed, because that theory implies that failure to end the dispersion would mean extinction....

Except, then, for these two extreme parties, the Jews remain true to their ancient belief: their attitude toward the Diaspora is subjectively negative, but objectively positive. Dispersion is a thoroughly evil and unpleasant thing, but we can and must live in dispersion, for all its evils and all its unpleasantness. Exodus from the dispersion will always be, as it always has been, an inspiring hope for the distant future; but... our survival as a people is not dependent upon it....

[I]t is precisely this positive attitude toward the Diaspora that gives the question its urgency.... [I]f the Jews believe that they can and must continue to live in dispersion, the question at once arises— how is it to be done?... The will to live not only persuades them to believe that it is possible to survive in dispersion; it also impels them, in the changing circumstances of successive epochs, to find always the most appropriate means of preserving and developing their national identity. Moreover, this watchful instinct is always anticipating events, always providing in advance against the future. When Titus besieged Jerusalem, we are told, the defenders always had a new rampart ready in the rear before the one in front of it was overthrown. So it is with our national survival. And now that all but the willfully blind can see the old rampart tottering to its fall, we are bound to ask ourselves: Where is the new rampart that is to secure our existence as a people in dispersion?

The Nationalists answer: national autonomy. . . .

If we are to decide how far autonomy is a satisfactory answer to our problem, we must first of all define the scope of the problem itself. To judge from the current controversy on this matter, there appear in fact to be two different schools of thought. It is common ground among the Nationalists that we must find some new means of maintaining our distinctive national life in the Diaspora; but, on close examination, we find that while some of them are looking for a pattern of national life that will be as complete and self-contained as the ghetto life of our forefathers, others are convinced, in their heart of hearts, that that is an impossible ideal. These latter ask for nothing more than the possibility of developing our national life up to the limit of what is in practice attainable, and with no more than the unavoidable minimum of truncation and circumscription. . . .

[W]e must ask the further question: To what extent is it a solution? Is national autonomy put forward as a final answer to our problem, holding out a promise of full and complete national life in the Diaspora? Or is it offered merely as the best that can be had in the circumstances, it being recognized that a complete national life in the Diaspora is impossible except in the ghetto which we have left forever? . . .

To sum up, then: If national autonomy in the Diaspora is put forward as a completely satisfactory solution of our problem, it has to promise to normalize the life of the scattered and atomized Jewish people. It has to undertake to provide the Jewish people with both the opportunity and the necessary strength of will to deploy its creative faculties to the maximum extent in the development of its specific national culture. . . . It has to guarantee the possibility of educating all the individual members of the people . . . on the lines of the national culture, so as to ensure that when they reach maturity they will find within the circle of the national life so wide a range of intellectual interests, and such ample scope for practical activity, that they will feel neither the need nor the desire to desert that sphere for another.[19]

Exile in the East

Rina Shani (1937–83), Israeli poet turned spiritual guru, felt disconnected from the land of her birth, the national Jewish homeland. Her feelings of alienation likely stemmed from a difficult childhood and were nurtured by the 1960s counterculture in Europe and America. In 1975 she left for the United States, returning to Israel after a couple of years, only to leave for India in the early '80s before her untimely death.

Overtly referencing Judah Halevi's poem in the title of hers, Shani draws a sharp contrast between his longing for Zion and her feeling of exile at home. Violent imagery of dismemberment and dislocation and terms from the military sector permeate her verse, which Riki Traum reads as Shani's reaction to the Six-Day War and its aftermath.[20]

> RINA SHANI, "I AM IN THE EAST AND MY
> HEART IS IN THE EAST" (1970)
>
> Fire opened from a field, a tired soul beaten
> toward a wall of dust, to the green line, red line, line of
> fire opened from north, sick evil from east,
> harsh plot from south, a soul extinguished, a heart
> sprayed over a sandbag, a leg torn from its home
> a body from its place, a vaporous sea carried westward
> no weeping, no refugee, on boiling water,
> a wide border, a hard shell floating
> in the western edge too what you expect, consuming[21]

The Neuroses of Exile

Best known as a novelist, Abraham B. Yehoshua (1936–2022) also wrote plays and essays. A fifth-generation Jerusalemite (on his father's side), he studied Hebrew literature and philosophy at the Hebrew University, had a long career teaching comparative literature at Haifa University, and received many literary prizes, including the Israel Prize for literature, the National Jewish Book Award, the Prix Médicis Étranger, and the Viareggio Prize for Lifetime Achievement.

Yehoshua did not accept the idea that Jewish life in the Diaspora had significant validity. He controversially defined Diaspora Judaism as "masturbation" in conversation with editors and reporters at the *Jerusalem Post*, and insisted in a 1981 essay "Israel: Problem or Solution" that "the question of the *Golah* (Exile) is the most important and profound question a Jew must pose to himself when trying to probe the essence of the Jewish people"—a stance he powerfully expressed in this later essay as well.[22]

A. B. YEHOSHUA, "EXILE AS A NEUROTIC SOLUTION" (1986)

There are two attitudes toward the *golah*. One regards the *golah* as an accident that befell the Jewish people, a tragedy wrought upon the Jews by the nations of the world. According to this view the *golah*, although it lasted for a long time, is essentially transient, and the nation yearns for its redemption. It simply awaits more favorable conditions that will enable its return. All roads lead either to Israel or to assimilation. When peace comes and with it some respite, then the *golah* will gradually disintegrate and the nation will stream to Israel. This conception ignores the basic fact that the dispersion was not forced upon us; it was, rather, something we forced on ourselves. It should not be viewed as an accident or a tragedy, but rather as a distortion—a basic deviant trait in our national makeup—and that is why any solution must be different from what is commonly imagined.

The other attitude views the *golah* as a permanent, almost natural state. If one accepts this view, it is remarkable that other nations do not also maintain diasporas worthy of the name, scattered throughout many countries. People with this attitude sense the depth of the Jewish people's need for the *golah*, how closely woven the *golah* is to the essence of the Jew, and they try to see exile as a legitimate and normal state. As a consequence of this attitude the question sometimes arises: why bother to have a state? And even when the necessity for an independent national center is not rejected, there is a duality in which the *golah* and the center are seen as equal in value. This framework of ideas ignores the simple fact that the *golah* was the source of the most terrible disasters to befall the Jewish people; that because of the *golah* the nation was almost completely wiped out in our generation; that in spite of the existence of the State of Israel, the *golah* constitutes a threat to a large community of Jews in the Soviet Union and is likely to pose a grave threat to the Jews in South America; and that the *golah* is the root cause for that infamous Jewish fate which is given in any discussion on Jewish questions. . . .

The essence of our life in Israel is different from that of *golah* life. Spiritual life in the *golah* is like that of a man who has built his house on the water's edge, is preoccupied with the question of whether water will inundate his home, and is engaged with efforts to keep it out. We in Israel, on the other hand, are like a man who has removed his house from the erosive powers of the waves. The problem of the water no longer preoccupies him. He is able to build his house, cultivate his land, and create something new. . . .

The great debate between Israel and the *golah* must be resumed at once, without hypocrisy, with all its fierceness and honesty.[23]

Ambivalence

In her 2013 article "Out of Exile: Some Thoughts on Exile as a Dynamic Condition," Eva Hoffman (see chapter 9) writes of changing attitudes toward exile: of the ways in which it has come to be valued, particularly by writers, in the postmodern era, and also how it can become a convenient excuse for remaining detached from one's own community. In expressing such ambivalence, she engages with A. B. Yehoshua's view of exile as an unhealthy choice: whether for the collective, as a temptation that "leaves you free to be un-implicated in the mundane problems and conflicts of the place where you actually live," or for the individual, where "the posture of detachment can turn into a kind of willful separatism; the energy of critical distance into a mannerism."

EVA HOFFMAN, "OUT OF EXILE: SOME THOUGHTS ON EXILE AS A DYNAMIC CONDITION" (2013)

Historically, "exile" used to be thought of as a tragic or a pitiable condition; but recently, it has been redefined as somehow interesting, morally heroic, even glamorous. The exilic position is isomorphic with exactly those qualities which are privileged in a certain vein of postmodern theory: marginality, alterity, the de-centered identity. On a more lived level, the situation of the outsider, while hardly easy, has its consolations, and even its comforts. It provides not only a ready-made identity, but an explanation for one's existential condition, and its discontents. For a writer, there are the considerable advantages of the oblique vantage point, a perspective from which nothing can be taken for granted, and everything is strange and new. Indeed, the position of the writer—at least the modernist writer—maps easily onto the position of the outsider, and some writers have famously chosen exile, precisely for the bonus of that sharp angle of vision, the bracing coolness of distance and defamiliarisation.

For a while, exile can be a wonderful stimulus to perception and imagination. It can also be an existential challenge and a moral task, but I have come to think that if the "exilic position" is maintained for too long, it can become not fertile, but arid; not a prod to creativity, but an instrument of fixity.[24]

Affirmation

A leading influential rabbi in mid-thirteenth-century Spain, Moses ben Nahman, frequently known as Nachmanides or Ramban, served as chief rabbi of Catalonia, wrote important works on talmudic law, and was especially known for his commentary on the Pentateuch, which responded to the commentaries of both Rashi and Abraham ibn Ezra.

A turning point in his life occurred in 1263 when King James I of Aragon summoned him to represent Judaism in a public debate with Christian intellectuals. The crucial question was whether Christian doctrines could be supported by passages in the Talmud. For our purposes, what he said before the king in Barcelona is less relevant than his conception of exile in the literary report of the event he penned shortly thereafter.[25]

For Nachmanides, Jewish suffering stems from being in exile. Jews are derided and taunted by the non-Jews they are forced to live amidst, and exist at the mercy of the benevolence of the kings they live under, who may or may not provide them safety. He reasons, however, that as it is more difficult to be Jewish when in exile, the reward is greater too.

Ironically, he left exile: the strong attacks on Christian beliefs in his written account of the public debate in Barcelona (the text, excerpted here, but not those remarks) led to pressure for him to leave the country. He settled in Jerusalem, where he remained for the rest of his life.

MOSES BEN NAHMAN, "DISPUTATION OF BARCELONA" (1263)

I said, "My lord king, bear with me [a little]. The essence of our judgment, truth, and justice does not depend upon the Messiah. You are worth more to me than the Messiah. You are king, and he is king. You are a gentile king, and he is a Jewish king, for the Messiah is but a king of flesh and blood like you. When I worship my Creator in your dominion, exiled, suffering, and under subjugation, *the shame of the nations* (Ezek. 36:15), who taunt me always, my reward is abundant, for I bring a whole offering to God from my physical being. Because of that, I shall increasingly merit life in the world to come. However, when a king of Israel, of my own faith, will rule over all the nations, and I have no choice but to abide the law of the Jews, my reward will not be as abundant."[26]

Holier in Exile

Dov Baer, the Maggid of Mezritch (1704?–72), was a disciple and then successor of the Baal Shem Tov, the founder of the Hasidic movement.

The passage below is framed by a novel piece of homiletical exegesis. The opening three Hebrew words are usually translated as "Stay far away from a wicked neighbor." In typical Hasidic style, the preacher takes a simple, familiar phrase from the classical literature and gives it a new twist that nonetheless is firmly rooted in the text. In this case, the Maggid breaks down the traditional syntax of the three words "Stay far away" and reconstructs it anew. There is no "evil neighbor"; the *shakhen* is the indwelling presence of the Divine (*Shekhinah*). "Evil" becomes the direct object of the transitive verb *harḥek*, "remove," meaning "set at a distance." Though "evil" is directly juxtaposed to "neighbor" in the sentence, the goal is to set distance between them. Evil thoughts must be set at a distance, lest they cause God to be separated from us. The proper translation would therefore be "Keep evil far away from the Divine Presence."[27]

For Dov Baer, exile is not impediment to holiness, but indeed facilitates its attainment. Using the common analogy of a king to stand in for God, the Maggid of Mezritch explains how it is easier to encounter God in exile and thus "achieve the Holy Spirit" than it was in the days when the Temple was standing.

> DOV BAER (THE MAGGID OF MEZRITCH),
> "HARḤEK MISH'KHEN RAʿ" (CA. 1760–80)
>
> הרחק משכן רע. This means that it is easier to achieve the Holy Spirit in our time, a time of exile, than it was in the days when the Temple was still standing. To understand this, consider how difficult it would be to approach a king in his royal palace, as compared to when he is traveling through the countryside. While he is on the road or at an inn, anyone can approach him, even a simple farm lad who would never be permitted to enter the palace. In the same way, God will immediately inspire and dwell within someone who thinks about communion with God now, in our time of exile. For this reason, it is important to remove ourselves from evil desires and evil thoughts, so that God will not be separated from us. Rather, whatever we do should be for the sake of God's name. Thus הרחק משכן רע: remove all evil from the one who dwells within you.[28]

Autonomy in Exile

Born in Belorussia in 1860, Simon Dubnow became one of the most influential writers of Jewish history, authoring the seminal ten-volume work *History of the Jews* (1925–29, translated into English forty years later). His reading of Jewish history—that the Jewish people's survival as a nation was due to their independence, despite exile and dispersal—led to his political and ideological engagement.

Dubnow is the dominant personality associated with autonomism, a movement that believed in the perpetuation of Jewish life in the (European) Diaspora, as long as Jews maintained self-rule. In policy terms, the Bund and other socialist Jewish parties adopted variations on autonomism, but the Holocaust effectively ended the movement. Dubnow himself was killed by the Nazis in December 1941.

This article is clearly meant as a response to Ahad Ha'am's "Negation of the Diaspora" (see above), which proposed "a spiritual center in the land of Israel which will serve as a national point of attraction for the Diaspora" (as cited in Dubnow's essay). As a strong proponent of Jewish life in the Diaspora, Dubnow conceded the benefit of a spiritual center in the Land of Israel, but not an exclusive center. Rather, he believed, the dialogue between the two centers (Ahad Ha'am's in Palestine, and his in the Diaspora) would contribute to the "national development of Judaism."

Most importantly for this section, at the end of the essay he turns his attention to the question of a national language. He proposes continuing the tradition of diglossia, substituting Yiddish ("jargon") for Aramaic and preserving Hebrew: "We must not destroy with our own hands the power of our folk language to compete with foreign languages.... Such destruction would amount to suicide."

> SIMON DUBNOW, "THE AFFIRMATION OF THE DIASPORA" (1909)
>
> In the Diaspora, we must strive, within the realm of the possible, to demand and to attain national-cultural autonomy for the majority of the nation. In the land of Israel we will achieve it only for a minority

of the nation which, at present, is insignificant but which can greatly increase in the future. In order to strengthen the Diaspora we will use the weapons of national struggle which served us for thousands of years and which are adapted to the world view of our time. You ask what wall we shall erect in place of the fallen ghetto walls? Every period has its own architecture, and the powerful vital instinct will unmistakably tell the people what style to use for building the wall of national autonomy which will replace the former religious "fence to the fence,"[29] and will not at the same time shut out the flow of world culture. . . . [T]hose who do not negate the Diaspora have no alternative but to direct their efforts toward building up the Diaspora on the basis of autonomy. The spiritual center in the land of Israel, while exerting a force of its own for a minority, will serve the majority only as one of the factors in the strengthening of our people. . . .[30]

Among the forces which are the basis of our autonomy in the Diaspora, I also set aside a place for the powerful force of the folk language used by seven million Jews in Russia and Galicia, which for several generations now fulfills the function of a spoken language, the language of instruction in the school (the *ḥeder* and yeshiva), and . . . also a language of literature. . . .

The Hebrew language is our natural leg, but it is only one leg, not two; the second was cut off by the exile, which removed the language from living use by the masses of the people and confined it to the fields of literature, religion and, in some measure, to education. In place of the missing leg came an artificial leg, Yiddish. On those two legs our people has stood and survived for many generations, just as in former years it stood on the linguistic dualism of Hebrew and Aramaic. Do those nationalists who affirm the Diaspora wish to remove the artificial leg, which, for some time now, has gained the strength of a natural leg, and not to use it to get a firm foothold in national life? This would mean to pronounce a verdict of instantaneous disintegration on the people if they were so unwise as to listen to such a dangerous suggestion.

When the language problem is posed in all its ramifications and when it is . . . from the general national viewpoint, then there will be no place for such errors in this matter. Insofar as we recognize the merit of national existence in the Diaspora, we must also recognize the merit of Yiddish as one of the instruments of autonomy, together with Hebrew and the other factors of our culture.[31]

Jewish Exceptionalism

Rabbi Judah Leon Magnes (1877–1948) was an American Reform rabbi who considered himself a Zionist but whose Zionism was markedly different from the majority of Zionists.

He was a pacifist, and unlike many rabbis who abandoned pacifist commitments when the United States went to war in 1917, Magnes retained his pacifism throughout this life. The negative response to this position among American Jews who had entered the war made it more difficult for him to serve American congregations, and in 1922 he decided upon a new life in Palestine. In 1925 he became chancellor of the newly established Hebrew University in Jerusalem, and thirteen years later he became its president, a position he would hold until the end of his life.

Devoting himself to both Zionism and pacifism, Magnes insisted that Zionism did not require a "Jewish state," but was fully compatible with a binational state. In fact, the land's sanctity for three religions precluded the exclusive realization of either Jewish or Arab nationalism in Palestine. Despite his many attempts, neither the Jewish Yishuv leadership nor Arab leaders in Palestine agreed to move forward with his binationalist agenda. Yet he continued to persevere, even to advocate binationalism with U.S. President Truman in May 1948 at the price of Israel's founding.

The following essay originally appeared in a pamphlet printed in English, Hebrew, and German and published in Jerusalem in 1930. The American historian Daniel P. Kotzin explains:

> In the pamphlet's very title Magnes drew attention to the conflict between the Zionist effort to normalize the Jewish people and his claim that the Jewish people are a unique nation. The title *Like All the Nations?* referred to a biblical passage (2 Samuel 7:23) that declares

NEGATION, AMBIVALENCE, AFFIRMATION

Israel is a unique nation in the eyes of God. But Magnes's title also made reference to Theodore [sic] Herzl's attempt to normalize the Jewish nation, to make it like all other nations, by giving it a territory and a state. In the main article in the pamphlet, Magnes addressed the tension between the Herzlian effort to normalize the Jewish nation and his own belief in Jewish exceptionalism.[32]

Magnes's essay takes a middle stance, agreeing with Herzl et al. that the Jews need a homeland in order not to be a ghost nation and also with the opposing view that grants value to the Diaspora. He writes that the Diaspora is not only a present-day reality, but one that can be made even more beneficial by the establishment of a (binational) state in Palestine.

JUDAH MAGNES, "LIKE ALL THE NATIONS?" (1930)

This is a day of ferment throughout the world, also within Judaism.[33] The materials are there and are in the hands of the Potter. Palestine can perhaps help fashion this clay more than any one factor. But it is a living Jewish people everywhere that Palestine must serve. It is a people of useful citizens permeating the life of hundreds of communities, and yet giving evidence of the changelessness of that mystic phenomenon—their continued existence as a body set apart and separate. They are scattered, yet are one; they are unorganized, yet held together through spiritual bonds more subtle than organization. One sees this people in all the lands of its exile continuing to yield out of its body individuals of mind and spirit in the arts and sciences, and common soldiers for groups whose goal is the betterment of our human lot. The dispersion of this people, the Diaspora, is a marvelous instrumentality for the fulfillment of its function as a teacher. The dispersion is an irrevocable, historical fact, and Palestine can be a means of making this fact into an even greater blessing.

Unfortunately, one hears most of that Zionism which is not born of a positive, hopeful relationship toward the tremendous, unique fact of the Diaspora but of despair. It is a Zionism that loathes the ghetto (which it identifies with the dispersion), and that is so in despair of the future of Diaspora Judaism, and that in its own way loves Jews and Judaism so passionately that the further existence of Jews and Judaism is thought impossible if the present-day Palestine be not made ready to act as savior.

Palestine is the center of this organism, but by no means all of it. The dispersion and Palestine are both required for the fullest development of the Jewish people. This peculiar people could not be content with either, alone. This *sui generis* organism which we call the Jewish people has need of these all-embracing, complicated forms: an intensive center and a great periphery. The complete salvation and working power of Judaism is dependent upon both together.[34]

Coda

Poet, essayist, and Wellesley College professor Marjorie Agosin writes of her parents' exiles and her own. Her mother's side fled from Nazis in Vienna, only to settle among others in Osorno, Chile. Her father's side fled tsarist Russia by way of Istanbul and Marseilles; as Allende sympathizers, they were forced to leave Chile just before the coup, and came to settle in the United States. Her memoir of her father is aptly titled *Always from Somewhere Else*.

Agosin's own exile is rooted in her Jewish identity, experienced as an individual and assuaged by language. For her, as for many artists, exile becomes a productive force.

> MARJORIE AGOSIN, *A CROSS AND A STAR* (1995)
>
> My father used to say that it was very difficult being a Jew. I still think there is a lot of truth in his words, but more than anything there is a lot of beauty and good fortune. We survived, we took refuge in the last corner of the planet in that stretch of land lost between blizzards and tides. We survived exiles, foreign tongues, and jibes from the daily inferno. We were always the "others," those foreigners who believed in the Sabbath and prayed to an irate and invisible God. We were a people of solitude with a memory like tattoos.[1]

> MARJORIE AGOSIN, "I INVENTED A COUNTRY" (1994)
>
> I dream of my grandparents' house. In my dream I still see the steps leading to the closet beneath the kitchen where all the good things to eat were kept. It was magic. In my dreams I see my grandfather

waving goodbye to me from the balcony of his house the way I saw him that last time. I knew then looking back at him and waving that I would never see him again. He died four months later. Last month I dreamed I painted my kitchen a bright yellow and it turned into my grandmother's kitchen. Often I dream I am in my childhood home, walking toward a door. I open the door looking for someone, and it's me that I see on the other side. I go looking for someone that I loved and find myself there—a younger me.

In all this I have learned that women are deeper, stronger than men in their relationships. They are capable of intimacy without too much preparation, too much hedging and insurance. During the period of exile, the women who had never worked, never supported a family, women with little education picked up the pieces of their lives and started building. They were the pillars of the family structure. They held everything together.

As for me, I have learned a lot from exile. I learned to love my country with a passion. I have learned the nooks and crannies of my language and have come to use it to give structure to my inner life. I have also learned to broaden my horizons. The world has become a smaller place. I can feel good anywhere. I have an image of carrying a home on my shoulders by carrying my language with me. I can go to Yugoslavia or Argentina and feel fine because my home is my imagination.[2]

Source Acknowledgments

Biblical citations throughout are taken from *The JPS TANAKH: Gender-Sensitive Edition* (Philadelphia: Jewish Publication Society, 2023).

1.
Midrash Tanḥuma, Pekudei 3 (5th–9th century), translated by the editors.
Moses ben Maimon (Maimonides), *Guide of the Perplexed*, translated and annotated by M. Friedländer (New York: Hebrew Publishing, 1946–60).
Don Isaac Abravanel, *Perush ʿal ha-Torah* on Genesis 3 (Jerusalem: Sefarim Torah ve-Daʿat 1964), book 1, 115a, translated by the editors.
Amos Neufeld, "Exile," *Jewish Spectator* 53, no. 2 (Summer 1988): 13.

2.
Ezekiel Landau, "Exile in Egypt versus Exile in Persia" (1782), in Marc Saperstein, *Jewish Preaching, 1200–1800* (New Haven CT: Yale University Press, 1992), 362.
Midrash Tanḥuma, Yitro 5, translated by the editors.
Pesikta Rabbati 31:4, translated by the editors.
Yalkut Shimoni, Psalms, section 883 on Ps. 137, translated by the editors.
Israel Mattuck, "How Shall We Sing," Montague Centre Collection, London Central Synagogue, UK.
Amir Gilboa, "By the Waters of Babylon," translated by Robert Alter, in "A Poet of the Holocaust," *Commentary* (November 1973), https://www.commentary.org/articles/robert-alter-2/a-poet-of-the-holocaust/, original Hebrew in *Shirim Baboker Baboker* (Tel Aviv: Hakibbutz Hameuchad, 1953), 28.
Lea Goldberg, "Night," in "Shirei Sof haDerech," poem C (Lamdeni, Elohai), *Shirim*, volume B (Tel Aviv: Sifriat Poalim, 1973), 154. ©All rights to Lea Goldberg's poems reserved to Hakibbutz Hameuchad Publishers Ltd.
Yehuda Amichai, "If I Forget Thee, Jerusalem," translated by Assia Gutman, in *Poems of Jerusalem*. Copyright 1988 by Yehuda Amichai. Used by permission of HarperCollins Publishers and the Estate of Yehuda Amichai by arrangement with the Deborah Harris Agency.
Yalkut Shimoni, Be-ḥukkotai, 6:6, translated by the editors.

SOURCE ACKNOWLEDGMENTS

Yalkut, Zechariah, in *The Yalkut on Zechariah*, by Simeon Darshan, translated with notes by Edward G. King (Cambridge: Deighton, Bell, 1882), 35, 37–38.
Shir ha-Shirim Rabbah 3:1, no. 1.
Eikhah Rabbah, Lam. R. proem 17, Lam. R. 3:14, no. 5.
Profiet Duran (the Ephodi), "Epistle of Lamentation, Grief and Consolation," in Marc Saperstein, "A Sermon on the Akedah," *Exile and Diaspora—Studies in the History of the Jewish People: Presented to Professor Haim Beinart*, edited by Aharon Mirsky, Avraham Grossman, and Yosef Kaplan (Jerusalem: Ben-Zvi, 1991).
Judah ben David ibn Yahya, "Me'orah," in *Hebrew Scholarship and the Medieval World*, edited by Nicholas de Lange (Cambridge: Cambridge University Press, 2001). Reproduced with permission of the Licensor through PLSclear.
Don Isaac Abravanel, "Letter to Yehiel of Pisa, October 4, 1482," in B. Netanyahu, *Don Isaac Abravanel: Statesman and Philosopher* (Philadelphia: Jewish Publication Society, 1968), 29.
Don Isaac Abravanel, *Ma'yenei ha-Yeshu'ah* (commentary on the book of Daniel) (Amsterdam, 1647), 349, translated by the editors.
Don Isaac Abravanel, *Zevah Pesah* (commentary on the Passover Haggadah), Psalm 116 of the *Hallel* (Verlag: Constantinople David and Samuel ibn Nahmias, 1505), translated by the editors.
Abraham Saba, "A Debate over Which Exile Is Worse" (Christianity or Islam). Published as *Eshkol ha-Kofer al Megillat Ester*, edited by Eliezer Segal (Drohobycz, Poland, 1903), 66. Translation is by Barry Dov Walfish in *Esther in Medieval Garb* (Albany NY: SUNY Press, 1993), 137–38.
Abraham P. Mendes, "The Sorrows and Consolation of Jerusalem," *Sermons* (London: John Chapman, 1855), 146–47.

3.

Pesikta Rabbati 30:2, translated by the editors.
"A Derashah on the Haftarah for the Ninth of Ab," in Vera Basch Moreen, *In Queen Esther's Garden: An Anthology of Judeo-Persian Literature*, Yale Judaica Series (New Haven CT: Yale University Press, 2000), 207–9.
David Einhorn, "For the Anniversary of the Destruction of Jerusalem," *Olat Tamid: Book of Prayers* (new translation by Emil G. Hirsch from the German original, 1921). Copyright 1896 by Julie Einhorn, part 1, 141–46.
Mordecai Ze'ev Feierberg, "Whither," in *Whither? and Other Stories*, translated by Hillel Halkin (New Milford CT and London: Toby Press, 2004), 174–85. Used with permission of the Toby Press LLC.
Aminā (Binyamin ben Misha'el), *Commentary on the Book of Esther*, in Vera Basch Moreen, *In Queen Esther's Garden: An Anthology of Judeo-Persian Literature* (New Haven CT: Yale University Press, 2000), 214–15.

SOURCE ACKNOWLEDGMENTS

Abba Hillel Silver, "But Mordecai Bowed Not Down," Cleveland, March 8, 1936, in *Therefore Choose Life* (Cleveland OH: World, 1967), 277–81.

4.

B. *Megillah* 29a, translated by the editors.

Zohar I, 84b–85a, in Isaiah Tishby, *The Wisdom of the Zohar* (Oxford: Oxford University Press, 1989), 414–16. Reproduced with permission of the Licensor through PLSclear.

R. Nachman of Breslau, "The Lost Princess," in Howard Schwartz, *Reimagining the Bible: The Storytelling of the Rabbis* (New York: Oxford University Press, 1998), 135–36. Reproduced with permission of the Licensor through PLSclear.

Isaac ben Yedaiah, "Commentary on the Aggadot of the Talmud," in Marc Saperstein, *Decoding the Rabbis: A Thirteenth-Century Commentary on the Aggadah* (Cambridge MA: Harvard University Press, 1980), 135.

Saul Levi Morteira, "Dust of the Earth" (ca. 1623). Translated in Marc Saperstein, *Exile in Amsterdam: Saul Levi Morteira's Sermons to a Congregation of "New Jews"* (Cincinnati: Hebrew Union College Press, 2005), 380–92. Used with permission of Hebrew Union College Press; permission conveyed through Copyright Clearance Center, Inc.

Saul Levi Morteira, "Giv'at Sha'ul" (Amsterdam, 1645). Translated as "Guarded Him as the Pupil of His Eye" in Marc Saperstein, *Exile in Amsterdam: Saul Levi Morteira's Sermons to a Congregation of "New Jews"* (Cincinnati: Hebrew Union College Press, 2005), 447–88. Used with permission of Hebrew Union College Press; permission conveyed through Copyright Clearance Center, Inc.

Menasseh ben Israel, "To His Highnesse the Lord Protector of the Commonwealth of England, Scotland, and Ireland," translated in Paul Mendes-Flohr and Yehuda Reinharz, *The Jew in the Modern World* (New York: Oxford University Press, 1995), 10.

Berr Isaac Berr, "Letter of a Citizen to His Fellow Jews" (1791), in Paul Mendes-Flohr and Yehuda Reinharz, *The Jew in the Modern World*, 2nd ed. (New York: Oxford University Press, 1995), 119.

Hayyim Nahman Bialik, "In the City of Slaughter," in Israel Efros, ed., *Complete Poetic Works of Hayyim Nahman Bialik* (New York: Histadruth Ivrith of America, 1948).

5.

Sanhedrin 37b, translated by the editors.

Zohar III, 115a–b, *The Wisdom of the Zohar*, 3 vols. (Oxford: Oxford University Press, 1989), 1: 421–22. Reproduced with permission of the Licensor through PLSclear.

Don Isaac Abravanel, *Perush ʿal ha-Torah*, vol. 3, Leviticus (Jerusalem: Hotsa'at Sefarim Bene Arba'el, 1964), 173b–174a; vol. 5, Deuteronomy (Jerusalem: Hotsa'at Sefarim Bene Arba'el, 1964), 262b–263a, translated by the editors.

SOURCE ACKNOWLEDGMENTS

Hermann Adler, *Naftulei Elohim: A Course of Sermons on the Biblical Passages Adduced by Christian Theologians in Support of the Dogmas of Their Faith* (London: Trübner, 1869), 42–45.

Alexander Altmann, "Sermon for Rosh Hashanah 5695" (1934). Published in *Predigten an das Judentum von heute* (Berlin: Joachim Goldstein Verlag, 1935), 13–14, translated by the editors.

Augustine, "Reply to Faustus the Manichean," in *Disputation and Dialogue: Readings in the Jewish-Christian Encounter*, edited by Frank Talmage (New York: Ktav, 1975).

Tanḥuma, Bereshit 9, translated by the editors.

Israel Brunn, *She'elot u-Teshuvot* (Responsa), nos. 265, 166 (Salonika, 1798), in *An Introduction to the History and Sources of Jewish Law*, edited by N. S. Hecht, B. S. Jackson, S. M. Passamaneck, D. Piatelli, and A. M. Rabello (Oxford: Clarendon, 1996), 347–50. Reproduced with permission of the Licensor through PLSclear.

Don Isaac Abravanel, *Sefer Naḥalat Avot*, Pirkei Avot 1.11, translated by the editors.

Moses Cordovero, *The Palm Tree of Deborah*, translated by Louis Jacobs (London: Vallentine Mitchell, 1960), chap. 9, "Malkhut," 115–16.

Israel of Koznitz, "Avodat Yisrael to VaYetzei," in Normal Lamm, *The Religious Thought of Hasidism: Text and Commentary* (New York: Yeshiva University Press, 1999), 528–29.

6.

Dunash ibn Labrat, "Reply to an Invitation to a Feast," translated by the editors.

Benjamin of Tudela, "Exilarch," translated as "The Itinerary of Benjamin of Tudela" by Nathan Adler (1907).

Solomon Levi, *Divrei Shlomo* (1573), in Marc Saperstein, *"Your Voice like a Ram's Horn": Themes and Texts in Traditional Jewish Preaching* (Cincinnati: HUC Press, 1996).

Aaron Berechiah of Modena, "Shemot," *Derashot Ma'avar Yabbok* (Jerusalem: Ahavat Shalom, 2001), 63, translated by the editors.

Saul Levi Morteira, "The People's Envy," in Marc Saperstein, *Jewish Preaching* (New Haven CT: Yale University Press, 1980).

Charles Reznikoff, "Babylon: 539 B.C.E.," from *The Poems of Charles Reznikoff: 1918–1975*, edited by Seamus Cooney. Copyright © 2005 by the Estate of Charles Reznikoff. Reprinted with the permission of The Permissions Company, LLC on behalf of Black Sparrow/David R. Godine, Publisher, Inc., godine.com.

Myron Ernst, "Exile," *Midstream*, May 1988, published by the Theodore Herzl Foundation, once associated with WIZO.

SOURCE ACKNOWLEDGMENTS

7.

Yitzhak Baer, *Galut* (New York: Schocken, 1947).

Eliezer Berkovits, "Galut, or the Breach between the Torah and Life—the Real Problem" and "Galut and Eretz Israel," in *Towards Historic Judaism* (Oxford: East and West Library, 1943), 25–36, 76–81.

Eliezer Berkovits, "Galut," in *Faith after the Holocaust* (Brooklyn: Ktav, 1973), 120–24.

Isaac ben Yedaiah, *Commentary on the Aggadot of the Talmud* (late 13th century), from Escorial Hebrew manuscript, translated by the editors.

Judah Leib (Leon) Pinsker, *Auto-Emancipation*, translated in Arthur Hertzberg, *The Zionist Idea* (Philadelphia: Jewish Publication Society, 1959, 1997), 184–86. Reprinted from *Road to Freedom*, by Leo Pinsker, edited by B. Netanyahu, translated by David Blondheim.

Amy Levy, "Captivity," in *A London Plane-Tree and Other Verse* (London: T Fisher Unwin, 1889).

Hayyim Nahman Bialik, "Indeed This People Is Grass," in *Songs from Bialik*, edited by Atar Hadari (Syracuse: Syracuse University Press, 2000), 108–9.

Joseph Hayyim Brenner, "Self-Criticism," reproduced from *The Zionist Idea*, edited by Arthur Hertzberg (Philadelphia: Jewish Publication Society, 1997).

Jacob Klatzkin, "Boundaries," reproduced from *The Zionist Idea*, edited by Arthur Hertzberg (Philadelphia: Jewish Publication Society, 1997).

Max Nussbaum, "To Travel and to Flee" (1939), in Marc Saperstein, *Agony in the Pulpit* (Cincinnati: HUC Press, 2018).

Natan Zach, "An Exile Poem," in *Keivan she-Ani ba-Sevivah* (Tel Aviv: Hakibbutz Hameuchad, 1966), translated by the editors.

Eli Amir, *Tarnegol Kapparot [Scapegoat]*, translated by Dalia Bilu (London: Weidenfield & Nicholson, 1987).

Otto Weininger, *Sex and Character* (New York: Putnam's Sons, 1906), 187–91.

Joshua Sobol, *Soul of a Jew: The Last Night of Otto Weininger* (London: W. Heinemann, 1982).

8.

Moses ibn Ezra, "Ad An ba-Galut" and "Ahar Yemei ha-Shaharut," reproduced from *Selected Poems of Moses ibn Ezra*, translated by Solomon Solis-Cohen, edited by Heinrich Brody (Philadelphia: Jewish Publication Society, 1934, 1961).

"An Anonymous Chronicle of the 1492 Expulsion." Hebrew edition: Joseph R. Hacker, publisher, *Zion* 44 (1979). English edition: *The Expulsion 1492 Chronicles*, edited by David Raphael (Carmi House Press, 1992), 46–50.

Y. L. Gordon, "In the Depths of the Seas," in Harry H. Fein, *A Harvest of Hebrew Verse: Poems of the Cultural Renaissance and National Revival* (Boston: Bruce Humphries, 1934), 41–44.

SOURCE ACKNOWLEDGMENTS

Bābā'ī ibn Lutf, "How the Grand Vizier Found a Pretext against the Jews of Isfahan and Drove Them out of Their Homes," in Vera B. Moreen, *Iranian Jewry's Hour of Peril and Heroism: A Study of Bābāī ibn Lutf's Chronicle (1617–1662)* (New York: American Academy for Jewish Research, 1987).

Isaac Bashevis Singer, *Love and Exile: The Early Years—a Memoir* (London: Jonathan Cape, Penguin Books, 1986), 256–58.

Andre Aciman, *Out of Egypt: A Memoir* (New York: Picador, 2007), 300, 314–15, 327, 338, 339.

Dina Elenbogen, "Exile: Losing the Motherland," *Tikkun*, March 1999.

Sophia Parnok, "Hagar," from Noam Sienna, ed., *A Rainbow Thread* (2019). Reprinted with the permission of Print-O-Craft Press.

Lea Goldberg, "Fragment," from "Bamidbar," Poem A ("Sgor Hachol Vehaeven"), *Hashirim Hagnuzim* (Bnei Brak, Israel: Sifriat Poalim, 2019), 279. ©All rights to Lea Goldberg's poems reserved to Hakibbutz Hameuchad Publishers Ltd.

Edward W. Said, "Palestine, Then and Now: An Exile's Journey through Israel and the Occupied Territories," *Harper's Magazine*, December 1992, 47–55.

9.

Anton Shammas, "On Exile and Literature," *Agra* 2 (1986), 67–70.

Eva Hoffman, *Lost in Translation: A Life in a New Language* (New York: Dutton, 1989).

Haviva Pedaya, "A Man Walks," in *Diyo Adam* (Tel Aviv: Hakibbutz Hameuchad, 2009), translated by the editors.

Salman Masalha, "I Write Hebrew," translated by Vivian Eden, *Ariel: The Israel Review of Arts and Letters* 104 (Jerusalem: Israeli Foreign Affairs Ministry, 1997).

Giora Leshem, "My Mother's Tongue Is Not My Mother Tongue," translated by Karen Alkalay-Gut.

10.

Daniel al-Kumisi, "Appeal to the Karaites of the Dispersion to Come and Settle in Jerusalem," in Leon Nemoy, *Karaite Anthology* (New Haven CT: Yale University Press, 1952).

Jehudah Halevi, "My Heart Is in the East," in *Selected Poems of Jehudah Halevi*, translated by Nina Salaman (Philadelphia: Jewish Publication Society, 1928).

Heinrich Heine, "Jehudah ben Halevy," in *Complete Poems*, translated by Edgar Alfred Bowring (London: George Bell & Sons, 1908).

Theodor Herzl, *Der Judenstaat*, in *A Portrait for This Age*, edited by Ludwig Lewisohn, translated by Sylvie D'Avigdor (The Jewish State) and Maurice Samuel (the passages from the diaries); revised by Ben Halpern and Moshe Kohn (Cleveland: World, 1955).

SOURCE ACKNOWLEDGMENTS

Moses Leib Lilienblum, "Derekh Teshuvah," in Lucy S. Dawidowicz, *The Golden Tradition: Jewish Life and Thought in Eastern Europe* (New York: Holt, Rinehart & Winston, 1967), 128-29.

Ahad Ha'am, "The Negation of the Diaspora," reproduced from *The Zionist Idea*, edited by Arthur Hertzberg (Philadelphia: Jewish Publication Society, 1997).

Rina Shani, "I Am in the East and My Heart Is in the East" ["Ani Bamizraḥ ve'Libi Bamizraḥ"], in *Shalom le-Adoni Hamelekh* [Farewell to a king] (Tel Aviv: Am Oved, 1970), 46, translated by the editors. Reproduced by permission of Tamar Gabay-Eitan.

A. B. Yehoshua, "Exile as a Neurotic Solution," in *Diaspora: Exile and the Contemporary Jewish Condition*, edited by Étan Levine (Tel Aviv.: Shapolsky Books, 1986).

Eva Hoffman, "Out of Exile: Some Thoughts on Exile as a Dynamic Condition," *European Judaism: A Journal for the New Europe* 46, no. 2 (Autumn 2013): 55–60.

Moses ben Nahman (Nachmanides), "Disputation of Barcelona," *Kitvei Ramban*, edited by Charles Chavel, 2 vols. (Jerusalem: Mosad ha-Rav Kook, 1963), 1:310, translated by the editors.

Dov Baer (the Maggid of Mezritch), "Harḥek mish'khen raʿ," in *Maggid Devarav le-Ya'aqov*, edited by Rivka Schatz Uffenheimer (Jerusalem: Magnes Press, 1990), 70

Simon Dubnow, "The Affirmation of the Diaspora," reproduced from *The Zionist Idea*, edited by Arthur Hertzberg (Philadelphia: Jewish Publication Society, 1997).

Judah Magnes, "Like All the Nations?," reproduced from *The Zionist Idea*, edited by Arthur Hertzberg (Philadelphia: Jewish Publication Society, 1997).

Coda

Marjorie Agosin, *A Cross and a Star: Memoirs of a Jewish Girl in Chile*, translated by Celeste Kostopulos-Cooperman (Albuquerque: University of New Mexico Press, 1995).

Marjorie Agosin, "I Invented a Country," in Mahnaz Afkhami, *Women in Exile* (Charlottesville: University Press of Virginia, 1994), 140-49.

Notes

Introduction
1. Ravnitsky and Bialik, *Sefer ha-Aggadah*; English translation by Braude, *Book of Legends*.

1. Exile as Human Condition
1. Eisen, *Galut*, xiv.
2. Simpson, *Oxford Book of Exile*, vii.
3. See Ravnitzky and Bialik, *Book of Legends*, 575–76.
4. Maimonides, *Guide for the Perplexed*, part 1, chap. 2, 38.
5. Abravanel, *Perush ʿal ha-Torah*, 1:115a.
6. Amos Neufeld, "Exile," *Jewish Spectator*, Summer 1988, 13.

2. Exile in Ancient History
1. *The JPS TANAKH: Gender-Sensitive Edition.*
2. Saperstein, *Jewish Preaching*, 361–63.
3. The reference is to the Austrian emperor Joseph II and the famous "Edict of Tolerance" promulgated on January 2, 1782, several months before this sermon was delivered. A convenient though abridged text of the edict is in Mendes-Flohr and Reinharz, *Jew in the Modern World*, 34–36. The full sermon can be found in Saperstein, *Jewish Preaching*, 361–73.
4. *The JPS TANAKH: Gender-Sensitive Edition.*
5. Collected in Ravnitsky and Bialik, *Book of Legends*, 148.
6. The Assyrian king Sennacherib conquered the Northern Kingdom of Israel in 722 BCE. He imposed a siege on Jerusalem in 701 but failed to capture the city; the biblical account credits divine intervention by an angel. Later he was murdered by two of his sons.
7. Apparently based on the phrase "the lowest of men" (*shefal anashim*) in Daniel 4:14.
8. *Pesikta Rabbati* 31:4.
9. Collected in Ravnitsky and Bialik, *Book of Legends*, 149.
10. For full information about Mattuck's life and work, see Fox, *Israel Isidor Mattuck*.

NOTES TO PAGES 24-33

11. From the papers at the Liberal Judaism headquarters at Montagu Centre, London, UK.
12. Cf. Bargad's translation: "Who is the stutterer here, / Wild animals, and how do you [dare to] stutter?" The poet plays upon three associated Hebrew roots: *'alag* (stutter), *la'ag* (mock), and *lahag* (talk nonsense, gibberish). Bargad, *"To Write the Lips of Sleepers,"* 144.
13. Trans. Robert Alter.
14. Gideon Ticotsky points out that the poem also refers to a song popular in the Second Aliyah period, "Sing to us poets / only songs that awaken / sing us songs of Zion!" (Yisrael Dushman, 1911), also clearly a reference to the psalm. See Ticotsky, *Representations*, 76–77.
15. Goldberg, *Shirim bi-Tel Aviv*, 219. First published in *Me'asef Davar* 5716 (1955–56): 219B.
16. Amichai, *Poems of Jerusalem*, 12–13.
17. *Yalkut Shimoni, Be-ḥukkotai*, 6:6.
18. King, *Yalkut on Zechariah*, 35, 37–38.
19. *Shir ha-Shirim Rabbah* 3:1, no. 1.
20. Lam. R. proem 17, Lam. R. 3:14, no. 5.
21. The talmudic passage presents a long conservation between God and Abraham in the context of the destruction of the Temple by the Babylonians. Abraham defends the Jews; God cites biblical passages about their sinfulness but promises that "Israel will flourish at the end of time."
22. The context is of course the massive attacks against the Jews of Christian Spain in 1391. Many Jews agreed to convert to Christianity in order to save their lives (see Baer, *History*, 2:150–58).
23. The phrase *ha-'ones hagamur* would appear to reflect the canon-law term "absolute compulsion (*coaction absoluta*)," which invalidates baptism. According to canon law, however, baptism accepted because of fear and threats of violence would not be in this category, which applies only to those who are baptized against their will and despite their ongoing protests.
24. Saperstein, "Sermon on the Akedah," 103–24.
25. Following the talmudic statement (b. *Shabbat* 156a and elsewhere) "ein mazal le-Yisra'el" ("there is no constellation for Israel" [i.e., that determines the fate of Israel]).
26. Cf. Jer. 8:23.
27. Cf. Jer. 8:20.
28. The traditional date for the destruction of the Temple, and thus the beginning of the "long exile," was 68 CE, indicating that the poem would have been written in 1428.

29. This may be, as Van Bekkum suggests, simply playing with round numbers that have no precise chronological significance. If the number was intended to be taken seriously, it would suggest a tradition that the first Christian churches dated from the year 38 CE (thirty years before the destruction of the Temple) and have remained protected ever since.
30. De Lange, *Hebrew Scholarship*, 164–65.
31. Abravanel's terminology is misleading throughout this passage. Isabella was not a royal "consort," but the queen of Castile; indeed the Edict of Expulsion is issued by "King Ferdinand and Queen Isabella, by the grace of God, King and Queen of Castile, Leon, Aragon, Sicily" and other specified realms. Abravanel certainly knew this, and his insulting diminution of the status of Isabella appears to reflect a personal animus toward the queen as the initiator of the expulsion. On this trend among contemporary Jewish writers, see Yosef Hayim Yerushalmi's formulation: "With virtual unanimity the Jewish writers clearly differentiate between the king and the queen, and heap almost all the blame upon the latter" (*Lisbon Massacre*, 53–56).
32. Abravanel, introduction to commentary on 1 Kings.
33. The occasion of this letter was the death of the recipient's wife (Netanyahu, *Don Isaac Abravanel*, 29). "Weep not for the dead" is a topos in Jewish ethical and homiletical literature, but it usually highlights the peace and reward of the deceased. The assertion that Jewish life in exile is so dismal that it is better for a Jew to be dead than alive goes considerably beyond the requirement of the occasion and genre to provide some form of comfort.
34. Netanyahu, *Don Isaac Abravanel*, 29.
35. See b. *Sanhedrin* 5a.
36. *Ma'yenei ha-Yeshu'ah*, 349.
37. *Zevaḥ Pesaḥ*, Psalm 116 of the *Hallel*, the editors' translation.
38. For a stunning articulation of this, applied to the unique well-being of the Amsterdam community, see the sermon in Saperstein, *Exile in Amsterdam*, 402–4.
39. For a review of many sources, see Septimus, "Hispano-Jewish Views" 43–65.
40. Maimonides, "Epistle to Yemen," 241–42.
41. Joshua Soncino was rabbi of the Sephardi Great Synagogue in Constantinople; died in 1569. Soncino, *Naḥalah li-Yhoshua*, 45a, col. 2.
42. Walfish, *Esther*, 138.
43. Most historians would maintain that the level of anti-Jewish violence was in general higher in Christian Europe than in Islamic lands, especially during the period between 1096 and 1500.
44. Compare the story told by an early fifteenth-century Jewish preacher cited in Saperstein, *Jewish Preaching*, 96, and the sources for this common motif ("words worse than wounds") in n. 15.

45. Another strange assertion (that Jews in Islamic lands do not understand the language of their neighbors), perhaps referring more to recent emigrants from the Iberian Peninsula to the Maghreb.
46. Saba, *Eshkol ha-Kofer al Megillat Ester*, Esther 3:8,66; cited in Walfish, *Esther*, 137–38.
47. Meaning "internal with regard to a country or people." Mendes, following a rabbinic tradition, sees internal Jewish conflict as the cause of disaster.
48. Gessius Florus, the last procurator of Judea, starting from 64 CE, is described by a modern historian as "the perverse climax of a long line of corrupt and vicious officials" (Zeitlin, *Rise and Fall*, 2:230, based on Josephus, *Wars of the Jews*, bk. 2, 14, 2).
49. Cestius Gallus, the Roman legate of Syria, who had led the Roman Twelfth Legion to suppress the incipient Jewish revolt and was decisively defeated at Bet Horon on November 25, 65 CE, a date commemorated in the *Megillat Ta'anit*. See Josephus, *Wars of the Jews*, bk. 2, 19, and Zeitlin, *Rise and Fall*, 2:243–47.
50. Note the ambivalence in the description: the preacher seems to exult in the notion of the love of liberty inspiring the heroic valor of the Jewish rebels, yet he concedes at the outset that the uprising is "pregnant with evil" consequences for the Jewish people.
51. Cf. Josephus, *Wars of the Jews*, bk. 6, 3, 4.
52. Josephus, *Wars of the Jews*, bk. 6, 4, 2–5: "As the flames went upward, the Jews made a great clamour, such as so mighty an affliction required."
53. This sentence, and the following, express concisely what the historian Salo Baron has termed "the lachrymose conception of Jewish history." See Baron, *History and Jewish Historians*, 84, 96, and frequently elsewhere in his work.
54. The sword and the fire perhaps evoke the massacres of the First Crusade and the persecution by the Iberian inquisitions, two familiar emblems of Jewish suffering in exile.
55. Mendes, *Sermons*, 146–47.

3. Exile and Holidays

1. The last verse is repeated in the published translation presumably to end on a positive note, as per tradition. *JPS TANAKH: Gender-Sensitive Edition*.
2. The Masoretic text should be translated, *For your sake I have sent to Babylon*. The Rabbis here and in the Talmud (b. *Megillah* 29a) read the verse as if it were vocalized differently to make a passive or reflexive form: "I have been sent to Babylon."
3. *Pesikta Rabbati* 30, 2.
4. Moreen, *In Queen Esther's Garden*, 210.

5. Heb. *kelippot* (shards, shells), a term associated especially with Lurianic Kabbalah (cf. Scholem, *Kabbalah*, especially 138–39) [original endnote].
6. Aram., *sitra ahra* (the domain of dark emanations and dark powers), another kabbalistic term associated especially with Lurianic Kabbalah (cf. Scholem, *Kabbalah*, 123–28) [original endnote].
7. Moreen, *In Queen Esther's Garden*, 207, 208–9.
8. See Wachs, *American Jewish Liturgies*, nos. 76–80, 207–8, 518, 1087.
9. Meyer, *Response to Modernity*, 254.
10. Similar to the sermon of Abraham P. Mendes (see chapter 2 herein), this is a powerful formulation of Baron's aforementioned "lachrymose conception of Jewish history," presenting the entire experience of the Jews in exile as a series of uninterrupted persecutions.
11. Echoing 2 Sam. 1:23 and the liturgy.
12. This sentence is the first to reverse the traditional bleak presentation of exile. Above, he had written that the Jews in exile were "like sons disowned by their father," but now the shift is made to the idea of the Diaspora as a mission.
13. Note the teleological formulation: the subsequent establishment of synagogues (or "temples") scattered throughout the world was not just the consequence but the *purpose* for which God ordained the destruction of the Temple in Jerusalem.
14. Echoing Mic. 6:7.
15. Echoing Isa. 53:2–3 and 5, based on the assumption that the "suffering servant" described in that last passage is a personification of the Jewish people, whose suffering brings healing to the sinful afflictors.
16. Referring to Zech. 8:18, in which the fast days associated with the Babylonian assault on Jerusalem are commanded to be transformed into days of rejoicing with the return to the Land of Israel. Einhorn applies the transformation to the contemporary Diaspora, a process reminiscent of Sabbati Zevi's order in the summer of 1666 that the Ninth Day of Av be celebrated as a day of rejoicing in the advent of the Messiah.
17. A jibe at the incipient Zionist movement, or the earlier movement of Hovevei Zion, which fostered the return of Jews to the Land of Israel.
18. Einhorn, *Olat Tamid*, part 1, 141–46.
19. See Mintz, *Banished*, 57–58.
20. Translator's note: "to reenact the battles for the Temple fought on the Ninth of Av."
21. In the original, *Taytsch Chumesh*, the term used for a large number of translations of the Pentateuch (and sometimes the Five Scrolls, including Lamentations) into Judeo-German with expansions from the midrash and legendary material. The most famous was *Tsenah u-Re'enah*.

NOTES TO PAGES 58-70

22. In the original Hebrew, "to read in the evening the Scroll of Lamentations and *Churbn Beis ha-Mikdash*," a Yiddish narrative of the destruction based on rabbinic *aggadot*; see, e.g., *Tsenah u-Re'enah*, 792–806.
23. Again the word *aḥer*, alluding to the paradigmatic heretic.
24. All traditional expressions of mourning for the Ninth Day of Av, a total reversal of the ordinary.
25. This is one of the most poignant depictions of the loss of faith and (to use Pascal's phrase) "the misery of man without God" in modern Hebrew literature. The contrast between the God of Aristotle and the God of the Patriarchs and prophets is characteristic of Judah Halevi (e.g., *Kuzari* 1, 11), but the author also seems to reveal the influence of a celebrated passage in Blaise Pascal's *Mémorial*: "God of Abraham, God of Isaac, God of Jacob. Not the God of the philosophers." Cf. on this passage Mintz, *Banished*, 85–87.
26. A common phrase in kabbalistic and mystical literature. The original Hebrew continues with a phrase from the Zohar, "and to bring about a stirring on High."
27. The image of the Jew as spiritual soldier in the battle to bring the Messiah against the forces of evil is a central motif early in the book; see Feierberg, "Whither?," 155–57, 159–62; Mintz, *Banished*, 82–83.
28. Feierberg, "Whither?," 174.
29. *The JPS TANAKH: Gender-Sensitive Edition*.
30. Kay Khosrow is a character in the *Shahnameh*, the Persian epic of kings. He was the son of Siavash.
31. King Solomon's vizier (according to Moreen); Asaph the Jew (also known as Asaph the doctor) has been associated with the legendary Asif ibn Barkhiya of Arabian folklore.
32. Muslim term—generally Shi'i—for the Messiah.
33. Moreen, *In Queen Esther's Garden*, 214–15.
34. Silver, *Therefore Choose Life*, 277–81.

4. Divine Presence in Exile

1. By the remains of the flow of influence that descended upon Israel, per Tishby, *Wisdom of the Zohar*.
2. To the domain of "the other side" (*sitra ahra*), the realm of evil, per Tishby, *Wisdom of the Zohar*.
3. Guardian angel, per Tishby, *Wisdom of the Zohar*.
4. When incense is offered to God, a unifying link is effected among the *sefirot* (varied manifestations of the Godhead in kabbalistic thought), bridging the gap between the totally hidden and unknowable God and our world. When the *sefirot* offered incense to the pagan gods, this served to link the *Shekhinah* with "the other side." See Tishby, *Wisdom of the Zohar*.

5. The *sefirot*, varied manifestations of the Godhead in kabbalistic thought, bridge the gap between the totally hidden and unknowable God and the our world, per Tishby, *Wisdom of the Zohar*.
6. The Rabbinic view is that each nation has a guardian angel (*sar*), which determines the fortune of that nation in history. Yet the power of these guardian angels is ultimately derived from God through contact with the Divine Presence (*Shekhinah*).
7. The Rabbinic view is that prophecy occurs only in the Land of Israel or (as in Ezekiel's case) for the sake of the Land of Israel. See Lauterbach, *Mekhilta de-Rabbi Ishmael*, 1:4, 6–7. The following sentence about Jonah may be based on this passage.
8. Translation based on Tishby, *Wisdom of the Zohar*, 1:414–15.
9. Schwartz, *Reimagining the Bible*, 135–36.
10. I.e., earning one's livelihood through crafts requires many hours devoted to work, leaving little time for the study of Torah necessary to preserve Jewish identity in the dispersion.
11. Saperstein, *Decoding the Rabbis*, 135.
12. This book was published several times in the sixteenth century: in Constantinople (1543), Ferara (1556), and Friburg (1583). For other statements indicating a belief in a huge population of Jews scattered throughout the world, see Biale, *Cultures of the Jews*, 413, 519. For a very different polemical use of the material in Benjamin's *Travels*, see Glaser, "Invitation to Intolerance," 342n77.
13. For precedents of this idea, see Levi ben Abraham, "Livyat Ḥen," 147n90; Gerondi, *Derashot ha-Ran*, 6 (on the Tower of Babel); Abravanel, *Yeshu'ot Meshiḥo*, 11a; Usque, *Consolation*, 227: "By scattering you among all peoples, He made it impossible for the world to destroy you, for if one kingdom rises against you in Europe to inflict death upon you, another in Asia allows you to live." See also Mordecai Dato's teachings, cited in Jacobson, *Bi-Netivei Galuyot u-Ge'ulot*, 144.
14. Note Morteira's characteristic recapitulation, signaling to the listeners that one section of his sermon structure is ending and helping them remember the components included within it.
15. Cf. Zohar 2, 16b: "Why is Israel subjected to all nations? In order that the world may be preserved through them."
16. Saperstein, *Exile in Amsterdam*, 380–92.
17. Compare Menasseh ben Israel's statement in his *Conciliator*, 2:185, question 29: "Among all the nations of the world, only the Israelites can be really termed noble, for the honourable titles they enjoy were conferred by [God]." Two decades later, in his "Humble Addresses" (1655), he writes that one of the three qualities that make a foreign people "well-beloved amongst the Natives of a

land where they dwell" is "the Nobleness and purity of their blood." Later in this work, he states that the "nobility of the Jews . . . is enough known amongst all Christians" that there is no need to discuss it in detail. Both passages are cited by Kaplan, "Political Concepts," 50–51.

18. Echoing Genesis 34:9, where Hamor the Hivite makes a similar proposal.
19. The view that the gentiles' cordial interaction with Jews leads to assimilation and the disappearance of the Jewish population is reminiscent of Spinoza's claim (*Theologico-Political Treatise*, 46) that the population of "New Christians" in Spain "so speedily assimilated to the Spaniards that after a short while no trace of them was left."
20. This claim that hatred of Jews is unnatural, and that God providentially reversed the natural sociological order by making gentiles hate Jews in order to ensure their survival, bears natural comparison with Spinoza's assertion (*Theologico-Political Treatise*, 45) that Jews are preserved in their separate identity by the hatred of the gentiles, as historical experience shows. For fuller annotation on this passage, see Saperstein, *Exile in Amsterdam*, 481n83.
21. I.e., God implanted an unnatural hatred of the Jews in the hearts of the gentiles, but their hostility toward the Jews went beyond what God intended, requiring a form of providential protection against excessive danger.
22. Saperstein, *Exile in Amsterdam*, 476–84.
23. I.e., divine providence bestowed upon the Jews a "natural instinct" toward successful economic activity, but the Jews themselves activated this potential given their need for economic survival in the lands of their dispersion.
24. "Canaanite" in the final verse of Zechariah was understood to mean "trader" or "merchant," based on Hosea 12:4. Thus the conclusion is that in the Messianic Age, Jews will no longer exercise their talent for "merchandizing." This skill solely enabled them to survive economically in the exile, when the purchase of real estate was unadvisable given the frequent need for emigration.
25. Mendes-Flohr and Reinharz, *Jew in the Modern World*, 10.
26. See, for example, the striking formulation by Jacob Rader Marcus: "The medieval age comes to an end for Western Jewry with the proclamation of political and civil emancipation in France in September, 1791" (Mendes-Flohr and Reinharz, *Jew in the Modern World*, xxv). The text below corroborates this view from a contemporaneous perspective. For a recent study questioning the importance of the decree to which Berr is responding, see Schechter, *Obstinate Hebrews*, 151–53.
27. Undoubtedly a reference to the French National Assembly's "Declaration of the Rights of Man and of the Citizen," passed on August 26, 1789.
28. The author chooses paradigms of persecutors only from antiquity, and not such familiar Roman villains as Vespasian and Hadrian.

29. Berr goes on to discuss the second main topic of his letter: "what remains to be done, on our part, to become truly happy, and how we may be able to show, in some measure, our grateful sense for all the favors heaped upon us." By this he refers to demonstrating Jewish gratitude not to God, Whom he holds as ultimately responsible for the great event, but to the French Assembly. He then outlines the changes in Jewish behavior that will be necessary to fulfill the Jews' responsibilities given their new status. For the full letter see Tama, *Transactions*, 11–29.
30. Efros, *Complete Poetic Works of Hayyim Nahman Bialik*, 1:129–43.

5. Exile as Penance and Atonement

1. Sanhedrin 37b.
2. William Davidson Talmud, Sanhedrin 37b, Sefaria, Sefaria.org/Sanhedrin37b.13.
3. Translation based on Tishby, *Wisdom of the Zohar*, 1:421–22; see also Matt, *Zohar*, 158–60.
4. Abravanel, *Perush ʿal ha-Torah*, 3:173b–174a (editors' translation).
5. Abravanel, *Perush ʿal ha-Torah*, 5:262b–263a (editors' translation).
6. In one of the sermons, he described Societies for Promoting Christianity among Jews as turning "bad Jews into worse Christians" (April 25, 1868), 2.
7. Adler, *Naftulei Elohim*, 42–45.
8. A rather painfully optimistic evaluation of the present and future for German Jewry. Despite the strong repudiation of Jewish life in *Golus* and the apparent endorsement of Zionism as the authentic solution to Jewish suffering, when he left Germany Altmann spent the rest of his life in England and the United States.
9. Altmann, *Predigten*, 13–14 (editors' translation).
10. *The JPS TANAKH: Gender-Sensitive Edition.*
11. Augustine, in Talmage, *Disputation*, 30–31.
12. Original editor's interpolation: apparently Nissan had been seated. The first blow left him unable to rise. Simḥah's coup de grâce left Nissan dying on the floor.
13. The respondent summarizes the most pertinent material in what must have been a document recording the testimonies sent by the questioner. After the testimony implicating Naḥman and Simḥah, further testimony is reported, perhaps for the defense: Simḥah was drunk (and possibly unaware of what he was doing), Nissan (the victim) was ignorant and unobservant, and actually initiated the violent confrontation.
14. Confession is not admissible in Jewish law as a proof of guilt, and is therefore introduced here only as proof that Simḥah was not so drunk that he did not know what he had done.

15. Original editor's note: i.e., the meditation that describes God as merciful—*raḥum*—and a pardoner of sins; this occurs immediately before the commencement of the formal liturgy, the call to worship.
16. For evidence of this humiliating penitential ritual in early seventeenth-century Amsterdam, see Acosta, *Example of a Human Life*, 91. Acosta indicates that the flogging was not just symbolic; at least on one occasion he was publicly given thirty-nine lashes "according to the Jewish custom" (91).
17. An additional piece of information not included in the summary of the "Question."
18. Original editor's interpolation: i.e., hostages held by gentiles. Israel of Brunn was himself twice imprisoned by governmental authorities, once as a hostage to ensure the Jews of Regensburg paid a special "crown tax" and the second time because an apostate accused him of being involved in the murder of a Christian child. Bazak, *Jewish Law*, xxxix.
19. Original editor's interpolation: i.e., the quorum for worship, see b. *Makkot* 23a. For an example of exile as punishment for killing being lightened when there existed compelling reasons to believe it was not intentional, see the Responsum of Meir ben Gedaliah (Maharam) of Lublin in Saperstein and Marcus, *Jews in Christian Europe*, 609–11. See also Hecht et al., *Introduction*, 347–50.
20. Abravanel, *Sefer Naḥalat Avot*, 72–74 (editors' translation).
21. Cordovero, *Palm Tree*, 115–16.
22. *Avodah Zara* 8a.
23. Lamm, *Religious Thought*, 528–29.

6. Life in Exile

1. *The JPS TANAKH: Gender-Sensitive Edition*.
2. Dunash ibn Labrat, "Reply to an Invitation to a Feast," newly translated by the editors.
3. Benjamin of Tudela, *Itinerary of Benjamin of Tudela*, 99–102.
4. Saperstein, *"Your Voice Like a Ram's Horn,"* 29.
5. Cf. Exod. Rabbah 1:28, Lev. Rabbah 32:5, and parallels: "R. Huna stated in the name of Bar Kappara, [the People of] Israel were redeemed from Egypt on account of four things: because they did not change their names, they did not change their language, they did not go tale-bearing, and none of them was found to have been immoral." Maharal of Prague cites Midrash *Tanḥuma Balaq* 16 as "They did not change their names, they did not change their style of clothing" (*Netzaḥ Yisra'el*, 126a).
6. For this preacher, the increase in population and the spreading in space noted in Exod. 1:11 are positive qualities showing God's favor.
7. Unlike the other transformations, this is rather intricate: apparently Shimshon (Samson), the god of the sun (*shemesh*), becomes Dio Febo, "the god Phoebus

[Apollo]," the god of light. Diofebo was not uncommon as an Italian name; the use of the Hebrew name Uri ("my light") as an equivalent for Feibush appears to be analogous.

8. On the names of Italian Jews, see Roth, *Jews in the Renaissance*, 19-20; Bonfil, *Jewish Life*, 240-41. The preacher's own grandmother (the wife of a rabbi) was named Fioretta, and her sister Diana; his mother's name was Imperia. See Modena, *Autobiography*, 79.
9. On legal requirements for Italian Jews to wear distinctive hats, see Ravid, "From Yellow to Red," 179-210; and other clothing, Cassen, *Marking the Jews*.
10. It is not clear how to translate this anomalous phrase. The preacher seems to be referring to a legal requirement that Jewish community records be kept not in Hebrew but in the vernacular language, and he sees this as a punishment for Jewish neglect of the Hebrew language. In 1631 the Venetian senate ordered a translation of the Jewish community's entire *Libro Grande* into Italian because a "theological jurisconsult" of the government condemned one statute contained in it, but the preacher could not be referring to this for obvious chronological reasons. See Malkiel, *Separate Republic*, 31-33.
11. Aaron Berechiah, *Derashot Ma'avar Yabbok*, 63 (editors' translation).
12. See the discussion of this verse by Leibowitz, *Studies in Shemot*, 1:13 and 20-21.
13. See Solomon Alami's critique of Spanish Jewry in the early fifteenth century: "Because we have built here in Exile, upon the ruins of our holy temple, luxurious houses and beautiful and spacious chambers, we have been banished from our homes to the field and the dung gate" ("Iggeret Musar," quoted in Baer, *History*, 2:241).
14. Note the twofold explanation of the sin: theologically, it is conduct inappropriate in exile, arousing God's anger; sociologically, it arouses the hostility of gentile neighbors in the host country.
15. Ostentatious dress was a subject of both communal regulation and social criticism in most European countries. For an overview, see Baron, *Jewish Community*, 2:301-7. For the Spanish tradition, see the statutes passed by the synod at Valladolid in 1432 (Baer, *History*, 2:269) and ibn Verga, *Shevet Yehudah*, 47. Extravagance of attire was also a constant theme in Christian preaching of social criticism from the twelfth to the seventeenth century.
16. According to this view, the Israelites did not have to suffer real slavery. It became necessary because they failed to learn the proper lesson from their experience of forced labor under taskmasters, a lesser degree of servitude.
17. Saperstein, *Jewish Preaching*, 272-85.
18. Ps. 137:1-2.
19. Gen. 50:20.
20. Exod. 16:3.

21. Joel 1:4.
22. Deut. 28:38.
23. 1 Sam. 17:50.
24. Reznikoff, *In Memoriam*, 11–14.
25. Myron Ernst, "Exile," *Midstream*, May 1988, 6.

7. Internalized Exile

1. Baer, *Galut*, 9–10.
2. Baer, *Galut*, 122–23.
3. Berkovits, *Towards Historic Judaism*, 33.
4. Berkovits, *Towards Historic Judaism*, 77–78.
5. The quotation is taken from Baer, *Galut*, 26; no source is provided there.
6. From the *Musaf* service of the High Holy Days, festivals, and the new month.
7. See *Berakhot* 59a.
8. Berkovits, *Faith after the Holocaust*, 120–24.
9. On this author and his work, see Saperstein, *Decoding the Rabbis*.
10. B. *Sanhedrin* 75a.
11. In this excerpt, bracketed biblical citations follow paraphrased references, while parenthesized biblical citations follow quotations.
12. B. *Ketubot* 61b, 62a. The context is a discussion of how frequently the husband must have sexual relations with his wife to meet his responsibility to fulfill his wife's "marital rights" (*'onatah*, Exod. 21:10). The frequency depends upon the husband's occupation.
13. In the original context of Proverbs, the verse *Stolen water is sweet, and bread eaten in secret is pleasurable* (9:17) is presented as the false enticement with which Folly ensnares the ignorant. The commentator, explaining the Talmud's use of the verse, recasts it into a psychological truth about human behavior.
14. Ben Yedaiah, *Commentary on the Aggadot of the Talmud* (manuscript, editors' translation).
15. Hertzberg, *Zionist Idea*, 184–86.
16. Levy, *London Plane-Tree*, 62–63.
17. Klausner, *Haim Nahman Bialik*, 49.
18. This may refer to the poet's disappointment over the lack of a popular Jewish response to pre-Herzl Zionist writers such as Judah Leib Pinsker. Here and in the following verses Bialik uses the biblical language of "God's voice" thundering, but not in a traditionalist, fundamentalist sense. God's voice, in Bialik's era, demands the negation and repudiation of the exile.
19. Better, "a foolish people" (*am eviyl*), but not "idle" in its preoccupation with the "idols of gold"—contemporary materialism is held to be a manifestation of the paradigmatic Golden Calf disgrace.

20. Better, "schooled in the rod and the whip" (*limmud shevet va-shot*), referring to the people, the subject of the following phrase.
21. Better, "than its immediate concerns" (*milvad de'agat ha-yom*), rather than thinking of the future.
22. The language evokes the traditional messianic expectation by echoing one of the benedictions of the *Amidah* prayer.
23. Bialik, *Songs from Bialik*, 108–9.
24. The historian and political scientist Zeev Sternhell characterized Brenner as "the greatest Hebrew writer of his time (some say of all time)." Sternhell, *Founding Myths*, 38.
25. Hertzberg, *Zionist Idea*, 310–11.
26. Hertzberg, *Zionist Idea*, 322–25.
27. This last sentence is obviously a contemporary reference to the SS *St. Louis*, which departed from Hamburg in May 1939 with some 937 Jewish refugees, bound for Havana, only to be informed that the Cuban government had altered its immigration policy and would not allow nearly all the passengers to disembark.
28. Saperstein, *Agony in the Pulpit*, 453–54. Menachem Mendel was the name of many important rabbis, but here it alludes to a Sholem Aleichem character who repeatedly attempts to get rich, only to fail abysmally.
29. Zach, *Keivan she-Ani ba-Sevivah*, 52; 2 Kings 2:23. Also in Mendele Mokher Sefarim (S. Y. Abramovitch), "Burned Out," 17–27. So too, the sounds of the Hebrew phrase *'aleh kereach*, translated here as "Go away, old fool" (literally "Go up, baldy"), echo *Allah Karim*, Arabic for "God is great."
30. Ballas, *Ha-Ma'abarah*, 76.
31. Amir, *Tarnegol Kapparot*, 121–22.
32. Amir, *Tarnegol Kapparot*, 125.
33. Weininger, *Sex and Character*, 187–91.
34. Sobol, *Soul of a Jew*, 76.
35. Sobol, *Soul of a Jew*, 82.

8. Medieval and Modern History

1. See reference to the Anakites in Num. 13:22,33; Deut. 2:11; Josh. 15:13–14; Judg. 1:20.
2. Cf. Ps. 137:5.
3. A stream in the Golan Heights that—together with the Dan and Banias—would become the Jordan River.
4. Ibn Ezra, *Selected Poems of Moses ibn Ezra*, 2–5, 10.
5. Scholar of Ottoman Jewry and Hebrew University professor emeritus Joseph Hacker has identified the author of this excerpt as "Rabbi Abraham ibn Yaish, a

prominent Iberian exiled scholar who lived in Istanbul" from a 1505 colophon. Personal communication, February 20, 2023, with editor Nancy Berg.
6. Cf. Num. 11:3, Deut. 9:22.
7. Raphael, *Expulsion 1492 Chronicles*, 46–50.
8. Fein, *Harvest of Hebrew Verse*, 41–44.
9. Āṣaf is the name of King Solomon's prime minister in Islamic lore. It is a frequently used appellation for a Muslim grand vizier in Islamic literature [original note].
10. Probably referring to periodic prohibitions in various Muslim lands against new buildings or repairs of non-Muslim abodes and religious houses of worship. [According to Moreen] there is no evidence that such a prohibition [was] in effect at this time [original note].
11. Moreen, *Iranian Jewry's Hour*, 182, 185–91.
12. The Swedish explorer Sven Hedin was known for many expeditions to Central Asia. Roald Amundsen, from Norway, was famous for his expeditions to the South and North Poles. Robert Falcon Scott, a British Royal Navy officer who led expeditions to Antarctica, died together with other members of his party after having reached the South Pole in 1912. Singer was then ten years old; news of Scott's death seems to have had a strong impact on the future writer.
13. Seagate (or Sea Gate) is a private gated community at the far western end of Coney Island at the southwestern tip of Brooklyn, New York.
14. This was called the "heart of Jewish Warsaw."
15. Singer is recording his feelings in 1935, when the Dachau concentration camp and the Siberian labor camp were the worst catastrophes imaginable.
16. Andre Aciman, "In a Double Exile," *New York Times*, April 13, 1995.
17. Lit. "slaughterhouse"; invokes both the smell of the leather suitcases taken from storage for the about-to-be-exiled to pack their lives as well as the ignominious end of their existence in Egypt. From the French *abattre*, "to beat down."
18. Aciman, *Out of Egypt*, 300, 314–15, 327, 338, 339.
19. BkMk Press at the University of Missouri–Kansas City, 2015.
20. Dina Elenbogen, "Exile: Losing the Motherland," *Tikkun*, March 1999, 80.
21. *Beerlachai-royi*, lit. "the one who lives and sees me" (Gen. 16:14), is the name Hagar gives to the well by which she gives birth to Ishmael.
22. Sienna, *Rainbow Thread*, 247–48.
23. See, for example, Goldberg's poem "Oren" (Pine), in which she writes of "the heartache of two homelands."
24. See Rachel Tzvia Back, "Toward the 'Whole Fragment,'" *Nashim* 25 (2013): 120.
25. See, for example, Emile Habiby, "Your Holocaust, Our Catastrophe," *Tel Aviv Review*, January 1988, 332–36.
26. Edward W. Said, "Palestine, Then and Now: An Exile's Journey through Israel and the Occupied Territories," *Harper's Magazine*, December 1992, 47–55.

9. Language as the Locus of Exile

1. *The JPS TANAKH: Gender-Sensitive Edition.*
2. Shammas's essay, written for a conference, was published in Hebrew in 1985. Shammas translated it into English for this volume.
3. Hoffman, *Lost in Translation*, 120–21.
4. Hoffman, *Lost in Translation*, 216–17.
5. Wordplay; the line reads "'ivriyut 'ivruiti 'arviyuti."
6. The slogan of the Battalion for the Defense of Language, a militant group led by students from the Herzliya Gymnasium (high school) in Tel Aviv in the 1920s who promoted the use of Hebrew in the Yishuv (prestate settlement of Jews in the Land of Israel).
7. Pedaya, "A Man Walks," in *Diyo Adam.*
8. The village of Al-Maghar is also the birthplace of the poet Na'im al-Araidi. It gained notoriety in February 2005 when Druze physically attacked members of the Christian community in response to a rumor—later found to be untrue—that Christian youth had posted indecent photographs of young Druze girls on the internet.
9. Masalha, "I Write in Hebrew," 104.
10. Giora Leshem and the English-language poet Karen Alkalay-Gut have translated each other's poems. Leshem's poem appears in English translation on Karen Alkalay-Gut's blog, March 18, 2011, karenalkalay-gut.com/diarymarch152011.html.

10. Negation, Ambivalence, Affirmation

1. Nemoy, *Karaite Anthology*, 35–37. A fuller version of this text can be found in Nemoy, "Pseudo-Qūmisīan Sermon," 49–105.
2. Carmi's "domain" in line 4 expresses the ambiguity of the Hebrew, which means both "territory" and "rope."
3. Halevi, "*Selected Poems*," 347.
4. Heine, *Complete Poems*, 470–503.
5. Herzl, *The Diaries of Theodor Herzl*, 2:581.
6. Private letter to Moritz Benedikt dated 1892, as cited in Brownfeld, "Zionism and Anti-Semitism," 49.
7. Lewisohn, *Theodor Herzl.*
8. Mintz, *Banished*, 8; see 29–54.
9. The entry repeats the substance of a passage written some two weeks earlier (28 Elul): both refer to the mandate of an official Russian state communiqué "to gather and submit to the proper location precise information together with presumptions of guilt on the question: which aspects of the economic activity of the Jews cause injury to the lives of the principal [or original,

native] inhabitants" (Mintz, *Banished*, 51). The reference is to the instructions to the special provincial commissions in the imperial ukase of August 22, 1881 (Dubnow, *History*, 2:272).

10. Here the author may have been echoing (and ironically endorsing) some of the sentiments expressed in a report by the Vilna Provincial Commission established in the wake of the pogroms: "For the Jew, there is no fatherland, no state, no laws except their caste laws, no authority except that of their *kahal*. They represent a mobile state within the states against which they are waging permanent and relentless economic warfare." Goldstein, *Dostoyevsky and the Jews*, 130.

11. At the time Lilienblum was writing, the word "antisemitism" was a relatively recent neologism, first popularized by Wilhelm Marr in German in 1879. Lilienblum understands it to highlight the "Semitic" identity of the Jew, which is by definition alien in Europe, as he proceeds to explain at the end of the paragraph.

12. Typically of European proto-Zionists, the existing population of the Land of Israel was not taken seriously, producing the Zionist slogan "a land without a people for a people without a land."

13. For most of those who had given up hope for a future in Eastern Europe, emigration to the United States was a far more appealing option. The author repudiates the idea that this will be different from the millennial experience of alienation in exile.

14. Or "of renaissance, revival, resurrection," imagery drawn from Isa. 26:19.

15. This is a dramatic repudiation of the Haskalah's ideological principle that the solution to the alienation of Jews from their neighbors lies in a transformation of their educational curriculum to produce mastery of subjects deemed important by the host society. In the preceding entries, the author juxtaposed material from his gymnasium studies (including Latin classics, mathematical problems, and Russian geography) with biblical texts (see Mintz, *Banished*, 51–53). Central to the Zionist analysis was the dictum that Jews could do nothing to transform themselves that would resolve the problem of their alienation in exile.

16. Dawidowicz, *Golden Tradition*, 128–29.

17. Ahad Ha'am, "First Zionist Congress," 542.

18. Ahad Ha'am, *Al Parashat Derakhim*, 2:127.

19. Hertzberg, *Zionist Idea*, 270–77.

20. Traum, "Disruptive Nativity," 208.

21. Shani, *Shalom le-Adoni Hamelekh*, 46.

22. JPost editorial, "Leaving Israel," *Jerusalem Post*, October 16, 2014, jpost.com/Opinion/Leaving-Israel-379021; Yehoshua, *Between Right and Right*.

23. Levine, *Diaspora*, 16–35.
24. Hoffman, "Out of Exile," 57–58.
25. On these issues, which have been studied extensively for more than a century, see, most recently, the discussion of the literary character of Nachmanides's account in Chazan, *Barcelona and Beyond*, 39–79, 100–141.
26. Ben Nahman, *Kitvei Ramban*, 1:310.
27. See also Saperstein, *Leadership and Conflict*, 265–66; Saperstein and Berg, "'Arab Chains,'" 301–26.
28. Dov Baer, *Maggid Devarav*, 70; translation based on Dan, *Teachings of Hasidism*, 132–33. Cf. Buber, *Tales of the Hasidim*, 1:103, who introduces the element of the king's being "driven from his realm" without any basis in sources that the present editors could find.
29. Pinson, *Nationalism and History*, 371n33 explains: "The reference is to the rabbinic principle of 'placing a fence around the Torah,' which meant setting up precautionary measures, in addition to those prescribed by Scripture, in order to prevent man from even getting near possible violations of divine law."
30. Pinson, *Nationalism and History*, 186–87.
31. Pinson, *Nationalism and History*, 190.
32. Kotzin, *Judah L. Magnes*, 236.
33. At the end of his introduction to the text in *The Zionist Idea* Arthur Hertzberg writes: "There had been bloody outbreaks by the Arabs in August 1929, triggered by wild tales that the Jews intended to seize the Mosque of Omar and throw it down in order to clear its site for the rebuilding of the Temple" (443). The specific day to which Magnes refers in the first sentence is not clear.
34. Hertzberg, *Zionist Idea*, 445–46.

Coda

1. Agosin, *A Cross and a Star*, 177–78.
2. Afkhami, *Women in Exile*, 148–49.

Bibliography

Aaron Berechiah of Modena. *Derashot Ma'avar Yabbok*. Jerusalem: Ahavat Shalom, 2001.
Abramson, Glenda. *The Oxford Book of Hebrew Short Stories*. Oxford: Oxford University Press, 1996.
Abravanel, [Don] Isaac. *Haggadah shel Pesach im Sheni Perushim: Zevaḥ Pesaḥ* . . . Brooklyn NY: Y. Vider, 1978.
——— . *Ma'yenei ha-Yeshu'ah* ("Wells of Salvation," commentary on Daniel). Ferrara, 1551.
——— . *Perush 'al ha-Torah*. 5 vols. Jerusalem: Bene Arba'el, 1979.
——— . *Sefer Naḥalat Avot*. New York: Hubert, 1953.
——— . *Yeshu'ot Meshiḥo*. Koenisberg, 1861.
Aciman, Andre. *Out of Egypt*. New York: Picador, 2007.
Acosta, Uriel. *An Example of a Human Life*. Translated by Helen Lederer. Readings in Modern Jewish History. Cincinnati OH: Hebrew Union College–Jewish Institute of Religion, 1958.
Adler, Herman. *Naftulei Elohim: A Course of Sermons on the Biblical Passages Adduced by Christian Theologians in Support of the Dogmas of Their Faith*. London: Trübner, 1869.
Afkhami, Mahmaz. *Women in Exile*. Charlottesville: University Press of Virginia, 1994.
Agosin, Marjorie. *A Cross and a Star: Memoirs of a Jewish Girl in Chile*. Translated by Celeste Kostopulos-Cooperman. Albuquerque: University of New Mexico Press, 1995.
Ahad Ha'am. *Al Parashat Derakhim*. Berlin: Judischer Verlag, 1921.
——— . "The First Zionist Congress." In *Ten Essays on Zionism and Judaism*, 70–78. London: George Routledge & Sons, 1922.
Altmann, Alexander. *Predigten an das Judentum von heute*. Berlin: Joachim Goldstein Verlag, 1935.
Amichai, Yehuda. *Poems of Jerusalem*. New York: HarperCollins, 1988.
——— . *The Poetry of Yehuda Amichai*. New York: Farrar, Straus & Giroux, 2015.
Amir, Eli. *Tarnegol Kapparot*. Tel Aviv: Am Oved, 1983.

BIBLIOGRAPHY

Ashkenazi, Jacob Ben Isaac. *Tsenah u-Re'enah*. Cracow: J. M. Nick, 1907.
Bacher, Wilhelm. "Elégie d'un poète judéo-persan contemporain de la persecution de Schah Abbas II." *Revue des études juives* 48, no. 95 (1904): 94–105.
Back, Rachel Tzvia. "Toward 'the Whole Fragment.'" *Nashim* 25 (2013): 114–28.
Baer, Yitzhak F. *Galut*. New York: Schocken Books, 1947.
———. *A History of the Jews in Christian Spain*. Translated by Louis Schoffman. Philadelphia: Jewish Publication Society, 1961–66.
Ballas, Shimon. *Ha-Ma'abarah*. Tel Aviv: Am Oved, 1964.
Bargad, Warren. *"To Write the Lips of Sleepers": The Poetry of Amir Gilboa*. Cincinnati OH: Hebrew Union College Press, 1994.
Baron, Salo. *History and Jewish Historians: Essays and Addresses*. Philadelphia: Jewish Publication Society, 1964.
———. *The Jewish Community: Its History and Structure to the American Revolution*. Philadelphia: Jewish Publication Society, 1942.
Bazak, Jacob. *Jewish Law and Jewish Life*. New York: UAHC, 1979.
ben Avraham, Levi. *Livyat Ḥen: The Work of Creation*. Edited by Howard Kreisel. Jerusalem: World Union of Jewish Studies, 2004.
Benjamin of Tudela. *The Itinerary of Benjamin of Tudela: Travels in the Middle Ages*. Malibu CA: J. Simon, [1983].
ben Nahman, Moses/Nachmanides (Ramban). *Kitvei Ramban*. Edited by Charles Chavel. Jerusalem: Mosad ha-Rav Kook, 1963.
Berg, Nancy E. *Exile from Exile: Israeli Writers from Iraq*. Albany NY: SUNY Press, 1996.
Berkovits, Eliezer. *Faith after the Holocaust*. Brooklyn NY: Ktav, 1973.
———. *Towards Historic Judaism*. Oxford: East and West Library, 1943.
Biale, David. *Cultures of the Jews: A New History*. New York: Schocken Books, 2006.
Bialik, Hayyim Nahman. *Songs from Bialik*. Edited by Atar Hadari. Syracuse NY: Syracuse University Press, 2000.
Bonfil, Simon. *Jewish Life in Renaissance Italy*. Translated by Anthony Oldcorn. Berkeley: University of California Press, 1994.
Brownfeld, Allan C. "Zionism and Anti-Semitism: A Strange Alliance through History." *Washington Report on Middle East Affairs* 48–50 (July–August 1998).
Buber, Martin. *Tales of the Hasidim*. 2 vols. New York: Schocken Books, 1964.
Carmi, T., ed. *The Penguin Book of Hebrew Verse*. New York: Penguin Books, 1981.
Cassen, Flora. *Marking the Jews in Renaissance Italy: Politics, Religion, and the Power of Symbols*. Cambridge: Cambridge University Press, 2017.
Chazan, Robert. *Barcelona and Beyond: The Disputation of 1263 and Its Aftermath*. Berkeley: University of California Press, 1992.
Cordovero, Moses. *The Palm Tree of Deborah*. Translated by Louis Jacobs. London: Vallentine Mitchell, 1960.

BIBLIOGRAPHY

Dan, Joseph. *The Teachings of Hasidism*. New York: Behrman House, 1983.

Dawidowicz, Lucy S. *The Golden Tradition: Jewish Life and Thought in Eastern Europe*. New York: Holt, Rinehart & Winston, 1967.

DeKoven Ezrahi, Sidra. *Booking Passage: On Exile and Homecoming in the Modern Jewish Imagination*. Berkeley: University of California Press, 2000.

De Lange, Nicholas. *Hebrew Scholarship and the Medieval World*. Cambridge: Cambridge University Press, 2001.

Dov Baer, the Maggid of Mezritch. *Maggid Devarav le-Ya'aqov*. Edited by Rivka Schatz Uffenheimer. Jerusalem: Magnes Press, 1990.

Dubnow, Simon. *History of the Jews in Russia and Poland: From the Earliest Times to the Present Day*. Translated by Israel Friedlaender, 3 vols. Philadelphia: Jewish Publication Society, 1916–20.

Efros, Israel, ed. *Complete Poetic Works of Hayyim Nahman Bialik*. New York: Histadruth Ivrith of America, 1948.

Einhorn, David. *Olat Tamid: Book of Prayers for Jewish Congregations*. New translation from the German original. N.p., 1921.

Eisen, Arnold M. *Galut: Modern Jewish Reflection on Homelessness and Homecoming*. Bloomington: Indiana University Press, 1986.

Feierberg, Mordecai Ze'ev. "Whither?" In *Whither? and Other Stories*, translated by Hillel Halkin. New Milford CT: Toby, 2004.

Fein, Harry H. *A Harvest of Hebrew Verse: Poems of the Cultural Renaissance and National Revival*. Boston: Bruce Humphries, 1934.

Fox, Pam. *Israel Isidor Mattuck: Architect of Liberal Judaism*. London: Vallentine Mitchell, 2016.

Gerondi, Nissim ben Reuben. *Derashot ha-Ran*. Jerusalem: Mossad HaRav Kook, 2008.

Glaser, Edward. "Invitation to Intolerance: A Study of the Portuguese Sermons Preached at the Autos de Fé." *HUCA Annual* 27 (1956): 327–85.

Goldberg, Lea. *Shirim*. Tel Aviv: Hakibbutz Hemeuchad–Sifriat Poalim, 2004.

Goldstein, David I. *Dostoyevsky and the Jews*. Austin: University of Texas Press, 1976.

Halevi, Jehudah. *Selected Poems of Jehudah Halevi*. Translated by Nina Salaman. Philadelphia: Jewish Publication Society, 1928.

Hecht, N. S. et al., eds. *An Introduction to the History and Sources of Jewish Law*. Oxford: Clarendon, 1996.

Heine, Heinrich. *Complete Poems*. Translated by Edgar Alfred Bowring. London: George Bell & Sons, 1908.

Hertzberg, Arthur. *The Zionist Idea: A Historical Analysis and Reader*. Philadelphia: Jewish Publication Society, 1997.

Hess, Moses. *Rome and Jerusalem*. Translated and edited by Rabbi Maurice J. Bloom. New York: Philosophical Library, 1958.

Hoffman, Eva. *Lost in Translation*. New York: Dutton, 1989.

——. "Out of Exile: Some Thoughts on Exile as a Dynamic Condition." *European Judaism: A Journal for the New Europe* 46, no. 2 (Autumn 2013): 55–60.

ibn Ezra, Moses. *Selected Poems of Moses ibn Ezra*. Translated by Heinrich Brody and Solomon Solis-Cohen. Philadelphia: Jewish Publication Society, 1945.

ibn Verga, Solomon. *Shevet Yehudah*. Edited by Shaul Robinzon. Jerusalem: Schocken Books, 1946.

Jacobson, Yoram. *Bi-Netivei Galuyot u-Ge'ulot*. Jerusalem: Mosad Bialik, 1996.

Josephus, Flavius. *The Wars of the Jews*. Translated by William Whiston. Philadelphia: J. Grigg, 1829.

The JPS TANAKH: Gender-Sensitive Edition. Philadelphia: Jewish Publication Society, 2023.

Kaplan, Yosef, "Political Concepts in the World of the Portuguese Jews of Amsterdam during the Seventeenth Century: The Problem of Exclusion and the Boundaries of Self-Identity." In *Menasseh ben Israel and His World*, edited by Yosef Kaplan, Henry Méchoulan, and Richard H. Popkin, 45–62. Leiden: Brill, 1989.

King, Edward G. *The Yalkut on Zechariah*. Cambridge, UK: Deighton, Bell, 1882.

Klausner, Yosef. *Haim Nahman Bialik ve-Shirat Ḥayav*. Tel Aviv: Dvir, 1951.

Kotzin, Daniel. *Judah L. Magnes: An American Jewish Nonconformist*. Syracuse NY: Syracuse University Press, 2010.

Lamm, Norman. *The Religious Thought of Hasidism: Text and Commentary*. New York: Yeshiva University Press, 1999.

Lauterbach, Jacob Z. *Mekhilta de-Rabbi Ishmael*. Philadelphia: Jewish Publication Society, 1976.

Leibowitz, Nehama. *Studies in Shemot*. Translated by Aryeh Newman. Jerusalem: World Zionist Organization, 1986.

Levine, Etan, ed. *Diaspora: Exile and the Contemporary Jewish Condition*. Tel Aviv: Steimatzky & Shapolsky, 1986.

Levy, Amy. *A London Plane-Tree and Other Verse*. London: T. Fisher Unwin, 1889.

Lewisohn, Ludwig, ed. *Theodor Herzl: A Portrait for This Age*. Translated by Sylvie D'Avigdor (The Jewish State) and Maurice Samuel (the passages from the diaries). Revised by Ben Halpern and Moshe Kohn. Cleveland OH: World, 1955.

Maimonides, Moses (Ben Maimon). "The Epistle to Yemen." In *The Jews of Arab Lands: A History and Source Book*, edited by Norman Stillman, 241–42. Philadelphia: Jewish Publication Society, 1979.

——. *Guide for the Perplexed*. Translated and annotated by M. Friedländer. New York: Hebrew Publishing, 1946–60.

Malkiel, D. J. *A Separate Republic: Mechanics and Dynamics of Venetian Jewish Self-Government 1607–1624*. Jerusalem: Magnes, 1991.

Marcus, Jacob Rader. *The Jew in the Medieval World.* Rev. ed. Cincinnati OH: Hebrew Union College Press, 1999.

Masalha, Salman. "I Write in Hebrew." Translated by Vivian Eden in *Ariel: The Israel Review of Arts and Letters,* no. 104. Jerusalem: Israeli Foreign Affairs Ministry, 1997.

Matt, Daniel. *Zohar: The Book of Enlightenment.* New York: Paulist Press, 1983.

Mendele Mokher Sefarim, "Burned Out." In Abramson, *Oxford Book of Hebrew Short Stories.* Oxford: Oxford University Press, 1996.

Mendes, Abraham P. *Sermons.* London: John Chapman, 1855.

Mendes-Flohr, Paul, and Yehuda Reinharz. *Ideas of Jewish History.* Detroit MI: Wayne State University Press, 1987.

——. *The Jew in the Modern World.* New York: Oxford University Press, 1980.

Meyer, Michael A. *Response to Modernity: A History of the Reform Movement in Judaism.* New York: Oxford University Press, 1988.

Mintz, Alan. *Banished from Their Father's Table: Loss of Faith and Hebrew Autobiography.* Bloomington: Indiana University Press, 1989.

Mirsky, Aharon, Avraham Grossman, and Yosef Kaplan, eds. *Exile and Diaspora— Studies in the History of the Jewish People: Presented to Professor Haim Beinart.* Jerusalem: Ben-Zvi, 1988.

Modena, Leon. *Autobiography of a Seventeenth-Century Venetian Rabbi: Leon Modena's "Life of Judah."* Edited by Mark R. Cohen. Princeton NJ: Princeton University Press, 1988.

Moreen, Vera Basch. *In Queen Esther's Garden: An Anthology of Judeo-Persian Literature.* New Haven CT: Yale University Press, 2000.

——. *Iranian Jewry's Hour of Peril and Heroism: A Study of Bābāī ibn Luṭf's Chronicle (1617–1662).* New York: American Academy for Jewish Research, 1987.

Nemoy, Leo. *Karaite Anthology.* New Haven CT: Yale University Press, 1952.

——. "The Pseudo-Qūmisīan Sermon to the Karaites." *Proceedings of the American Academy for Jewish Research* 6 (1976): 49–105.

Netanyahu, Benzion. *Don Isaac Abravanel: Statesman and Philosopher.* Philadelphia: Jewish Publication Society, 1953.

Pedaya, Haviva. *Diyo Adam.* Tel Aviv: Hakibbutz Hameuchad, 2009.

Pinsker, Judah Leib (Leon). *Auto-Emancipation: An Appeal to His People by a Russian Jew.* New York: Maccabaean, 1906.

Pinson, Koppel S., ed. *Nationalism and History: Essays on Old and New Judaism.* Philadelphia: Jewish Publication Society, 1958.

Raphael, David T., ed. *The Expulsion 1492 Chronicles.* North Hollywood CA: Carmi House, 1992.

Ravid, Benjamin. "From Yellow to Red: On the Distinguishing Head Covering of the Jews of Venice." *Jewish History* 6, no. 12 (1992): 179–210.

BIBLIOGRAPHY

Ravnitsky, Y. H., and H. N. Bialik. *Sefer ha-Aggadah*. Krakow: Fisher, 1907–10.
Reznikoff, Charles. *In Memoriam: 1933*. New York: Objectivist Press, 1934.
———. *Poems 1918–1936: Volume 1 of the Complete Poems of Charles Reznikoff*. Edited by Seamus Cooney. Santa Barbara CA: Black Sparrow, 1977.
Roskies, David G., ed. *The Literature of Destruction: Jewish Responses to Catastrophe*. Philadelphia: Jewish Publication Society, 1988.
Roth, Cecil. *The Jews in the Renaissance*. Philadelphia: Jewish Publication Society, 1959.
Saba, Abraham. *Eshkol ha-Kofer al Megillat Ester*. Edited by Eliezer Segal. Drohobycz, Poland: n.p., 1903.
Saperstein, Marc. *Agony in the Pulpit: Jewish Preaching in Response to Nazi Persecution and Mass Murder, 1933–1945*. Cincinnati OH: Hebrew Union College Press, 2018.
———. *Decoding the Rabbis: A Thirteenth-Century Commentary on the Aggadah*. Cambridge MA: Harvard University Press, 1980.
———. *Exile in Amsterdam: Saul Levi Morteira's Sermons to a Congregation of "New Jews."* Cincinnati OH: Hebrew Union College Press, 2005.
———. *Jewish Preaching, 1200–1800*. New Haven CT: Yale University Press, 1989.
———. *Leadership and Conflict: Tensions in Medieval and Early Modern Jewish History and Culture*. Liverpool, UK: Littman Library of Jewish Civilization in association with Liverpool University Press, 2014.
———. "A Sermon on the Akedah from the Generation of the Expulsion and Its Implications for 1391." In *Exile and Diaspora*, edited by Aharon Mirsky, Avraham Grossman, and Yosef Kaplan, 103–24. Jerusalem: Yad Ben Zvi, 1991.
———. *"Your Voice Like a Ram's Horn": Themes and Texts in Traditional Jewish Preaching*. Cincinnati OH: Hebrew Union College Press, 1996.
Saperstein, Marc, and Nancy E. Berg. "'Arab Chains' and 'The Good Things of Sepharad': Aspects of Jewish Exile." *AJS Review* 26, no. 2 (November 2002): 301–26.
Saperstein, Marc, and Jacob Rader Marcus. *The Jews in Christian Europe: A Source Book, 315–1791*. Cincinnati OH: Hebrew Union College Press, 2016.
Schechter, Ronald. *Obstinate Hebrews: Representations of Jews in France, 1715–1815*. Berkeley: University of California Press, 2003.
Scholem, Gershom. *Kabbalah*. New York: Dorset, 1987.
Schwartz, Howard. *Reimagining the Bible: The Storytelling of the Rabbis*. New York: Oxford University Press, 1998.
Schwarz, Leo. *Memoirs of My People*. Philadelphia: Jewish Publication Society, 1960.
Septimus, Bernard. "Hispano-Jewish Views of Christendom and Islam." In *In Iberia and Beyond*, edited by Bernard Cooperman, 43–65. Newark: University of Delaware Press, 1998.

Shani, Rina. *Mivchar Shirim* [Selected poems]. Edited by Riki Traum. Tel Aviv: Hakibbutz Hameuchad, 2019.

——— . *Shalom le-Adoni Hamelekh* [Farewell to a king]. Tel Aviv: Am Oved, 1970.

Sienna, Noam, ed. *A Rainbow Thread*. Philadelphia: Print-O-Craft, 2019.

Silver, Abba Hillel. *Therefore Choose Life*. Cleveland OH: World, 1967.

Simpson, John, ed. *The Oxford Book of Exile*. Oxford: Oxford University Press, 1985.

Singer, Isaac Bashevis. *Love and Exile: The Early Years—a Memoir*. New York: Penguin Books, 1986.

Sobol, Joshua. *Soul of a Jew*. London: W. Heinemann, 1982.

Soncino, Joshua. *Naḥalah li-Yhoshua*. Constantinople, 1731.

Sternhell, Zeev. *The Founding Myths of Israel*. Translated by David Maisel. Princeton NJ: Princeton University Press, 1998.

Stillman, Norman. *The Jews of Arab Lands: A History and Source Book*. Philadelphia: Jewish Publication Society, 1979.

Talmage, Frank Ephraim, ed. *Disputation and Dialogue: Readings in the Jewish-Christian Encounter*. New York: Ktav, 1975.

Tama, M. Diogene. *Transactions of the Parisian Sanhedrim*. London: Charles Taylor, 1807.

Ticotsky, Giddon. "The Representations of Eretz-Israel Landscapes in Leah Goldberg's Poetry as an Arena of Dealing with Ideological and Literary Norms." [In Hebrew.] Master's thesis, The Hebrew University of Jerusalem, 2006.

Tishby, Isaiah. *The Wisdom of the Zohar*. Oxford: Oxford University Press, 1989.

Traum, Riki. "Disruptive Nativity." In *Since 1948: Israeli Literature in the Making*, edited by Nancy E. Berg and Naomi B. Sokoloff, 208. Albany NY: SUNY Press, 2020.

Usque, Samuel. *Consolation for the Tribulations of Israel*. Translated by Martin A. Cohen. Philadelphia: Jewish Publication Society, 1964.

Wachs, Sharona. *American Jewish Liturgies: A Bibliography of American Jewish Liturgy from the Establishment of the Press in the Colonies through 1925*. Cincinnati OH: Hebrew Union College–Jewish Institute of Religion, 1997.

Walfish, Barry Dov. *Esther in Medieval Garb*. Albany NY: SUNY Press, 1993.

Weininger, Otto. *Sex and Character*. London: W. Heinemann and New York: G. P. Putnam's Sons [1906?].

Yehoshua, Abraham B. *Between Right and Right*. Translated by Arnold Schwartz. New York: Doubleday, 1981.

——— . "Exile as a Neurotic Solution." In *Diaspora: Exile and the Contemporary Jewish Condition*, edited by Etan Levine, 15–35. New York: Shapolsky Books, 1986.

BIBLIOGRAPHY

Yerushalmi, Yosef Hayim. *The Lisbon Massacre of 1506 and the Royal Image in the Shebet Yehudah.* Cincinnati OH: Hebrew Union College–Jewish Institute of Religion, 1976.

Zach, Natan. *Keivan she-Ani ba-Sevivah.* Tel Aviv: Hakibbutz Hameuchad, 1966.

Zeitlin, Solomon. *The Rise and Fall of the Judaean State.* Philadelphia: Jewish Publication Society, 1962.

Zipperstein, Steven J. *The Jews of Odessa: A Cultural History, 1794–1881.* Stanford CA: Stanford University Press, 1991.

Index

Aaron, 49, 50
abasement, 95
Abraham, 20, 49, 71, 136, 137, 154, 197; blessing of 184; covenant with, 87, 120; lands of, 183; seed of, 31–32, 53
Abravanel, Don Isaac, 8–9, 35–39, 91, 105
Aciman, Andre, 178–79
Adam, 99, 189, 192; and Eve, 5–10, 71, 86, 98, 101, 188
Adler, Hermann, xvi, 52, 93–95
Agnon, S. Y., 148, 193
Agosin, Marjorie, 229–30
Ahad Ha'Am, 56, 151, 214–15, 224
Ahasuerus, King, 63–64, 77
Alfonso V of Portugal, 35
Alhambra Decree, 162
alienation, 143, 212, 218, 254nn13, 15
al-Kumisi, Daniel, 204–5
Amichai, Yehudah, 12, 26–27
Amina (Benyamin b. Misa Il Kasani), 64–65
Amir, Eli, 156–58
Amos, 9, 96, 135
Amsterdam, xvii, 74, 80, 110
Anan ben David, 204
Andalusia, xvii, 109, 113, 114, 162
Antigone, 184
Antiochus, 83

antisemitism, 142–43, 211, 254n11; consequences of, 141; countering, 75, 203; and Dreyfus affair, 209–10; inevitability of, 131–32, 143, 159; intractability of, 141, 213
apostasy, 31, 138
Aristotle, 60, 139, 244
assimilation, 141, 151, 152, 216, 219, 246; countering, 153; to escape persecution, 138; failure of, 209–10; and intermarriage, 75; spiritual, 97
atonement, exile as, 55, 86, 102, 103–6, 132
Augustine (of Hippo), 100
autonomism and autonomy, 38, 134, 215, 217, 224–26

Baal Shem Tov, 71, 222
Babylon / Babylonia, 123–29; conquest of, 43; kingdom of, 29, 49
Babylonian exile, 12, 15–28, 30, 32, 92, 207; descendants of, 46, 124; failure to return from, xv, xviii; rabbinic account of, 20–23; Second; 156–57; settling in, xviii, 110–13; Shekhinah in, 69
Baer, Dov (Magid of Mezrich), xviii, 107, 222–23
Baer, Yitzhak, 131

265

INDEX

Baghdad, 109, 113, 115, 116, 156, 158
banishment, 1, 71, 81, 86, 131, 162, 171
ben Israel, Menasseh, 80–81, 245 n. 17
Benjamin of Tudela, 109, 115–16
ben Naḥman, Moses, xvii, 221, 222
ben Yedaiah, Isaac, 73–74, 138–39
Berechiah, Aaron, 118–19
Berkovitz, Eliezer, 133–35
Berr, Berr Isaac, 82–83, 246n26, 247n29
Bialik, Haim Nachman, xix, 83–84, 145–47
Brenner, Yosef Hayyim, 148–49, 159, 251n24
Brunn, Israel, 102

Cain, 86, 89, 98–99, 100, 101, 171, 188–89
captive, Babylonian, xvii, 124, 143
Chaldeans, 17, 18, 23, 89
Christendom, 162. See also Edom (as Christendom)
confusion, 33, 153, 175, 192, 194
consolation, 31, 42–43, 54, 65, 150; exile as, 221; Shekhinah as, 68
conversion: argument for, 93, 94; as escape, 138; forced, 32, 40, 65, 162, 167, 174; Heine's, 207
Cordovero, Moses, 106
Cromwell, Oliver, 80
Crusades, 161, 172
Cyrus, King, xviii, 15, 125, 127

Daniel, 36, 239 n7
Dante Alighieri, 190, 191, 192, 194
David, 22, 49, 89
death, exile as, xx, 2, 10, 179
desert, 73, 97, 126, 275–76, 297, 298; wanderings in, 71, 184, 208
destruction, 35, 77, 108; angels of, 3; of First Temple, 92; of Jerusalem, 10, 53, 209; of Second Temple, 28, 107, 240n28, 241n29; self-, 122, 244; and Shekhinah's banishment, 10, 71; of Temple, 12, 27, 32, 110, 119, 137, 160; and Tisha B'av, xvi, 19, 45, 57–62
diaspora, 131, 204, 219–20; Hellenistic-Roman, 132; life in, 66, 67, 214, 224–26, 227; and Messiah, 203. See also *galut*
diglossia, 224
dispersal, 74–80, 188, 203, 224. See also scattering
Dov Baer, xviii, 107, 222–23
Dreyfus Affair, 209–10
Dubnow, Simon, 224, 253–54n9
Duran, Profiet (the Ephodi), 30–31

Eden, Garden of: expulsion from, 1–3, 5, 7–9, 71, 86, 189; east of, 99; poetic references to, 11, 166
Edict of Tolerance (Toleranzpatent), 14, 239n3
Edom (as Christendom), 30, 39, 41, 206
Edomites, 20, 40
Egypt, xviii, 7, 178, 193; exodus from, xv, 88
Egyptian exile, 12, 13–15, 30–31, 69, 121, 122; life in, 118–20, 123, 125–26, 137, 248n5; and Passover, 36, 38, 45, 179. See Egypt, exodus from
Eichah. See Lamentations, Book of (*Eichah*)
Einhorn, David, 51, 52, 243n16
Eisen, Arnold, 1
Elenbogen, Dina, 180–82
Emancipation, 82, 97, 141, 211, 246n26; auto-, 142, 214
England: expulsion from, xvi, xvii, 46, 93, 161, 166; return to, 80, 170

266

enlightenment, Jewish. See *Haskalah*
envy, 110, 122, 150
Ephraim, 205
Eretz Israel, 134, 135, 152
Ernst, Myron, 110, 129
Esau, 117, 118
Esther, Book of, 46, 62, 66, 67; book of, 45, 62, 63–64; commentary on, 13, 40, 65
Ethiopian Jews, 180, 181–82
Euphrates (site of exile), 19, 22, 24
exceptionalism, 226, 227
exilarch, 38, 109, 115, 116–17
exiles, comparison of, 13, 39
exodus, from Egypt, xv, 88
expulsion. *See* England, expulsion from; France, expulsion from; Spain (Christian), expulsion from
Ezekiel, 39–197

Faustus, 100
Feierberg, Mordecai Ze'ev, 56–57, 244n27
Ferdinand and Isabella, 13, 35, 166–67, 170, 241n31
First Zionist Congress, 210, 214, 215
France: emancipation in, 246n26; expulsion from, xvi, xvii, xviii, 46, 91, 93, 161, 166
Freud, Sigmund, 159

galut, 26, 113, 133, 136, 137, 139; as bleak, xv, xvii, 136; definition of, 131; and Divine Presence, 138; negation of, xvi, 203, 214; repudiation of, 151–53; tragedy of, 134, 154–55; translation of, 131, 215. See also *golah*
galutiyut, xv, xvi, 131
garden, 17, 110–13, 129, 158; of Babylon, 125, 126, 127. *See also* Eden, Garden of

Germany, xvii, 46, 133, 153, 155
Gilboa, Amir, 12, 25
golah, 15, 215, 219–20
Goldberg, Leah, 12, 26, 184, 252n23
Golden Age of Spain. *See* Spain (Christian), Golden Age of
golden calf, 50, 250n19
Golus. See *galut*
Gordon, Y. L., 170
Grass, Gunter, 192
Greenberg, Uri Zvi, 190, 191
guilt, 47, 95, 103, 201, 202, 247n14, 253n9

Hagar, 83, 84, 252n21
HaLevi, Judah (Yehuda), 129, 143, 162, 206, 244n25
Hanukkah, 104
Hasidism, 71, 107, 222, 223
Haskalah, 212, 254n15
Hatikvah, 159
hatred of the Jews, 54, 56, 142, 143; God's, 167, 170; planted by God, xvii, 79, 80; as unnatural, 75, 79, 246nn20–21. *See also* antisemitism
Hebrew: estrangement from, 119, 197, 199; as ideological choice, 190–92, 199–200; preservation of 214, 224–26
Heine, Heinrich, 143, 206, 207
heresy: exile as punishment for, 105–6
Herzl, Theodor, 146, 159, 209–10, 214, 227
Hess, Moses, 210
Hibbat Tsiyon, 141, 146
Hoffman, Eva, 195–96, 220–21
holidays. *See specific holidays*
holiness, 61, 223
homeland, 153, 185; ancestral, 207; away from, 12, 131, 135, 154; Israel

267

INDEX

homeland (*continued*)
as, 180, 181, 218; language as, 190–94; return to, 13, 16, 144, 149; significance of, 152, 197, 227

ibn Ezra, Moses, 162–66, 206
ibn Labrat, Dunash, 109, 113–15
ibn Lutf, Ba'ba', 174
ibn Yaḥya, Judah, 32–35, 94
idolatry, 31, 32, 108, 137
imagination, 21, 109, 142, 221, 230
Inquisition, xvi, 242
Iraq, xviii, 19, 156–57, 196, 198
Isaac, 49, 60, 71, 87, 120, 244n25
Isaiah, 9, 39
Isfahan, 64, 174
Ishmael (as Muslim nation), 20–21, 39, 41
Ishmaelites, 20–21, 41
Israel, State of, xvi, 156, 180, 203, 220; and Arab citizens, 185, 187, 190, 191, 192
Israel of Koznitz, 107

Jacob, 43, 75, 77, 107, 117–18; children of, 170, 171; covenant with, 87; house of, 53; one of the patriarchs, 49, 60, 71, 120, 244n25; voice of, 127, 172
Jeconiah, 63, 89, 111
Jehoiachin, 15, 16, 17
Jehoiada, 112
Jehoiakim, 17
Jepthah's daughter, 170
Jeremiah, 39, 51, 110; advice of, xviii, 109, 110–12, 113, 129; Book of, 57, 110, 205
Jerusalem, 204, 205; away from, 129, 197; centrality of, 12, 45, 135; destruction of, 10, 53, 54, 60–61, 126–7; longing for, 19–20, 127, 181–82, 186, 207; return to, 191–4, 203, siege of, 15, 16–18, 43, 217; reunification of, 27
Jewish Question, 141, 158, 210–11, 217, 219
Job, Book of, 57
Jonah, 69, 70, 71
Joseph, 13, 20, 121, 122, 125
Joseph II, Emperor, 14, 239n3
Judah, 126, 168; community of, 11, 112; exiled, 16–18, 23, 33–35, 124–29; kingdom of, 18, 36, 47; tribe of, 34, 126, 128, 171. *See also* Jeconiah
Judeophobia. *See* antisemitism

Kabbalah (Jewish mysticism), 69, 71, 243nn5–6
Karaites, 203, 204–5
Kishinev pogrom (1903), 84
Klatzkin, Jacob, 151–53
Klausner, Joseph, 146

Lamentations, Book of (*Eichah*), 29, 33, 45, 46–48, 57–58, 85, 110
Landau, Ezekiel, 14–16
Leshem, Giora, 201
Levi, Solomon, 117–18
Levy, Amy, 143–45
Lilienblum, Moses Leib, 212–14
longing, 72, 127, 132, 180, 181, 206, 207, 218

Magnes, Judah, 226–28, 255n33
Maimonides (Moses ben Maimon), xviii, 1, 7–8, 39, 73, 139
Mani (and Manichaeism), 100
Maria Theresa, Queen, 14
martyrs, 54, 55, 95, 133, 212
Masalha, Salman, 199–200

Mattaniah. *See* Zedekiah (Mattaniah)
Mattuck, Israel, xvii, 23, 239n10
Megillat Eicha. *See* Lamentations, Book of (*Eichah*)
Megillat Esther. *See* Esther, Book of
Menachem Mendel(s), 155, 251n28
Mendes, Abraham P., 42–44, 52, 94, 242n47
Meyer, Michael, 52
Messiah, 24, 32, 72, 94, 222, 244nn26, 32; coming of, 66, 123, 203, 204, 243n6; and suffering, 53, 55, 136
Messianic age, 37, 97, 117–18, 146, 204, 246n24
Mishnah, 46, 137
Modena, Rabbi Judah Aryeh (Leon), 74, 118, 249n79
Mordecai, 62–63, 64, 67
Morteira, Saul Levi, xvii, xviii, 74–80, 120–23, 245n14
Moses, 39, 49, 50, 60, 179; covenant with, 88; law of, 205
mourning, 22, 30; dancing turned into, 47; and fasting, 46; for Jerusalem, 60, 61; ritual of, 118, 205; turned into rejoicing, 52–56; on Tisha B'Av, 42, 45, 57, 58
murder: exile as punishment for, 86, 102–5; in exile, 66, 92
Muslim rule, xvii, 69, 115, 174, 206

Nachmanides (Moses ben Nahman), xvii, 221, 222, 255n25
Naples, 8, 9, 35
Nebuchadenezzar, 15–17, 21–22, 63, 111, 170
negation of exile (*shelilat hagolah*), xvi, xix, 153, 158, 201, 203
Neufeld, Amos, 10
Ninth of Ab. *See* Tisha B'av

Noah, 71, 163
normalizing: exile, 28, 129, 134, 138, 217, 220; and the Jewish people, 226, 227
nostalgia, 185
Nussbaum, Max, 153–55

opportunity, exile as, 53, 76–77, 94, 133–36
Orpheus, 10
outsider, 183, 185, 212, 221

pacificism, 226
Pale of Settlement, 183
Palestine, xvii, 24, 67, 210, 214; as Arab homeland, 185–87, 192, 198; binational state in, 226–28; new home in, 26, 149, 155, 190, 226; and Second Temple, 132–33; spiritual center in, 224
Palestinians, 181, 185–87, 191–94, 213
parable, 48, 49, 90
Parnok, Sophia, 183–84
Passover, xv, 14, 38, 45, 178; Haggadah, 36; commentary on, 38–39; seder, 178–79
Pedaya, Haviva, 196–99
Persia, empire of, xvii, 28–29, 50, 67, 204; Jewish communities in, xviii, 14–15, 116, 174
persecution (in exile), 37, 68, 137–38; counter to, 42, 64, 210; Egyptian, 12; and Inquisition, xvi, 161, 242n54; Nazi, 132; pattern of, 24, 44, 117–18, 133, 211, 243n10; by Safavids, 174
Pesach. *See* Passover
Pharoah, 13, 14, 15, 123
philosemite, 159
pilgrimage, 45, 71

INDEX

Pinsker, Judah Leib "Leon," 141–43, 146, 159, 214, 250n18
Pirkei Avot, 105–6, 107
pleasures, 7, 13, 139–41, 150, 168, 173; of exile, 109, 113–15, 185, 187; of the Lord, 95
Po'alei Tzion, 148
Poland, xviii, 141, 157, 176–78, 195
Portugal: exile from, xvii, 9, 35, 74; forced conversions in, 40, 117; immigrants from, 74; refuge in, 40, 162
Prague, 14, 93
prosperity, 14, 43, 60, 110, 111, 116
punishment: Adam's, 7; of body, 92; Cain's, 89, 98, 99; exile as, xviii, 86; as necessary, 90, 189; for sins, 102, 119, 120, 188. *See also* heresy; murder
Purim, xvi, 45, 62–67, 104

Ravnitsky, xix
Reconquista, 162
redemption: by God, 32, 49, 79, 192; exile and, xix, 86, 157, 197; meriting, 95, 119; messianic, 34, 37–39, 66, 146; nation yearns for, 219; salvation and, 3; spiritual, xviii, 62; and suffering, 97, 133
remorse, 102, 103, 105
repentance, 31, 46, 83, 103–5, 132; Sabbath of, 75
restoration, xx, 32, 44, 52. *See also* redemption
Reznikoff, Charles, 110, 123–29
R. Nachman of Bratzlav, 71, 72–73
Rome, exile in, 28, 29, 43, 61
Rosh Hashanah, 75; sermon for, 96, 97, 131

Rothschilds, 93, 155
R. Yohanan, 22

Saba, Abraham, 40–41
Sabbath, 117, 153, 176, 229; observance of, 30; and specific Sabbaths, 14, 42, 48, 75
Said, Edward W., 183–87
Sakakini, Khalil, 193, 194
Salonika, 110–17
Sarah, 183, 184
scattering, 69, 131, 137, 216, 217, 227; by Chaldeans, 17; and exile of Rome, 28; and exile in Spain, 168, 170; as harsh, 33, 87, 137; as positive, 75–79, 80, 125, 245n13
Sefer Haggadah. *See Haggadah*
Serah Bat Asher, 175
Seraiah (chief priest), 18
Shabbat Naḥamu (Sabbath of Comfort), 43
Shammas, Anton, 190–94, 199
Shavuot, xv, 45
Shekhinah, xvi, 68; banishment of, 70–71; as consolation, 68; and evil, 223, 244n4; with exiles, 68, 69, 106; and guardian angels, 245n6; as guide, 61; impotence of, 84; as protection, xvi, 68, 107
shelilat hagolah. *See* negation of exile (*shelilat hagolah*)
siege of Jerusalem, 15, 16–17, 43, 89, 217, 239
sifrut hama'abarah (transit camp literature), 156
Silver, Abba Hillel, 66–67
Simpson, John, 1
sin, because of our sins (*mipnei hataeinu*), 119, 134, 135, 137

INDEX

Singer, Isaac Bashevis, 176–78
Six-Day War, 27, 218
slavery, 148, 249n16
slaves, 82, 88, 122, 140; abased by, 47; in Egypt, 2, 120, 125, 226
Sobol, Joshua, 158–60
Sokolow, Nahum, 56, 168
Solomon, 16, 18, 49, 140–41, 244n31
Soncino, Joshua (Ottoman rabbi), 40
Spain (Christian), 36, 132, 162, 240n22; and conversion, 167, 246n19; exile in, 7, 93, 161, 170, 208, 221; expulsion from, 9, 31, 35, 40, 45–46, 161, 166–70; Golden Age of, xv, 149, 206; as *Tabera*, 169
Spain (Muslim). *See* Andalusia
Sukkot, xv, 45

Tanḥuma, 2, 3, 20–21, 101, 248n5
Temple: destruction of, 12, 27, 32, 110, 119, 137, 160; destruction of First, 92; Mount, 114; destruction of Second, 28, 107, 240n28, 241n29
Tisha B'Av, xvi, 19, 45, 46–62
Titus, 43, 61, 217
Tokhecha, Night of (rebuke), 97
Toleranzpatent. *See* Edict of Tolerance (Toleranzpatent)
Torah, 1, 73, 75–78, 169; abandoned or mocked, 33, 34, 74, 115, 134; commentaries and study of, 8, 36, 45, 71, 245n10; keeping of, 2, 3, 4, 107, 152; scrolls, 23, 61

Tower of Babel, 86, 188, 189, 192, 245n13

Ukraine, 71, 148

vineyard, 122, 125, 128, 173

Walfish, Barry Dov, 40
wandering, 107, 152, 163; of Abraham, 154; and Arab exile, 191, 197, 199; of Cain, 86; desert as site of, 45, 71, 184; of Israel, 54, 56, 97, 148, 205
weeping, 22, 23, 54, 84–85, 137, 197, 199
Weil, Jacob, 102
Weininger, Otto, 158–59, 160

Yalkut Shimoni, 21, 28
Yehoshua, A. B., 219, 220
Yiddish, xv, 131, 214, 224, 225–26
Yiddishists, 214
Yom Kippur, 75

Zach, Natan, 155
Zechariah, 28, 246n24
Zedekiah (Mattaniah), 15, 16, 17, 111, 112
Zephaniah, 112, 113
Zionism, 65, 149, 151, 157
Zohar, 69, 89–90, 106, 244n56

INDEX

Biblical references:

Gen. 1:28, 142
Gen. 3, 5–7
Gen. 3:9, 8
Gen. 3:14, 9
Gen. 3:17–19, 9
Gen. 3:24, 10
Gen. 3:18, 8
Gen. 3:23, 8
Gen. 4, 98–99
Gen. 4:12, 100
Gen. 4:13, 101
Gen. 4:14, 89, 100
Gen. 4:15, 100
Gen. 4:16, 89, 101
Gen. 11:1–9, 189–90
Gen. 12:1, 136
Gen. 13:16, 75
Gen. 22:17, 184
Gen. 28:14, 75, 76, 78
Gen. 28:15, 78
Gen. 28:16–17, 107
Gen. 30:8, 93
Gen. 37:25–28, 20
Gen. 38:1, 20
Gen. 49:10, 38
Gen. 49:15, 149
Exod. 1:6, 121
Exod. 1:7, 120, 121
Exod. 1:8, 123
Exod. 1:8–14, 13
Exod. 1:11, 119
Exod. 1:12, 123
Exod. 1:14, 14
Exod. 11:5, 14
Exod. 14:14, 79
Exod. 19:6, 33
Exod. 23:24, 120
Exod. 25:8, 68
Exod. 32, 50
Exod. 38:21–40:38, 2
Lev. 24:18, 103
Lev. 25:10, 96
Lev. 26:28, 90
Lev. 26:31–45, 87–88
Lev. 26:33, 29
Lev. 26:36, 37
Lev. 26:38–39, 92
Lev. 26:44, 90–91
Deut. 2:5, 77
Deut. 4:20, 120
Deut. 10:18, 60
Deut. 15:15, 12
Deut. 23:21, 73
Deut. 28:36–37, 38
Deut. 28:61, 37
Deut. 28:64–49, 88
Deut. 28:66, 67
Deut. 28:68, 9
Deut. 30:3, 69
Deut. 30:15, 3
Deut. 32:39, 79
Josh. 16:10, 140
Jud. 9:4, 38
1 Sam. 1:2, 97
1 Sam. 2:8, 97
1 Sam. 2:27, 69
1 Sam. 4:21, 37, 38
2 Sam. 7:14, 75
2 Sam. 7:23, 226
2 Kings 24:8–25:21, 15–18
2 Kings 25:22, 16
Isa. 8:15, 31
Isa. 18:2, 7, 41
Isa. 29:13, 205
Isa. 40:1, 48
Isa. 40:6–8, 145, 147
Isa. 41:8, 32
Isa. 42:22, 76

INDEX

Isa. 42:24, 38
Isa. 43:14, 23, 49, 69
Isa. 44:5, 31
Isa. 49:3, 94
Isa. 52:13–53:12, 94
Isa. 53:10–12, 95
Isa. 53:3, 37, 95
Isa. 62:6–7, 205
Isa. 63:16, 49
Deutero-Isaiah 43:14, 21
Jer. 8:13, 50
Jer. 8:20, 39
Jer. 10:24, 141
Jer. 15:7, 29
Jer. 21:8–9, 89
Jer. 22:30, 89
Jer. 23:24, 70
Jer. 29, 111–13
Jer. 29:4–6, 129
Jer. 31:18, 205
Jer. 31:21–22, 205
Jer. 46:19, 107
Jer. 48:11, 139
Jer. 49:38, 49
Ezek. 12:3, 107
Ezek. 19, 143
Ezek. 23:15, 29
Ezek. 36:15, 222
Ezek. 37:11, 38
Hos. 3:4, 38
Amos 3:2, 135
Amos 3:6, 96
Obad. 1:20, 93
Jon. 1:3, 70
Zech. 1:17, 61
Zech. 6:1, 29
Zech. 6:2, 29
Zech. 14:21, 81
Ps. 10:7, 118
Ps. 49:13, 8

Ps. 69:13, 29, 30
Ps. 116:10–11, 38, 39
Ps. 120:2–7, 41
Ps. 124:1–2, 6, 77
Ps. 136:7, 33
Ps. 137, 12, 18–20, 23, 25, 26, 109, 207
Ps. 137:1, 21, 22
Ps. 137:4, 21, 22
Ps. 139:7–10, 101
Ps. 146:5, 107
Prov. 5:20, 140
Prov. 7:9, 140
Prov. 9:17, 139, 140, 141
Prov. 23:4, 141
Prov. 30:20, 140
Job 24:16, 140
Songs 3:1, 30
Lam. 1:5, 38
Lam. 1:19, 20
Lam. 2:18–19, 59
Lam. 3:1, 59
Lam. 3:6–7, 59
Lam. 3:10, 59
Lam. 3:14, 30
Lam. 4:2, 37
Lam. 5, 47–48
Lam. 5:5, 22, 23
Eccles. 6:10, 3
Esther 2:5–22, 63–64
Dan. 2:38, 29
Dan. 7:14, 37
Dan. 7:5, 29
1 Chron 16:20, 78
1 Chron 3:17, 89

In the JPS Anthologies of Jewish Thought Series

Exile and the Jews: Literature, History, and Identity
Edited by Nancy E. Berg and Marc Saperstein

Modern Musar: Contested Virtues in Jewish Thought
Geoffrey D. Claussen

Modern Conservative Judaism: Thought and Practice
Elliot N. Dorff
Foreword by Julie Schonfeld

Modern Orthodox Judaism: A Documentary History
Zev Eleff
Foreword by Jacob J. Schacter

A Kabbalah and Jewish Mysticism Reader
Daniel M. Horwitz

Modern Jewish Theology: The First One Hundred Years, 1835–1935
Edited by Samuel J. Kessler and George Y. Kohler

The Growth of Reform Judaism: American and European Sources
W. Gunther Plaut
Foreword by Jacob K. Shankman
New introduction by Howard A. Berman
New epilogue by David Ellenson
With select documents, 1975–2008

The Rise of Reform Judaism: A Sourcebook of Its European Origins
W. Gunther Plaut
Foreword by Solomon B. Freehof
New introduction by Howard A. Berman

The Zionist Ideas: Visions for the Jewish Homeland— Then, Now, Tomorrow
Gil Troy

To order or obtain more information on these or other Jewish Publication Society titles, visit jps.org.

www.ingramcontent.com/pod-product-compliance
Lightning Source LLC
Chambersburg PA
CBHW030336240426
43661CB00052B/1650